Quick Start Guide to FFmpeg

Learn to Use the Open Source Multimedia-Processing Tool like a Pro

V. Subhash

Apress®

Quick Start Guide to FFmpeg: Learn to Use the Open Source
Multimedia-Processing Tool like a Pro

V. Subhash
Chennai, Tamil Nadu, India

ISBN-13 (pbk): 978-1-4842-8700-2   ISBN-13 (electronic): 978-1-4842-8701-9
https://doi.org/10.1007/978-1-4842-8701-9

Managing Director, Apress Media LLC: Welmoed Spahr
Acquisitions Editor: James Robinson-Prior
Development Editor: James Markham
Coordinating Editor: Jill Balzano

Cover image designed by Freepik (www.freepik.com)

Distributed to the book trade worldwide by Springer Science+Business Media LLC, 1 New York Plaza, Suite 4600, New York, NY 10004. Phone 1-800-SPRINGER, fax (201) 348-4505, e-mail orders-ny@springer-sbm.com, or visit www.springeronline.com. Apress Media, LLC is a California LLC and the sole member (owner) is Springer Science + Business Media Finance Inc (SSBM Finance Inc). SSBM Finance Inc is a **Delaware** corporation.

For information on translations, please e-mail booktranslations@springernature.com; for reprint, paperback, or audio rights, please e-mail bookpermissions@springernature.com.

Apress titles may be purchased in bulk for academic, corporate, or promotional use. eBook versions and licenses are also available for most titles. For more information, reference our Print and eBook Bulk Sales web page at http://www.apress.com/bulk-sales.

Any source code or other supplementary material referenced by the author in this book is available to readers on GitHub (https://github.com/Apress). For more detailed information, please visit http://www.apress.com/source-code.

Printed on acid-free paper

*Dedicated to the creators and supporters of free
and open source software*

Table of Contents

About the Author

V. Subhash is an invisible Indian writer, programmer, and illustrator. In 2020, he wrote one of the biggest jokebooks of all time and then ended up with over two dozen mostly nonfiction books including *Linux Command-Line Tips & Tricks, CommonMark Ready Reference, PC Hardware Explained, Cool Electronic Projects,* and *How To Install Solar.* He wrote, illustrated, designed, and produced all of his books using only open source software. Subhash has programmed in more than a dozen languages (as varied as assembly and Java); published software for desktop (*NetCheck*), mobile (*Subhash Browser & RSS Reader*), and the Web (*TweetsToRSS*); and designed several websites. As of 2022, he is working on a portable JavaScript-free CMS using plain-jane PHP and SQLite. Subhash also occasionally writes for the *Open Source For You* magazine and CodeProject.com.

About the Technical Reviewer

Gyan Doshi has been with the FFmpeg project as a developer and maintainer since 2018. During this time, he has focused on FFmpeg filters, formats, and command-line tools. From his experience in video postproduction stages such as editing and motion graphics, Gyan has learned how FFmpeg can be used in multimedia workflows as a valuable addition or as a substitute for expensive tools. Aside from being engaged as a multimedia/FFmpeg consultant, Gyan also troubleshoots FFmpeg issues on online forums such as Stack Exchange and Reddit.

Gyan builds the official Windows binary packages of FFmpeg (`ffmpeg`, `ffprobe`, and `ffplay`) and other tools (`ffescape`, `ffeval`, `graph2dot`, etc.) and offers them for download from his website at `www.gyan.dev`.

Acknowledgments

The author would like to thank:

- The publisher Apress who insisted on not using any third-party video in the screenshots, as the author did in the original self-published book (*FFmpeg Quick Hacks*). Most screenshots in this Apress book were taken from the author's own videos. The rest used videos and images that were in the public domain (Archive.org, Pixabay.com, and Unsplash.com). This led to a rewrite of most of the content, and in the process, several mistakes were eliminated.

- The technical reviewer Gyan Doshi for pointing out several other mistakes and making valuable suggestions.

- Creators and supporters of *free and open source* projects.

- The author's family, friends, enemies and governments without whose help and encouragement this book would have been completed much ahead of its deadline.

Introduction

FFmpeg is a *free and open source program* for editing audio and video files from the command line. You may have already known FFmpeg as a nifty program that can do simple conversions such as:

```
ffmpeg -i some-video.mov same-video.mp4
ffmpeg -i song-video.mp4 song-audio.mp3
```

FFmpeg is much more capable than this, but it is this intuitive interface and support for a wide variety of formats that has won it millions of users.

The FFmpeg project was originally started by a French programmer named Fabrice Bellard in the year 2000. It is now being developed by a large team of open source software developers spread around the world.

This book can serve as an easy FFmpeg tutorial, hack collection, and a ready reference. However, it is not possible for one book to cover everything that FFmpeg can do. FFmpeg has a very huge online documentation with which you may have to craft your commands. While this book may seem more than enough for most users, the documentation will open up vastly more possibilities. DO NOT avoid going through the documentation.

Before you go further into the book, you should be aware that the FFmpeg project creates two types of software:

1. `libav` **libraries**: These are FFmpeg programming software or "libraries" that are used by programmers to create audio/video processing software such as media players, browser plug-ins, and audio/video editors. The `libav` libraries have been used to build some parts of popular software such as VLC, xine, Blender, and Kodi.

2. `ffmpeg` **command-line program**: This is the FFmpeg end-user software that most people can use. The `ffmpeg` *command-line program* internally uses the `libav` *libraries*.

In this book, we will ignore the `libav` *libraries* and instead focus on the `ffmpeg` *command-line program*.

Extra Resources for This Book

- All code snippets used in this book are available in a plain-text file, complete with chapter and section titles and comments. It is actually a MarkDown/ CommonMark file. You can easily convert it to an HTML, ODT, DOCX, or PDF file. Conversion instructions are in the text file.

- Videos of several code examples used in the book are available in an online video playlist.

Render audio waveforms over video — 'Quick Start...

The 'Quick Start Guide To FFmpeg' book

Links to these resources can be found at

- `www.apress.com/9781484287002` (domain + ISBN)

- `www.vsubhash.in/ffmpeg-book.html`

CHAPTER 1

Installing FFmpeg

In the Introduction, I mentioned that FFmpeg was an "end-user program."
It is actually three command-line end-user programs, or **executables**:

1. `ffprobe`

2. `ffplay`

3. `ffmpeg`

The executables for these programs are available for Linux, Mac,
Windows, and other operating systems (OSs). When you go to the FFmpeg
website (`www.ffmpeg.org`), you will have two download options:

- Either download **pre-built FFmpeg executables** to
  your computer

- Or download **FFmpeg source code** to your computer
  and build your own customized FFmpeg executables

If you are unfamiliar with building executables from source code (as
are most people), you should choose the first option.

FFmpeg for Microsoft Windows Users

The download options on the FFmpeg site for *pre-built FFmpeg executables*
change frequently, so this book will not be specific with instructions. Just
go to this page and navigate to one of the download sites.

```
https://ffmpeg.org/download.html
```

© V. Subhash 2023
V. Subhash, *Quick Start Guide to FFmpeg*, https://doi.org/10.1007/978-1-4842-8701-9_1

1

On the selected download site, you may be presented with a dizzying array of downloads. Spend some time reading the information given there, and pick the most appropriate download for you.

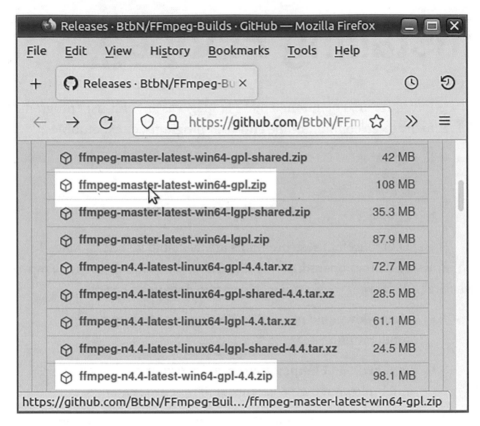

Figure 1-1. *This download page lists several download options for FFmpeg executables. Strangely, for FFmpeg, the latest master download is supposed to be more stable than the numbered release version*

Sometimes, there may be an *essentials* build and a *full* build. The *essentials* build may be enough for most people. If you want to use certain unusual features such as *frei0r* filters, you should choose the latter. As you never know what you might need in the future, I suggest that you choose the *full* build.

ffmpeg-git-essentials.7z	.ver	.sha256
ffmpeg-git-full.7z	.ver	.sha256

Figure 1-2. *There may be more than one "build" option for the downloads*

In the downloaded archives (zip or 7z files), you will find the executables: `ffprobe.exe`, `ffmpeg.exe`, and `ffplay.exe`.

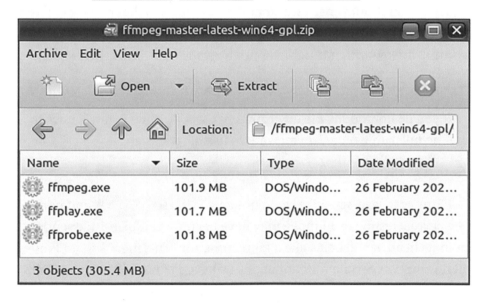

Figure 1-3. *The downloaded archive file contains three EXE files. Copy them to a folder specified in your PATH environment variable*

Copy the EXE files to some folder that is already included in your operating system's PATH environment variable. If you copy them to a new folder, then add the folder's full location to the PATH variable.

If you do not do the above, you will need to type the full path of the executable in your commands in the *Command Prompt* window.

3

Before modifying the PATH environment variable, take a backup of its value. Open the **Command Prompt** window and type this command.

```
echo %PATH% > PATH-BAK.TXT
```

Let us assume that you have extracted the EXE files to the folder `C:\MyInstalls\ffmpeg\bin`. Launch the **Command Prompt** window with Administrator privileges. Then, permanently suffix this folder's location to the PATH environment variable with this command.

```
SETX /M PATH "%PATH%;C:\MyInstalls\ffmpeg\bin"
```

Then, you should check whether the FFmpeg installation is accessible from the command-line without the full path. (Do this in a **Command Prompt** window with normal-user privileges.)

```
ffmpeg -version
```

If you do not modify the environment variable, then you will have to type the full path whenever you want to use the program.

```
C:\MyInstalls\ffmpeg\bin\ffmpeg -version
```

FFmpeg is case-sensitive so do not type `FFMPEG -VERSION` and hope to get a correct response. FFmpeg may have become platform-independent, but in its heart, it still beats like a Linux program. This means that FFmpeg will not support certain functionalities expected of native Windows/DOS programs. For example, you cannot type command switches (arguments) in uppercase (even if the command name can be typed in uppercase).

```
@ Causes error
FFMPEG -VERSION

@ Causes no error
FFMPEG -version
ffmpeg -version
```

Almost all command-line examples in this book assume a Linux environment. One-line commands will not require any change in Windows.

The Windows/DOS counterpart for the Linux null device (`/dev/null`) is NUL. This means that you should replace all instances of `2> /dev/null` in this book with `2> NUL`. This construct is used to prevent the commands from displaying text messages on the screen. `ffmpeg` outputs all its messages to *standard error*, which happens to be the screen. In case it outputs something to *standard output*, which also happens to be screen, and has to be blocked, the Linux remedy is to use `> /dev/null`. To do the same on your Windows computer, you will have to use `> NUL` instead.

In multiline commands, you will find a "\" (backslash) at the end of each line (except the last one), as is the practice in Linux.

```
# For 'nix users
ffmpeg -f lavfi \
       -i "testsrc=size=320x260[out0];
           anoisesrc=amplitude=0.06:color=white[out1]" \
       -t 0:0:30 -pix_fmt yuv420p \
       test.mp4
```

As a Windows user, you should use a caret (^) instead of the backslash (\ ).

```
@ For Windows users
ffmpeg -f lavfi ^
       -i "testsrc=size=320x260[out0]; ^
           anoisesrc=amplitude=0.06:color=white[out1]" ^
       -t 0:0:30 -pix_fmt yuv420p ^
       test.mp4
```

You should avoid writing anything after the backslash or the caret. Invisible trailing space(s) can also make a command to fail. (This happens often with copy-pasted commands.)

In a Linux `bash` terminal, the backslash is not required after a double-quotation mark has been opened, and you can continue on like that for more lines until the quotation is closed. In a Windows `cmd` terminal, all wrapping lines will have to end with a caret.

FFmpeg for Linux Users

If your Linux distribution has not installed FFmpeg by default, then use its default *software manager* or *package manager* to do so. Beware that the FFmpeg installed from software repositories used by Linux distributions are usually out of date.

The download sites linked by FFmpeg.org provide the latest builds with maximum support for external libraries. However, some Linux users like to build their executables from source. If you have a fast machine or a few hours to spare, start with the instructions on the *FFmpeg Wiki* site. Check their *source code compilation steps* specific to the Linux distribution that you use.

```
https://trac.ffmpeg.org/wiki/CompilationGuide
```

You can customize your FFmpeg build by enabling/disabling several build options. Instead of just blindly following the wiki, spend some time studying the `configure` script or its help output.

```
configure --help
```

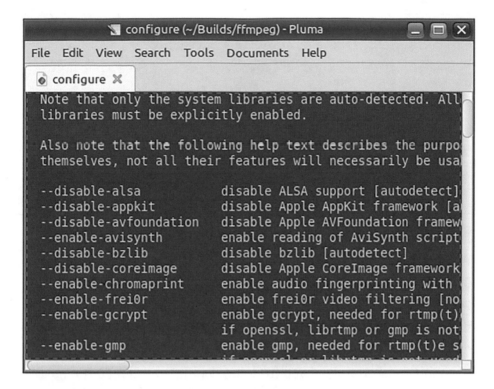

Figure 1-4. *The* configure *script, by default, will try to autodetect external libraries. You may have to manually enable those that are not autodetected*

In your Linux package manager app, try to search and install (*dev-*suffixed) developmental packages with similar names as the external libraries. You may not be able to install developmental packages for all of the libraries. But, for whatever libraries that you can install or have them already installed, add relevant -enable options to the configure compilation step. Here are a few:

```
...
--enable-chromaprint --enable-frei0r \
--enable-libbluray --enable-libbs2b --enable-libcdio \
--enable-libflite --enable-libfontconfig \
```

```
--enable-libfreetype --enable-libfribidi \
--enable-libmp3lame --enable-libsmbclient \
--enable-libv4l2 --enable-libvidstab \
...
```

Run the FFmpeg build statement with these changes, and eventually all three binary executable files will be created in your `$HOME/bin` directory. Then, secure the copy of the documentation from the `ffmpeg_build` directory so that you can read it whenever it is required.

☞   When I built FFmpeg version 5.1, I encountered some errors with the official wiki guide. The guide uses one long stringified command to install the FFmpeg binary executable files. This command is a combination of several commands that downloads the source and then configures, compiles, builds, and installs the executable files. If the configuration and compilation commands encounter any errors and you fix it, the command will restart the whole drama beginning with downloading the source. You do not have to endure that. Just continue with the `configure` step.

If you have an old OS where the latest FFmpeg executable does not run or cannot be compiled, go to `https://johnvansickle.com/ffmpeg/` and download pre-built statically linked executables (not including `ffplay`). On my old Ubuntu 10 *Fiendish Frankenstein* installation, I could not run the latest FFmpeg pre-built executable nor build the source, but these statically linked executables worked. (Even the C library is statically linked.) That is how I was able to finish the 2020 version of this book in the old OS.

FFmpeg for Apple Mac Users

With Apple moving from Intel x86 to ARM architecture, any specific instructions will be outdated when you read it. It is best that you consult the FFmpeg Wiki for the specific kind of Apple hardware that you are using.

```
https://trac.ffmpeg.org/wiki/CompilationGuide/macOS
```

Summary

Although originally designed as a Linux program, FFmpeg is also available for Windows and Mac operating systems. In this chapter, you learned how to obtain pre-built FFmpeg executables specific to your OS from the official FFmpeg site. You also learned how to build your own customized FFmpeg executables from source.

In the next chapter, you will learn how to start using the executables.

CHAPTER 2

Starting with FFmpeg

The FFmpeg project provides several end-user programs. This book will focus on three command-line programs – `ffprobe`, `ffplay`, and `ffmpeg`. You will be using `ffmpeg` most of the time, but `ffprobe` and `ffplay` can help you as well. In this chapter, you will gain an introduction to all three.

All three have an annoying "feature" – they display a build-information banner that is as big as the state of Texas. If you create the following aliases in your `$HOME/.bashrc` file, then you do not have to suffer the annoyance.

```
alias ffmpeg='ffmpeg -hide_banner '
alias ffplay='ffplay -hide_banner -autoexit '
alias ffprobe='ffprobe -hide_banner   '
```

☞   The `-autoexit` option for the `ffplay` command ensures that it makes a clean exit after playing a file instead of sticking around like it has crashed.

Some command examples in this book will have the suffixes `2>` `/dev/null` or `> /dev/null`. Such recourses were necessary to prevent information clutter.

© V. Subhash 2023
V. Subhash, *Quick Start Guide to FFmpeg*, https://doi.org/10.1007/978-1-4842-8701-9_2

ffprobe

If you want to find out useful information about an audio or video file, you need to use ffmpeg with the -i option. With ffprobe, you do not need the option.

```
ffmpeg -i tada.wav
ffprobe tada.wav
```

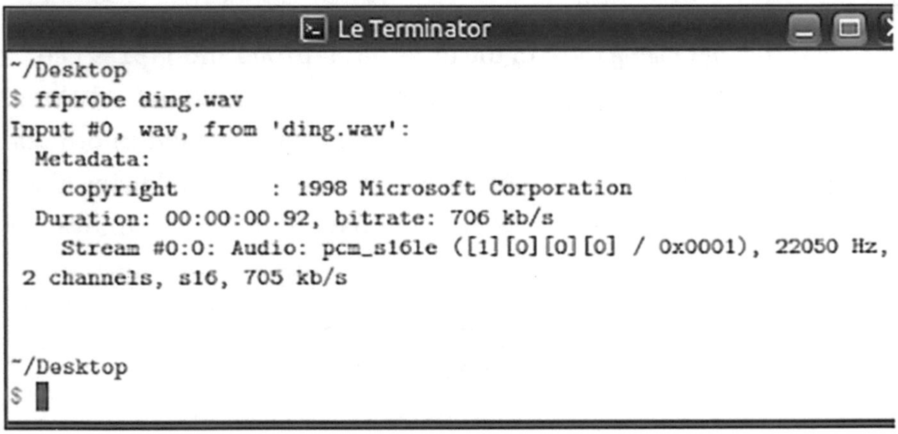

```
                          Le Terminator                    _  □  X
~/Desktop
$ ffprobe ding.wav
Input #0, wav, from 'ding.wav':
  Metadata:
    copyright        : 1998 Microsoft Corporation
  Duration: 00:00:00.92, bitrate: 706 kb/s
    Stream #0:0: Audio: pcm_s16le ([1][0][0][0] / 0x0001), 22050 Hz,
 2 channels, s16, 705 kb/s


~/Desktop
$ ▌
```

Figure 2-1. *ffprobe can be used to display information about what is contained in a multimedia file*

ffprobe can reveal much more information than this if you use the -show_streams option. You can filter the output of this command for use in your shell scripts. In a later chapter, you will find a sample output of this command.

```
ffprobe -show_streams somefile.mp4
```

ffplay

If you want to play a video file directly from the command line, just type ffplay and the file name. ffplay is a tiny media player. It does not have a context menu system or other interface. It responds to some keys and mouse clicks but does nothing more.

```
ffplay solar.mp4
```

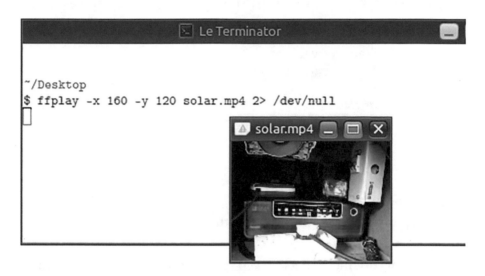

Figure 2-2. *ffplay can be used to play audio and video files*

To play an audio file without the (windowed) interface, say, as an audio notification in a shell script, you can use ffplay like this:

```
ffplay -autoexit -nodisp ding.wav
```

13

ffmpeg

The executables ffprobe, ffplay, and ffmpeg have several common command-line options (arguments, switches, or parameters). You can list most of them with the -h option.

```
ffmpeg -h
ffmpeg -h long
ffmpeg -h full > ffmpeg-help-full.txt
```

If you want to review some of the features supported by your installation of FFmpeg, try these:

```
ffmpeg -formats
ffmpeg -encoders
ffmpeg -decoders
ffmpeg -codecs
ffmpeg -filters
```

The output of these commands will give you a good overview of what FFmpeg can do. Sample output of these commands is available as annexures in this book.

You can dig out more specific help information with commands such as these:

```
ffmpeg -h demuxer=mp3
ffmpeg -h encoder=libmp3lame
ffmpeg -h filter=drawtext
```

Other FFmpeg End-User Programs

The FFmpeg project provides a few other command-line tools in addition to the three introduced in this chapter. Their purpose and usage are beyond the scope of this book. If you wish to do your own R&D, then you can find their files at www.gyan.dev/ffmpeg/builds/#tools.

Summary

In this chapter, you gained an introduction to the three FFmpeg executables. Before venturing into what FFmpeg can do for you, you need to learn a few things about multimedia formats and codecs. The next chapter will help you with that.

CHAPTER 3

Formats and Codecs

An MP3 audio file can be identified by its ".mp3" file extension. Similarly, an MP4 video file can be identified by the ".mp4" extension. The file extensions of multimedia files do not provide any kind of surety about the format. Even the format name is merely a notion. If you need to process audio and video content, you need to go beyond file extensions. You need to be familiar with multimedia concepts such as containers, codecs, encoders, and decoders. In this chapter, you will gain some basic information about all that and more.

Containers

Multimedia files such as MP4s or MP3s are just *containers* – containers for some audio and/or video content. An MP4 file is a container for some video content written using the *H.264 codec* and some audio content written using the *AAC codec*. It need not be like that for all MP4 files. Some MP4 files may have their video content written using the *Xvid codec* and the audio content written using the *MP3 codec*. Similarly, AVI, MOV WMV, and 3GP are popular containers for audio/video content. Codecs can differ from file to file even if their extensions are the same. A multimedia file may have the wrong extension because of some human error. You can expect all sorts of combinations in the wild.

When the codecs are not what is usually expected in a container, you may encounter annoying format errors in playback devices. Sometimes, you may be able to fix the error by simply renaming the file with the correct

© V. Subhash 2023
V. Subhash, *Quick Start Guide to FFmpeg*, https://doi.org/10.1007/978-1-4842-8701-9_3

extension. At other times, you will have to re-encode the file using *codecs* supported by the device. So, what does it mean when a device says it only supports certain "codecs"?

Codecs, Encoders, and Decoders

When audio and video recordings transitioned from analog to digital, equipment manufacturers developed algorithms to store audio waveforms and video frames in a scheme retrievable by computer software. Initially, these storage schemes were proprietary, and their documentation was not publicly available. With the rise in the popularity of digital media devices, interoperability and open standards became necessary.

When multimedia (audio or video) content is written or stored in a computer file, it is written in a specific retrievable format developed by the manufacturer of the multimedia equipment. The algorithm used to read or write multimedia content in a specific format became known as a **codec** (coder-decoder). The software used for writing the content using the codec became known as an **encoder**. The software used to read the written content became known as a **decoder**. A camera uses an *encoder* chip to store captured video. A TV uses a *decoder* chip to play the video from a USB drive. On a personal computer, the logic of encoder and decoder chips is installed as a *software codec*.

Raw audio or video requires a lot of space when stored on a computer file. The multimedia industry, led by camera manufacturers and computer companies, has developed several compression techniques to squeeze multimedia content on to as few bytes of storage as possible. The efficiency of the compression techniques varies. When the compression discards some content (assuming that the human ear or the eye would not miss it) for a dramatic decrease in the size of the file, the technique would be known as *lossy compression*. When no content was discarded, the technique was known as *lossless compression*. Lossless compression techniques are not used everywhere because of the high file-space requirement.

To suit real-world requirements, most codecs provide options to their algorithm so that a balance between file size reduction and detail loss can be specified on a preset or *ad hoc* basis. You will do the same when you use FFmpeg. For example, in the following command, to convert an uncompressed audio from a microphone recording to a lossy compressed audio format, several settings such as bitrate, number of channels, and sampling frequency are specified.

```
ffmpeg -i uncompressed-stereo.wav \
       -c:a libmp3lame -b:a 128k -ac 2 -ar 44100 \
       compressed.mp3
```

☞   You will learn more about these settings in later chapters, but for now just be aware that they are often required.

Demuxers and Muxers

I have been using FFmpeg for years without knowing what demuxers and muxers were. Even now, I cannot care less. Well… maybe a little. A *demuxer* is a software component that can read a multimedia input file so that a decoder can work on it. Similarly, a *muxer* writes data to a multimedia output file after it has been processed by an *encoder*. Between a decoder and encoder, some processing work may be done, or it may even pass directly to the other end. Here is all that you need to know:

- To write to a particular container format, the format's muxer is required.

- To read from a particular container format, a demuxer is required.

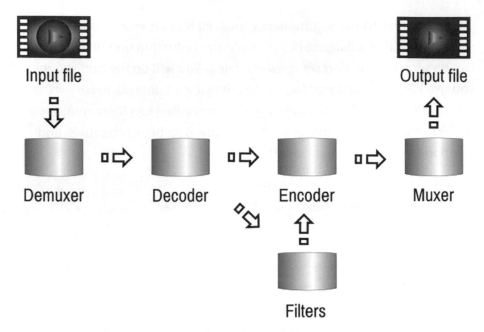

Figure 3-1. *This schematic shows how different components in
FFmpeg work together to give the output you want*

For example, to read and write to the MP4 format, an MP4 demuxer
and an MP4 muxer are required. FFmpeg automatically takes care of
muxers and demuxers so that you do not have to bother with them.
However, there may come situations when you do have to explicitly
address them.

```
~/Desktop
$ ffmpeg -h demuxer=gif
Demuxer gif [CompuServe Graphics Interchange Format (GIF)]:
GIF demuxer AVOptions:
  -min_delay          <int>        .D....... minimum valid delay between
  -max_gif_delay      <int>        .D....... maximum valid delay between
  -default_delay      <int>        .D....... default delay between frame:
  -ignore_loop        <boolean>    .D....... ignore loop setting (netsca|
```

Figure 3-2. *This demuxer help output provides a clue as to how to
create endlessly looping GIF animations*

Summary

In this chapter, you learned some theoretical concepts about multimedia formats, containers, and codecs. In the next chapter, we will delve deeper into the container and learn how to refer to its constituents from the command line using index numbers.

## CHAPTER 4

Media Containers and FFmpeg Numbering

In the previous chapter, you learned that a multimedia file is actually a container. On the inside, it encloses multimedia *streams* and *metadata*. In this chapter, you will learn what streams and metadata are and how you can access them from the command line. The sections in this chapter are arranged for easy access and completeness. It may not be possible for you to understand all of it on your first read. Return to this chapter a few times to get a full understanding.

Containers

A container can have several streams. A stream could be audio, video, subtitles, or a file attachment.

In an MP4 video file or container, you will usually find a *video stream* and an *audio stream*. In an MP3 file, you will find an audio stream and maybe some IDv3 tags (such as title, album, and artist) as metadata.

If you have one of those rare multi-angle DVDs, then each camera angle will be represented by a separate *video stream*. Multi-language videos will have an *audio stream* for each language. DVD subtitles for multiple languages are represented as individual *subtitle streams*. MKV files may have custom font files for displaying the subtitles. These font files will be represented as *file-attachment streams*.

In an audio stream, there can be several channels. A mono audio stream has only one channel. A stereo stream has two channels - left and right. A DVD movie's 7.1 surround sound stream has eight channels - front left, front right, center left, center right, rear left, rear right, and one LFE (low frequency effects).

FFmpeg identifies these streams, channels, and metadata **using index numbers** so that you can refer to them from the command line.

Container Internals

Logically, the internals of a multimedia file look like this. A container needs to have at least one stream. Everything else is optional. It is all right for a video file to not have album art, subtitles, custom fonts, or tags (global metadata), but one video stream and one audio stream are usually expected.

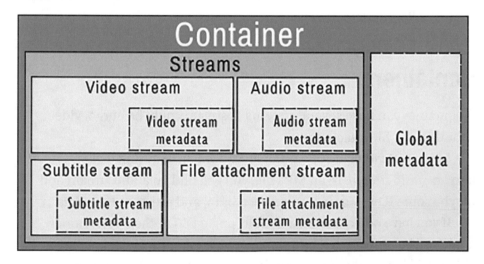

Figure 4-1. *Internals of a multimedia file container*

From this logical representation, you will note that a multimedia file container may have some global metadata and that each stream in the container can have stream-specific metadata too.

You can use `ffprobe` to display these details for any multimedia file.

```
~/Desktop/FasDrive
$ ffprobe "Flyte1 - Manic Monday (Album).mp3"
Input #0, mp3, from 'Flyte1 - Manic Monday (Album).mp3':
  Metadata:
    title            : Manic Monday (Album)
    album            : Greatest Hits
    artist           : The Bangles
    genre            : Pop
    date             : 1990
    comment          : Purchased by V. Subhash from Flipkart - Flyte
  Duration: 00:03:03.72, start: 0.025056, bitrate: 320 kb/s
    Stream #0:0: Audio: mp3, 44100 Hz, stereo, fltp, 320 kb/s
    Metadata:
      encoder        : LAME3.98r
    Stream #0:1: Video: mjpeg (Baseline), yuvj420p(pc, bt470bg/unkno
    Metadata:
      comment        : Cover (front)
```

Figure 4-2. *This is a sample* `ffprobe` *output for an audio file*

In this `ffprobe` output, the global metadata for the MP3 file shows ID3 tags such as title, album, and artist. It also includes a "comment" metadata that I added after I bought the music. The metadata for the audio stream shows that it was encoded using the LAME encoder by the music vendor. The album art is shown as a video stream but it has only one frame. More importantly, you should note that FFmpeg refers to the input files and streams using **index numbers starting from 0 (zero)**, instead of 1 (one).

Here is another example; this one is for a video file.

```
~/Desktop
$ ffprobe lucas.mkv
Input #0, matroska,webm, from 'lucas.mkv':
  Metadata:
    encoder          : libebml v1.0.0 + libmatroska v1.0.0
    creation_time    : 2020-02-19T20:30:08.000000Z
  Duration: 00:00:20.13, start: 0.000000, bitrate: 507 kb/s
    Stream #0:0: Video: h264 (High), yuv420p(progressive), 320x180 [SAR
1:1 DAR 16:9], 24 fps, 24 tbr, 1k tbn, 48 tbc (default)
    Stream #0:1: Audio: mp3, 44100 Hz, stereo, fltp, 128 kb/s (default)
    Stream #0:2: Subtitle: ass (default)
    Stream #0:3: Attachment: ttf
    Metadata:
      filename       : Florentia.ttf
      mimetype       : application/x-truetype-font
```

Figure 4-3. *This is a sample ffprobe output for a video file*

What does this output say?

- The MKV file is identified as the first input file (#0).

- It has **global metadata** for creation time but none for title, copyright, comments, etc.

- The first stream (#0:0) is a **video stream** and requires a H.264 decoder.

- The second stream (#0:1) is an **audio stream** and requires an MP3 decoder. The audio is in stereo, that is, it has two channels.

- The third stream (#0:2) is a **subtitle stream** and requires a decoder for the Substation Alpha (SSA) format.

- The fourth stream (#0:3) is a custom font for displaying the subtitles. It is stored as a **file-attachment stream**.

- The fourth stream also has some **stream-specific metadata** identifying the font file's name and mimetype. This is important because the SSA subtitles may refer to the font by this name.

☞   *Mimetype* is a more rigorous file-type definition (than file extensions) and is usually used by websites to identify downloads to web browsers.

Input and Output Files

An ffmpeg command can have multiple input and output files. The following command has two input files and one output file. (For now, ignore the line with the filter. Filters are explained in Chapter 7.)

```
ffmpeg -i solar.mp4 -i overlay.png \
       -filter_complex "overlay=370:260:" \
       watermarked-solar.mp4
```

☞   When specifying multiple input files, place options specific to one input file on the left side of -i option. Whatever specified after the file name applies to the next input file (-i) or (in its absence) the next output file.

☞   ffmpeg can also read from streams and write to them. The streams can be piped from/to another command and also transported over a network protocol. For more information, read the official documentation on *protocols*.

A video of my solar inverter and the cover image of one of my books are the input files. The command renders the image at 370 pixels from the left edge and 260 pixels from the top edge of the video.

Figure 4-4. *The output video is the input video with the overlaid input image*

The two **input files were specified using the** -i **option**. An MP4 video file is input file #0 and a PNG image file is input file #1. **The output file, as is always, has been specified last**.

```
~/Desktop
$ ffmpeg -i solar.mp4 -i overlay.png \
>        -filter_complex "overlay=370:260:" \
>        watermarked-solar.mp4
Input #0, mov,mp4,m4a,3gp,3g2,mj2, from 'solar.mp4':
  Metadata:
    comment         : MOV00127
  Duration: 00:01:36.93, start: 0.000000, bitrate: 390 kb/s
    Stream #0:0(und): Video: h264 (High) (avc1 / 0x31637661)
SAR 1:1 DAR 4:3], 351 kb/s, 24 fps, 24 tbr, 12288 tbn, 48 tb
    Metadata:
      handler_name    : VideoHandler
    Stream #0:1(und): Audio: aac (LC) (mp4a / 0x6134706D), 8
40 kb/s (default)
    Metadata:
      handler_name    : SoundHandler
Input #1, png_pipe, from 'overlay.png':
  Duration: N/A, bitrate: N/A
    Stream #1:0: Video: png, rgba(pc), 245x200 [SAR 11811:11
br, 25 tbn, 25 tbc
Stream mapping:
  Stream #0:0 (h264) -> overlay:main (graph 0)
  Stream #1:0 (png) -> overlay:overlay (graph 0)
  overlay (graph 0) -> Stream #0:0 (libx264)
  Stream #0:1 -> #0:1 (aac (native) -> aac (native))
Press [q] to stop. [?] for help
```

Figure 4-5. *The output of the command shows the index numbers used for the input files and streams*

The output of the command shows that the first stream in the first input file is a video stream and is numbered #0:0. The second stream in that file is an audio stream and is numbered #0:1. The first stream in the second input file (the PNG image file) is considered as a video stream even though it has only one (image) frame and is identified as #1:0.

You can refer to streams by their type. In the previous command, the streams were as follows:

- `0:v:0` (first file's first video stream) or `0:0` (first file's first stream)

- `0:a:0` (first file's first audio stream) or `0:1` (first file's second stream)

- `1:v:0` (second file's first video stream) or `1:0` (second file's first stream)

For this to become clear, spend some time studying the screenshot in Figure 4-5.

Suppose that a multi-language DVD video file had one video stream and two audio language streams. The streams can be referred as follows:

- `0:v:0` (first video stream) or `0:0` (first stream)

- `0:a:0` (first audio stream) or `0:1` (second stream)

- `0:a:1` (second audio stream) or `0:2` (third stream)

☞   In the output of `ffmpeg` commands, you will encounter index numbers ignoring the stream type. To make your FFmpeg commands somewhat fail-safe, I recommend that you refer to streams by their type instead.

As you may have guessed, the stream-type identifier for video is `v` and `a` for audio. There are others as given in Table 4-1.

Table 4-1. *Stream-type identifiers*

Stream type	Identifier
Audio	a
Video	v
Video (not images)	V
Subtitles	s
File attachments	t
Data	d

After displaying the information about the input files and streams, ffmpeg will list how the input streams will be processed and mapped to intermediate and final streams. Then, it will list the final output files and their streams. In a bash terminal, you can press the key combination Ctrl+S if you wish to pause and study this information. Otherwise, all of this information will quickly flash past your terminal as ffmpeg will then post a huge log of informational, warning, and error messages as it performs the actual processing of the input data.

Maps

With multiple input files, FFmpeg will use an internal logic to choose which input streams will end up in the output file. To override that, you can use the -map option. Maps enable you to specify your own selection and order of streams for the output file. You can specify stream mapping in several ways:

```
-map InputFileIndex
```
all streams in file with specified index

For example, -map 1 means
all streams in second (1) input file.

31

```
-map InputFileIndex:StreamIndex
```
the stream with specified index in file with specified index

For example, -map 0:2 means
third (2) stream in first (0) input file.

```
-map InputFileIndex:StreamTypeIdentifier
```
all streams of specified type in file with specified index

For example, -map 1:s means
all subtitle (s) streams in second (1) input file.

```
-map InputFileIndex:StreamTypeIdentifier:StreamIndex
```
among streams of specified type in file with specified index, the
stream with specified index

For example, -map 2:s:1 means
second (1) subtitle (s) stream in third (2) input file.

Information overload? Let me explain with an example. When I created
this stop-motion video a few years ago, I used a gramophone recording as
the background music. Typical of old record music, it had a lot of sound
artifacts. At that time, I did not know much about FFmpeg. So, I used
FFmpeg to extract the audio as an MP3 file but used the free *Audacity*
program to apply a *low-pass filter*. Then, I used FFmpeg again to swap the
original audio with the MP3 fixed by Audacity.

Figure 4-6. *The audio of this video had gramophone sound artifacts*

```
# Extract the audio
ffmpeg -i Stopmotion-hot-wheels.mp4 \
     -map 0:1 \
     Stopmotion-hot-wheels.mp3

# Apply low-pass filter to Stopmotion-hot-wheels.mp3
# using Audacity and export to Stopmotion-hot-wheels-fixed.mp3

# Swap the existing audio track with the mp3 fixed by Audacity
ffmpeg -i Stopmotion-hot-wheels.mp4 \
     -i Stopmotion-hot-wheels-fixed.mp3 \
     -map 0:0 -map 1:0 \
     -codec copy \
     Stopmotion-hot-wheels-fixed.mp4
```

☞   `-codec copy` or `-c copy` copies the streams as they are, instead of unnecessarily re-encoding or converting them again. It saves a lot of time.

In the first command, I included a map for the second stream (0:1) in the MP4 file and saved it as an MP3 file. (I assumed that the second stream was an audio stream. It need not be.) I then corrected errors in the MP3 file using Audacity. In the second command, the first input file (the MP4 file) had two streams – (0:0) and (0:1) – same as in the first command. (More assumptions.) The second input file (the "fixed" MP3) had one stream (1:0). In the second command, I used the first file's first stream (0:0) and the second file's first and only stream (1:0). Alternatively, I could have typed the command by mapping to the first file's first video stream (0:v:0) and the second file's first audio stream (1:a:0).

```
ffmpeg -i Stopmotion-hot-wheels.mp4 \
       -i Stopmotion-hot-wheels-fixed.mp3 \
       -map 0:v:0 -map 1:a:0 \
       -codec copy \
       Stopmotion-hot-wheels-fixed.mp4
```

☞   This alternative *fail-early* approach is safer, as it can protect you from typing mistakes.

The audio stream in the original MP4 (0:1) or (0:a:0) gets discarded because it was not included in any of the maps. If I wanted to retain the original audio stream, I can add another map for it as a second audio stream. The fixed audio track will be played by default by media players. I can manually select the second audio track with the remote or a menu option to hear the unfixed original audio.

```
ffmpeg -i Stopmotion-hot-wheels.mp4 \
       -i Stopmotion-hot-wheels-fixed.mp3 \
       -map 0:v:0 -map 1:a:0 -map 0:a:0 \
       -codec copy \
       Stopmotion-hot-wheels-fixed-n-restored.mp4
```

You can use maps when generating multiple output files with one command.

```
ffmpeg -i solar.mp4 \
  -map 0:1 -c:a libmp3lame -b:a 128k solar-high.mp3  \
  -map 0:1 -c:a libmp3lame -b:a 64k solar-low.mp3
```

The -map options provide a new set of streams available for options specified after them. Options such as -codec or -ac will only affect streams specified by the -map options before them, not the streams available in the input files.

Metadata

Metadata means data about data. When using FFmpeg, metadata is read by the demuxer and/or written by the muxer. The data is usually specified as **key-value pairs**. For a media file, the metadata can be global (for the entire file) or specific to a stream in the file. Each container format specifies a limited set of metadata keys. The MP3 format, for example, supports metadata keys such as title, artist, album, and copyright. You can specify metadata for individual streams as follows:

```
-metadata:s:StreamIndex or

-metadata:s:StreamTypeIdentifier:StreamIndex
```

This command sets metadata at the global/file/container level.

```
ffmpeg -i solar.mp4 -codec copy \
       -metadata title="Me Solar Inverter" \
       solarm.mp4
```

Figure 4-7. *The background video has no metadata, and the video player just displays the file name on the window title. In the foreground video, title metadata is available, and the video player displays that text instead of just the file name*

The `ffprobe` output in Figure 4-8 shows potentially incriminating information about a moonshiner MP3.

```
~/Desktop
$ ffprobe raisa.mp3
Input #0, mp3, from 'raisa.mp3':
  Metadata:
    major_brand    : mp42
    minor_version  : 0
    compatible_brands: isommp42
    title          : Musiki - Мужики
    encoder        : ███████
    artist         : Raisa Prikolnaya - Раиса Прикольная
  Duration: 00:02:50.71, start: 0.000000, bitrate: 136 kb/s
    Stream #0:0: Audio: mp3, 44100 Hz, stereo, s16p, 128 kb/s
    Stream #0:1: Video: png, rgb24, 640x360, 90k tbr, 90k tbn, 90k tbc
    Metadata:
      title        : Screenshot-HD-2015-YouTube-mp4-1.png
      comment      : Other
```

Figure 4-8. This *ffprobe* output shows that this inveterate pirate had downloaded a music video from Youtube and ripped the audio!

```
ffmpeg -y -i raisa.mp3 \
      -map 0 -c copy \
      -metadata:s:v:0 title='raisa.png' \
      raisa2.mp3          # Smooth!
```

This command makes no changes to the MP3 except for the value of the incriminating `title` metadata of the album art.

```
    Stream #0:1: Video: png, rgb24, 640x360 [SAR 3780:3780 DAR 16:9],
90k tbr, 90k tbn, 90k tbc
    Metadata:
      title        : raisa.png
      comment      : Other
```

Figure 4-9. This updated *ffprobe* output shows that the pirate has smoothly changed the metadata. Maybe he was doing researchez academique! Non? Nhyet?

Remember my stopmotion video with multitrack audio? I can use the `-metadata` option to give its audio streams an informative language name.

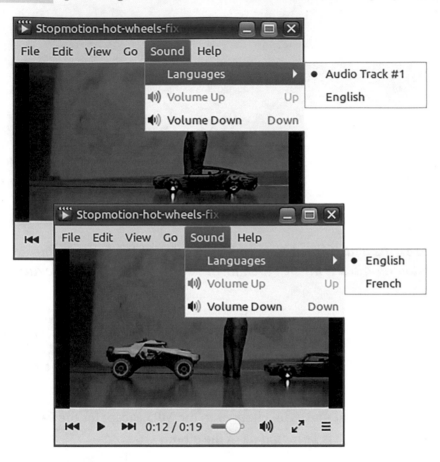

Figure 4-10. *If you do not specify a language name for an audio track, media players may make wrong assumptions*

```
ffmpeg -i Stopmotion-hot-wheels.mp4 \
       -i Stopmotion-hot-wheels-fixed.mp3 \
       -map 0:v:0 -map 1:a:0 -map 0:a:0 \
       -codec copy \
       -metadata:s:a:0 language="eng" \
       -metadata:s:a:1 language="fre" \
       Stopmotion-hot-wheels-fixed-n-restored.mp4
```

Remember that to set the language names for subtitle streams, the -metadata option should refer to subtitle streams, not audio streams.

```
-metadata:s:s:0 language="eng" \
-metadata:s:s:1 language="fre" \
```

The StreamIndex refers to the index of the stream IN THE OUTPUT FILE. The s after -metadata: identifies itself as metadata for a stream. Do not mistake it for subtitles. Also, remember that metadata is all about the output file. Do not use any numbering from the input file(s).

 Apart from streams (-metadata:s), metadata can be specified for DVD chapters (-metadata:c) and DVD programs (-metadata:p). They are not covered by this book.

 You can learn more about metadata in Chapter 10.

Metadata Maps

Have you noticed that when you convert MP3 files, the album art or the meta tags get lost? This is because of improper or no metadata mapping. Metadata can get lost when you convert files or create new files from multiple input files. The -map_metadata option helps you correctly route metadata from input files to output files. Its value is specified in a rather twisted manner. The **left is the destination** and the **right is the source**.

```
-map_metadata InputFileIndex:MetadataSpecifier or
-map_metadata:g InputFileIndex:MetadataSpecifier or
-map_metadata:MetadataSpecifier InputFileIndex:↵
MetadataSpecifier
```

> Where
>
> MetadataSpecifier is either g or s:StreamType (all streams) or
> s:StreamType:StreamIndex (some stream)

Yeah, it made my head spin too! Take your time. Nobody does metadata mapping on their first excursion into FFmpeg. Take the slow lane.

The following example copies global metadata from the second input file (-map 1) as the global metadata for the output file. This ensures that the MP3 tags are copied as the video's metadata.

```
ffmpeg -y -i raisa.png -i raisa.mp3  \
       -c:a copy -c:v mjpeg \
       -map 0 -map 1 \
       -map_metadata 1 \
       raisa.mp4
```

The next example copies global metadata from the second input file both globally (:g) and to the audio stream (:s:a). The global metadata from the second input file can be specified either as 1:g or simply as 1. Global output metadata can be typed as -map_metadata:g (as below) or simply as -map_metadata (as above).

```
ffmpeg -y -i raisa.png -i raisa.mp3  \
       -c:a copy -c:v mjpeg \
       -map 0 -map 1 \
       -map_metadata:g 1:g -map_metadata:s:a 1 \
       raisa.mkv    #Does not work with MP4
```

What is the advantage of this command? If someone decides to extract just the audio stream from the MKV, the metadata does not get omitted. The stream and the MKV (global) both have a copy of the metadata from the MP3 file. The original metadata will survive even in the extracted audio stream.

```
Input #0, matroska,webm, from 'raisa2.mkv':
  Metadata:
    title              : Musiki - Мужики
    MAJOR_BRAND        : mp42
    MINOR_VERSION      : 0
    COMPATIBLE_BRANDS: isommp42
    ARTIST             : Raisa Prikolnaya - Раиса Прикольная
  Duration: 00:02:50.74, start: 0.000000, bitrate: 131 kb/s
    Stream #0:0: Video: mjpeg, yuvj444p, 640x360 [SAR 1:1 DAR 16:9], 25
fps, 25 tbr, 1k tbn, 1k tbc (default)
    Stream #0:1: Audio: mp3, 44100 Hz, stereo, s16p, 128 kb/s (default)
    Metadata:
      title            : Musiki - Мужики
      MAJOR_BRAND      : mp42
      MINOR_VERSION    : 0
      COMPATIBLE_BRANDS: isommp42
      ARTIST           : Raisa Prikolnaya - Раиса Прикольная
```

Figure 4-11. *The global metadata has been duplicated to the audio stream metadata as well*

☞   The `-metadata` option overrides `-map_metadata` mapping.

Channel Maps

Audio streams can have one or more channels. Monaural audio has only one channel. Stereo music has two channels - left and right. DVD movies can have two or six or eight channels for playback on both stereo and surround speaker systems.

To pin down the channels exactly as you want in the output file, you need to use the `-map_channel` option. It can be specified as follows:

```
-map_channel
InputFileIndex.StreamIndex.ChannelIndex
```

> or as
>
> ```
> -map_channel -1
> ```
> if you want the channel muted.

The `-map_channel` options specify the input audio channels and the order in which they are placed in the output file.

Imagine that the audio channels in an MP4 file are mixed up. When you wear headphones, in either ear, the voices are heard for people on the opposite side in the video. You can fix it by the following:

```
ffmpeg -i wrong-channels.mp4 \
       -c:v copy \
       -map_channel 0.1.1 -map_channel 0.1.0 \
       fine-channels.mp4
```

In a stereo audio stream, the channel order is `0.1.0` (left) followed by `0.1.1` (right). When you use a channel map of `0.1.1` followed by `0.1.0`, the channels get switched.

For the next example, imagine that you are using headphones in a work environment. You want to have one ear for music and one ear for surroundings. You could mute one of the channels.

```
ffmpeg -i moosic.mp3 \
       -map_channel 0.0.0 -map_channel -1 \
       moosic4lefty.mp3
```

☞ No, you should not make it mono. Mono audio will be heard on both sides.

In some videos, the left and right audio channels are independent tracks. What these content creators do is place the original audio on one channel and the most annoying royalty-free music on the other. Instead of deleting the offending channel, you could move each channel to a separate audio stream while preserving the original stereo stream in a third stream.

```
ffmpeg -y -i zombie.mp4 \
        -map 0:0 -map 0:1 -map 0:1 -map 0:1 \
        -map_channel 0.1.0:0.1 -map_channel 0.1.1:0.2 \
        -c:v copy \
        zombie-tracks.mp4
```

The first stream in the output file will be the original video (0.0). The left channel (0.1.0) will be the second stream (0.1). The right channel (0.1.1) will be the third stream (0.2). The original stereo audio will become the fourth stream. (Yes, the second and third streams will be mono audio.)

What about the numbers after the colon? That is explained by the full definition for channel maps:

```
    -map_channel InputFileIndex.InputFileStreamIndex.⏎
    ChannelIndex:OutputFileIndex.OutputFileStreamIndex
```

How do you like them apples? The second part beginning with the colon is optional. It is for placing the mapped input audio channel on a specified output stream.

☞   Channel mapping numbers use dots, not colons. The colon is used only when you begin to specify the output stream.

☞   Channel mapping cannot be used to mix channels from multiple input files.

☞   When you make changes to the channels, the audio will be
converted again and this takes time. It will not be done quickly like
with `-c:a copy`.

Do Not Use the `-map_channel` Option

The `-map_channel` option, with its difficulties, is on its way out. The
FFmpeg version 5.1 (released in July 2022) shows this warning.

```
The -map_channel option is deprecated and will be removed.
It can be replaced by the 'pan' filter, or in some cases by
combinations of 'channelsplit', 'channelmap', 'amerge' filters.
```

With newer `ffmpeg` versions, the previous commands can be rewritten
using filters, which you will learn in a later chapter.

```
# Switch right and left channels of stereo audio
ffmpeg -i wrong-channels.mp4 \
       -c:v copy \
       -filter_complex "channelmap=map=FR-FL|FL-FR" \
       fine-channels.mp4

# Silence right channel
ffmpeg -i moosic.mp3 \
       -c:v copy \
       -filter_complex "pan=stereo|FL=FL|FR=0" \
       moosic4lefty.mp3

# Split channels to separate audio streams
# and also preserve existing audio stream
```

```
ffmpeg -y -ss 0:0:20 -t 0:0:20 -i zombie.mp4 \
     -c:v copy \
     -filter_complex "channelsplit[L][R]" \
     -map 0:v:0 -map '[L]' -map '[R]' -map 0:a:0 \
     -codec:a:0 aac -ac:a:0 1 \
     -codec:a:1 aac -ac:a:1 1 \
     -codec:a:2 copy \
     zombie-tracks.mp4
```

☞   The -codec and -ac options are limited to streams specified by the -map options specified before them.

Summary

In this chapter, you learned about how to access streams and metadata. You also learned how to pick and choose what streams and metadata you would like to have in the output file(s).

As mentioned in the beginning of this chapter, it is not necessary that you grasp every detail in this chapter on the first go. As you read forthcoming chapters, certain things mentioned in this chapter will become clearer. If not, you can always return to this chapter.

CHAPTER 5

Format Conversion

The main reason that so many people use `ffmpeg` is its amazing ability to convert files from one format to another. `ffmpeg` supports so many formats that I doubt there is any competition even from paid software. In this chapter, you will learn how to perform these conversions and customize them to extract the best quality from the source files.

No-Brainer Conversions

The default output format in many Linux multimedia programs is OGV and OGG files. Sadly, very few consumer electronic devices support these two formats. I use `gtk-recordMyDesktop` to screen capture my computer demos, and it creates OGV video files. Before I can play the files on my TV, I need to convert them to MP4 format.

```
ffmpeg -i video1.ogv video1.mp4
```

An Ogg ringtone will play fine on an Android phone but not on a feature phone, which usually only supports MP3 and MIDI ringtones. Converting Ogg to MP3 is easy with FFmpeg.

```
ffmpeg -i alarm.ogg alarm.mp3
```

FFmpeg can guess the output format based on the file extension you have used for the output file. It will automatically apply some good preset conversion settings (defaults). You can specify custom conversion settings too.

© V. Subhash 2023
V. Subhash, *Quick Start Guide to FFmpeg*, https://doi.org/10.1007/978-1-4842-8701-9_5

Conversion Options

Table 5-1 lists a few FFmpeg options that are useful when converting files. You will learn how to use them in the rest of this chapter.

Table 5-1. *Some FFmpeg conversion options*

Option	For
-y	Prevent prompting before overwriting any existing output file
-b:a	Set audio bitrate
-c:a	Specify audio encoder or decoder
-ar	Set audio sampling rate
-ac	Set number of audio channels
-b:v	Set video bitrate
-c:v	Specify video encoder or decoder
-r	Set video frame rate
-pass	Specify number of the encoding pass
-passlogfile	Specify prefix for multi-pass encoding log files
-f	Force specified format (or oss, alsa, rawvideo, concat, image2, null…)
-shortest	Stop all processing when any one output stream is completely processed
-vn	Do not process video
-an	Do not process audio
-sn	Do not process subtitles

Obsolete/Incorrect Options

FFmpeg is fault-tolerant to an extent but do not be sloppy in typing the options. You should avoid using `-r:a` instead of `-ar` (audio sampling rate). Instead of conventions such as `-acodec` and `-vcodec`, you should be using `-c:a` or `-c:v` instead. Support for such old practices may be removed in future.

Codec Option

The `-codec` option is used to specify an encoder (when used before an output file). When used before an input file, it refers to the decoder. (`ffmpeg` may have more than one decoder and encoder for a particular codec.) Choose the correct name from the output of the command `ffmpeg -encoders` or `ffmpeg -decoders`, and not from that of `ffmpeg -codecs`.

How do you know which codec (encoder name) you need to use for a particular format? For an MP3 file, you could try the following:

The `-codec` option can also be specified for all streams for a particular type, such as `-codec:a` for all audio streams or `-codec:s` for all subtitle streams or for a particular stream using its index. For each stream, only the last applicable `-codec` option will be considered. If you use the value `copy` for the encoder, `ffmpeg` will copy applicable streams as is without using an encoder.

How do you know which codec (encoder name) you need to use for a particular format? For an MP3 file, you could try the following:

```
ffmpeg -encoders | grep mp3
```

It may not be so straightforward with other formats. Browse through the full output of the command `ffmpeg -encoders` to become familiar with codec names. Sample output of this command is available in Annexure 3. Then, you will learn that H.264 and MPEG-4 codecs have something to do with MP4 files. You could also use `ffprobe` on existing file samples and find prospective codec names.

```
~/Desktop
$ ffmpeg -encoders | grep mp3
 A..... libmp3lame          libmp3lame MP3 (MPEG audio layer 3) (code
 A..... libshine            libshine MP3 (MPEG audio layer 3) (codec

~/Desktop
$ ffmpeg -encoders | grep mp4

~/Desktop
$ ffmpeg -encoders | grep mpeg4
 V.S... mpeg4               MPEG-4 part 2
 V..... libxvid             libxvidcore MPEG-4 part 2 (codec mpeg4)
 V..... mpeg4_v4l2m2m       V4L2 mem2mem MPEG4 encoder wrapper (codec
 V..... msmpeg4v2           MPEG-4 part 2 Microsoft variant version 2
 V..... msmpeg4             MPEG-4 part 2 Microsoft variant version 3

~/Desktop
$ ffmpeg -encoders | grep h26
 V..... h261                H.261
 V..... h263                H.263 / H.263-1996
 V..... h263_v4l2m2m        V4L2 mem2mem H.263 encoder wrapper (codec
 V.S... h263p               H.263+ / H.263-1998 / H.263 version 2
 V..... libx264             libx264 H.264 / AVC / MPEG-4 AVC / MPEG-4
 V..... libx264rgb          libx264 H.264 / AVC / MPEG-4 AVC / MPEG-4
 V..... h264_nvenc          NVIDIA NVENC H.264 encoder (codec h264)
```

Figure 5-1. ffmpeg *lists a lots of encoders, several pages full. You may miss some important ones if you make assumptions and filter the output. Use the command* ffmpeg -encoders | more *to conveniently browse the full output*

Sample Conversion with Custom Settings

If I wanted to convert a HD video downloaded from the Internet for playing on my old portable media player, I would use these settings.

```
ffmpeg -i net-video.mp4 \
       -s 320x240 \
       -c:v mpeg4 -b:v 200K -r 24 \
```

```
-c:a libmp3lame -b:a 96K -ac 2 \
portable-video.mp4
```

The output video stream uses MPEG4 codec with qvga (320x240) dimensions, 200K bitrate, and a 24 frames-per-second rate. The output audio stream uses MP3 codec (Lame encoder) with two-channel audio (stereo) and 96K bitrate.

☞   You will know what values to use for each setting only if you make it a habit to use `ffprobe` on new types of files that you encounter.

☞   The bitrate is how densely the audio or video content is stored in the container. The greater the compression, the lesser is the bitrate and file size, and so is the quality. You need to find a balance between quality loss and file size reduction.

Multi-pass Conversion

In multi-pass encoding, `ffmpeg` processes the video stream multiple times to ensure the output video is close to the specified bitrate. `ffmpeg` creates a log file for each pass. In the initial passes, the audio is not processed and video output is not saved (dumped on null device). In the final pass, however, you will have to specify the audio conversion settings and the output file. In the next example, the conversion from the previous section is performed using two passes.

This is the first pass.

```
ffmpeg -y -i net-video.mp4 \
       -s 320x240 -c:v mpeg4 -b:v 194k -r 24 \
```

```
            -f mp4 -pass 1 -passlogfile /tmp/ffmpeg-log-
            net-video \
            -an /dev/null
```

    Windows users should use NUL instead of /dev/null.

And, this is the last pass.

```
ffmpeg -y -i net-video.mp4 \
            -s 320x240 -c:v mpeg4 -b:v 194k -r 24 \
            -pass 2 -passlogfile /tmp/ffmpeg-log-net-video \
            -c:a libmp3lame -ac 2 -b:a 96K \
            portable-video.mp4
```

Multiple passes of the first kind may be required for achieving a particular bitrate. Use the same video conversion settings for all passes.

    When the streams meet the specified bitrates, you will also know exactly how big the file will be. Just multiply the bitrate with the duration of the video. The reverse is also true. You can target a particular file size (allowing for some deviation) by specifying a proportional bitrate for both the audio and video. Conversion with constant bitrate was popular when DVD videos were encoded (ripped off) to fit on a CD.

Conversion for Maximum Compression and Quality

Multimedia codecs provide a trade-off between speed, quality, and compression. Now that we have almost unlimited online and offline space, constant quality rather than constant bitrate is preferred. With the H.264 codec, you can achieve the required quality and compression in *one pass* using the `-crf` (CRF or Constant Rate Factor) option and by specifying a processing "preset." The `-crf` option affects quality.

```
x264 Presets      x264 Tune        x264 Profiles
~~~~~~~~~~~       ~~~~~~~~~        ~~~~~~~~~~~~~

ultrafast         film             baseline
superfast         animation        main
veryfast          grain            high
faster            stillimage
fast              psnr
medium            ssim
slow              fastdecode
slower            zerolatency
veryslow
placebo
```

Figure 5-2. *This extract from the output of an old script shows preset and tuning variables supported by the H.264 encoder*

```
ffmpeg -i solar.mp4 \
       -c:v libx264 -crf 21 -preset fast \
       -c:a copy \
       solar-CONVERTED.mp4
```

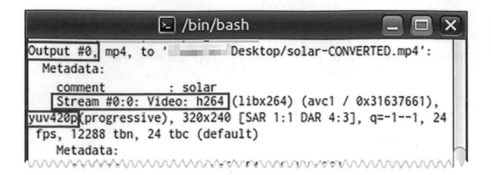

Figure 5-3. *The ffmpeg output stream details will tell you which pixel format has been used*

The CRF range is from 0 (lossless) to 63 (worst) for 10-bit pixel formats (such as yuv420p10le) and 0 to 51 for 8-bit pixel formats (such as yuv420p). You can determine the pixel format from the ffmpeg output of a similar file conversion. The median can be 21 for 8-bit encoder and 31 for 10-bit encoder.

What the heck is a pixel format? All that you need to know about pixel format (at this stage) is that it is a data-encoding scheme used to specify the colors of each pixel (dots) in a video frame. FFmpeg supports these pixel formats: monob, rgb555be, rgb555le, rgb565be, rgb565le, rgb24, bgr24, 0rgb, bgr0, 0bgr, rgb0, bgr48be, uyvy422, yuva444p, yuva444p16le, yuv444p, yuv422p16, yuv422p10, yuv444p10, yuv420p, nv12, yuyv422, and gray.

In addition to the processing preset, you can also specify a -tune option depending on the kind of video that you have selected. The values psnr and ssim are used to generate video quality metrics and are not normally used in production. zerolatency output can be used for streaming. fastdecode can be used for devices that do not have a lot of processing power. grain is to prevent the encoder from being confused by grainy videos.

Audio Conversion

This command uses the Lame MP3 encoder to convert an Ogg audio file to a 128K-bitrate two-channel (stereo) MP3 file.

```
ffmpeg -i alarm.ogg \
       -c:a libmp3lame \
       -ac 2 \
       -b:a 128K \
       alarm.mp3
```

☞   There is a better method for converting to MP3 files. You will find it in Chapter 11.

Audio Extraction

Some video files have great sound. Music videos are good examples. How do you extract their audio? Well, drop the video stream and copy the audio stream to an audio file.

```
# Matroska audio
ffmpeg -i music-video.mp4 -c:a copy music-video.mka
# MPEG4 audio - FFmpeg flounders
ffmpeg -i music-video.mp4 -vn -c:a copy music-video.m4a
```

☞   Without -vn, the video stream will get copied to the m4a file! Hurray for redundant options! Le paranoid survive!

Matroska audio or ".mka" files support several audio codecs. The ".m4a" files support AAC (MPEG4 audio) codec.

If you already know that the audio stream in the MP4 file has been encoded with MP3 codec (as they do sometimes), you can `-codec:a copy` the audio stream to a ".mp3" file. Most of the time, however, you will have to *encode* it to MP3. Files with extension ".mka" and ".m4a" are not supported by many playback devices. The following command converts the audio stream of the video file using the Lame encoder to create a two-channel (stereo) MP3 file encoded at 128K bitrate.

```
ffmpeg -i music-video.mp4 \
       -c:a libmp3lame -b:a 128K -ac 2 \
       music-video.mp3
```

You can simultaneously output audio in different bitrates using multiple `-map` options.

```
ffmpeg -i music-video.mp4 \
 -vn \
 -map 0:a -c:a libmp3lame -b:a 128K music-high.mp3 \
 -map 0:a -c:a libmp3lame -b:a 64K music-low.mp3
```

☞   As one understands, this is strictly for limited doomsday archival purposes…. Several films and music records have been lost to studio fires. Anything can happen. Cite the 2020 pandemic. 🤓

Extract Stills from a Video
(Video-to-Image Conversion)

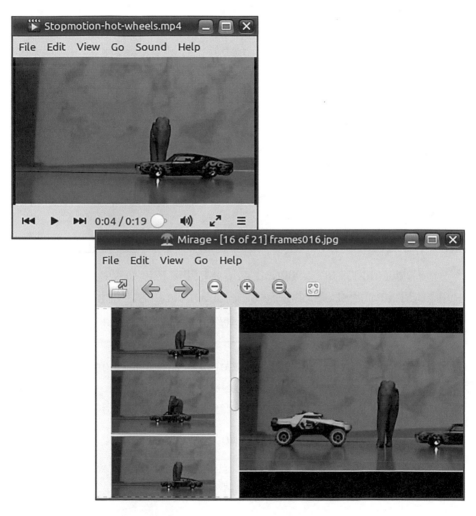

Figure 5-4. *A video and the still-image frames extracted from it*

To extract video frames as image files, you need to use the `-f image2` option. The numbering of the output images is specified in the name of the output file. The format mask of the output file is similar to that of the `printf` function in the C programming language. In the mask used in the next command, `%` is for character output, `0` is for padding with zeros instead of spaces, `3` is for the total number of digits, and `d` is for integer numbers.

```
# Extract images at the rate of 1 frame per second from
the video
ffmpeg -y -i Stopmotion-hot-wheels.mp4 \
       -r 1 \
       -f image2 \
       frames%03d.jpg 2> /dev/null
```

☞   Most videos are encoded with a frame rate of 24, 25, 30, or even 60 frames per second. Be careful with your extraction rate and length of the video, or you will quickly run out of space.

Use the `-r` option to restrict the number of images generated for each second of the source video. You can omit the `-r` option to extract all frames (and let it be determined by the frame rate of the source video) but

- Use small video clips as the source

- Use `-t` and `-ss` options (described in Chapter 6) to restrict the extracted duration of the source video

Image-Conversion Settings

Table 5-2 lists some FFmpeg conversion options that are useful when working with image files. Although this book will describe how to use them, more comprehensive information will be found in the official FFmpeg documentation.

Table 5-2. *ffmpeg image-conversion options and examples*

Option	Purpose
-f image2	Force conversion to and from images
-f image2pipe	Force image conversion for output piped over to another command
-loop 1	Repeat the processing of the input image indefinitely
-pix_fmt yuv420p	Use yuv420p pixel format when converting to image formats

Create Video from Images (Image-to-Video Conversion)

FFmpeg can also do the reverse by creating a video from several images (when they are numbered serially). The duration of the video depends on the number of images available and frame rate you have specified. If the -r option in the video-to-image conversion was higher (in the previous command), say between 12 and 30, a lot more images would have been extracted, and this video would have been smoother.

```
ffmpeg -r 1 -i frames%03d.jpg \
       -s qvga -pix_fmt yuv420p \
       Stopmotion-hot-wheels-reconstituted.mp4 2> /dev/null

ffplay -autoexit \
       Stopmotion-hot-wheels-reconstituted.mp4 2> /dev/null
```

☞   All input images should be of the same format and dimensions.

☞   The `-pix_fmt yuv420p` option is necessary to ensure such unusual video files play all right in most media player devices.

Create a Slideshow from Several Images

In the previous section, the output video ran out quickly because there were not many input images. If you want each input image to appear for longer than a second, then you need to specify a `-framerate` option for them as well. An input frame rate of 1/3 ensures that a frame plays for 3 seconds.

```
ffmpeg -y -framerate 1/3 -i image%02d.jpg \
        -filter:v \
            "scale=eval=frame:w=640:h=480:
            force_original_aspect_ratio=decrease,
            pad=640:480:(ow-iw)/2:(oh-ih)/2:yellow" \
        -pix_fmt yuv420p -r 24 \
        slide.mp4
```

☞   You will learn more about filters in Chapter 7.

The preceding command also takes care of images with irregular dimensions and ensures that they are resized appropriately.

Figure 5-5. *This video was created from several disproportionate images*

When you have input images in no particular naming sequence, then you can pipe them like this:

```
cat *.png | \
    ffmpeg -y -f image2pipe \
        -framerate 1/3 -i - \
        -filter:v \
```

```
    "scale=eval=frame:w=640:h=360:
    force_original_aspect_ratio=decrease,
    pad=640:360:(ow-iw)/2:(oh-ih)/2:black" \
-c:v libx264 -r 24 -s nhd -pix_fmt yuv420p \
slide2.mp4
```

Create a GIF from a Video

The ancient GIF format supports only 256 colors. You need to use
palettegen and paletteuse filters to downsample the source video to this
limited number of colors.

```
ffmpeg -y  -i bw.m4v \
    -filter_complex \
      "fps=7,scale=w=320:h=-1:flags=lanczos,split[v1][v2];
      [v1]palettegen=stats_mode=diff[p];
      [v2][p]paletteuse=dither=bayer:bayer_scale=4" \
    bw-4.gif
```

You need to experiment a lot with the filters to understand what will
work and what will not. A set of values that do well to optimize the file size
for one source video may do poorly for another video. GIF optimization is
extremely unpredictable. Learn more from this article:

```
https://engineering.giphy.com/how-to-make-
gifs-with-ffmpeg/
```

In an experiment with the production of a GIF file from a video, I
found that

- With a bayer_scale of 0 (with the dither=bayer
  mode), the animation is smooth but suffers from the
  appearance of a dotted texture. The file size is on the
  higher side.

- When moving to the highest value of 5 (default is 2), the frames are clearer but start to suffer from intermittent banding. The file size is smaller.

The results may be quite different for another video file.

If you are stuck with an older version of FFmpeg that does not have the `palettegen` and `paletteuse` filters, you can make FFmpeg output the frames to ImageMagick (`convert` or `magick`). (The hyphens in the following command refer to standard output and input.)

```
ffmpeg -y -i bw.m4v \
       -filter:v "fps=10,scale=w=320:h=-1:flags=lanczos" \
       -c:v ppm \
       -f image2pipe - | \
  convert -delay 10 - \
          -loop 0 \
          -layers optimize \
          bw.gif
```

APNG

A better alternative to GIF animations is APNG. This format has limited support from image-viewing and image-editing applications but has near-universal support from desktop and mobile web browsers. Like PNG and unlike GIF, APNG supports millions of colours. This means that its colours will not have to be downsampled and will be very close to those in the source content. APNG animation files are typically bigger than animated GIFs.

If you are converting GIF animations to APNGs, then ImageMagick is the tool you should use, not `ffmpeg`.

```
magick animated.gif animated.apng
```

The image frames in a GIF will already be downsampled to 256 colours. To create a richer animated PNG, try to use the source frames in PNG format.

```
magick -delay 200 -loop 0 \
        chapter-image-*.png \
        -units PixelsPerInch -density 72 -resize '>x300' \
        animation-unlikely-stories.apng
```

If you are converting a video to APNG, then you can use `ffmpeg`.

```
ffmpeg -i bw.m4v \
        -vf "scale=w=250:h=-2, hqdn3d, fps=6" \
        -dpi 72 -plays 0 \
        bw.apng
```

In this command, `-dpi` is an APNG encoder option and `-plays` is an APNG muxer option. The *high-quality denoise 3d* filter reduces blemishes introduced by the scaling filter. Learn more about these options from the official documentation or by typing:

```
ffmpeg -help muxer=apng
ffmpeg -help encoder=png
ffmpeg -help filter=hqdn3d
```

Create a Video Using an Image and an MP3

How do you play an MP3 in a media player that will only play MP4 files? Find a thumbnail or album art for the MP3 and churn it out as a video. The following command uses an image as a video stream encoded with MJPEG codec.

```
ffmpeg -i Blobfish_face.jpg -i blobfish.mp3 \
       -c:v mjpeg -c:a copy \
       -map 0:v:0 -map 1:a:0 \
       -disposition:v:0 attached_pic \
       "Weird Fins - 17 - The Blobfish.mp4"
```

This command generates only one image frame in the MP4. The image frame is not encoded as a regular video stream for the entire duration of the audio.

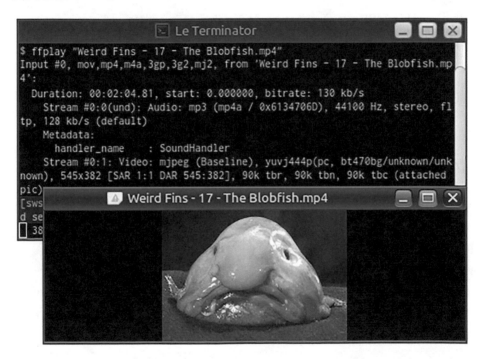

Figure 5-6. *This video does not really have any video, just one frame from an image*

However, not all media players will accept this trickery. On my computer, Totem media player does not show the image at all and plays it like a regular audio file. VLC displays the image because it uses FFmpeg internally. If your player shirks its duty, you will have to encode the image for the full duration of the audio.

```
ffmpeg -y -i  blobfish.mp3 \
  -loop 1 -framerate 12 -i Blobfish_face.jpg \
  -shortest -s qvga -c:a copy \
  -c:v libx264 -pix_fmt yuv420p \
  "Weird Fins - 17 - The Blobfish (no tricks).mp4"
# The album art image loops forever so the
# podcast audio creates the shortest output stream
```

☞   This MP3 was part of 18 MP3 files of the "Weird Fins" podcast published by the US NOAA. It got lost and buried when they redesigned their site. Some years ago, I recovered these files, tagged them and uploaded them to Archive.org.

Convert Online Videos to Audio

YouTube-DL is an open source command-line program that can download online videos for offline use. It supports several online video sites. Many journalists use it to grab still images for their articles about Internet videos. However, the entertainment industry has decided to challenge the legal status of this utility. The Electronic Frontier Foundation (EFF) and surprisingly GitHub (owned by Microsoft) have come up with a defense initiative for its survival.

```
https://youtube-dl.org
```

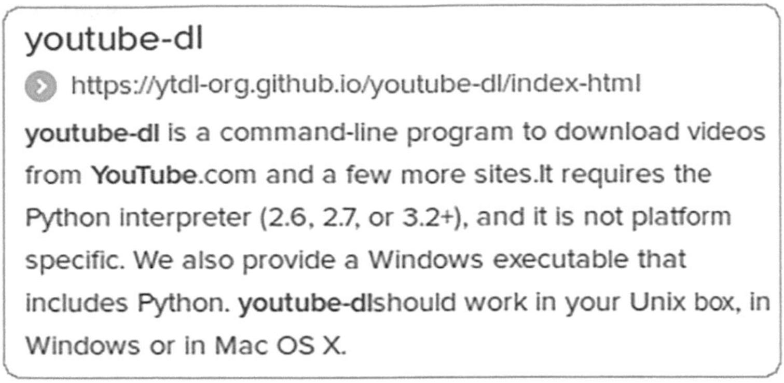

> ### youtube-dl
>
> 🔵 https://ytdl-org.github.io/youtube-dl/index-html
>
> **youtube-dl** is a command-line program to download videos from **YouTube**.com and a few more sites.It requires the Python interpreter (2.6, 2.7, or 3.2+), and it is not platform specific. We also provide a Windows executable that includes Python. **youtube-dl**should work in your Unix box, in Windows or in Mac OS X.

Figure 5-7. *This is a description of youtube-dl published by a search engine*

Assuming that your ~/bin directory is in the $PATH environment variable, you can install youtube-dl locally using the following:

```
wget https://yt-dl.org/downloads/latest/youtube-dl \
    -O ~/bin/youtube-dl

chmod +x ~/bin/youtube-dl

youtube-dl --version
```

☞   YouTube-DL will run from anywhere. You do not have to install the file to a privileged location like the site says.

☞   If youtube-dl does not run, maybe Python 3 is not in the PATH. Start it with /usr/bin/python3 youtube-dl ....

You can make youtube-dl use ffmpeg to convert the downloaded files. Many audio podcasts are posted to online video sites. To only listen to them in the Audacious media player, I use a command like this:

```
youtube-dl -f 140 -x \
           --audio-format mp3 \
           --exec 'audacious {} & ' \
           https://www.youtube.com/watch?v=yypDkqAErx0
```

youtube-dl will not only download and convert the audio (from AAC) to MP3 (using ffmpeg), but it will also launch a command when the conversion process is complete. That command can be for your media player. youtube-dl will replace {} in the command string with the name of the output (MP3) file.

Convert Text to Audio

If your ffmpeg executable has been built-in with support for the libflite text-to-speech synthesizer library, then you can convert text content to spoken words.

```
ffmpeg -f lavfi \
       -i "flite=textfile=speech.txt:voice=slt" \
       speech.mp3
```

This speech filter supports several voices. On my computer, it lists awb, kal, kal16, rms, and slt as available voices. Unfortunately, the female voice sounds a bit dopey.

```
ffprobe -f lavfi "flite=list_voices=1"
```

I like the male-only espeak utility better. The defaults are good, and you can change several settings.

Conversion Settings for Specific Storage Medium

If you use the -target option, certain conversion settings appropriate for the specified storage option will be applied. The values for this option can be vcd, svcd, dvd, dv, and dv50. They can be prefixed with ntsc, pal, or film for more specific targets. For the actual settings used by these targets, refer the official FFmpeg documentation.

```
ffmpeg -i movie.avi -target ntsc-dvd movie.mpg
```

☞   VCD (MPEG-1), DVD (MPEG-2), and DV (digital tape) are very old targets and consume more space than MPEG-4.

☞   If you want to extract still images from movies, optical media is usually the best source.

Summary

In this chapter, you learned how to convert multimedia content in the form of audio, video, image, and text. You also learned to customize conversion settings to suit different formats, coder/decoders, and mediums. In the next chapter, you will learn how to edit videos using ffmpeg.

CHAPTER 6

Editing Videos

I used to save DVDs as ISO files (whole-DVD backups) so that I could play them on my media player box. Each ISO took up several gigabytes (GBs) on my hard disk that I eventually ran out of space. Now, I use FFmpeg and store DVDs as MP4s of around just one GB.

While FFmpeg makes it very easy to convert multimedia files, as you learned in the previous chapter, storing them in their entity is not always feasible or required. Sometimes, you need just a few clips, not the whole shebang. You may want to combine parts of one video with parts of other videos. You can also downsize the videos to conserve space. In `ffmpeg` terms, you want to cut, concatenate, and resize videos. In this chapter, you will learn to do just that.

Resize a Video

You can resize a video using the `-s` option. The dimension of a video is usually specified as *WidthxHeight*. That is an "x" as in "x-mas" in the middle. When editing or converting videos, you will have to specify the video dimension using this syntax. The next command resizes a VGA-size (640x480) video to a VCD-size (352x288) video.

```
ffmpeg -i dialup.mp4 \
       -s 352x288 \
       dialup.mpg
```

© V. Subhash 2023
V. Subhash, *Quick Start Guide to FFmpeg*, https://doi.org/10.1007/978-1-4842-8701-9_6

FFmpeg supports certain easy-to-remember literals that you can use in place of the actual numbers for the -s option. They are listed in Table 6-1.

Table 6-1. *FFmpeg option and values for setting the dimensions of a video*

Option	For					
-s	Video dimensions (literal or actual)					
	Literal	Dimensions	Literal	Dimensions	Literal	Dimensions
	ntsc	720x480	uxga	1600x1200	hd1080	1920x1080
	pal	720x576	qxga	2048x1536	2k	2048x1080
	qntsc	352x240	sxga	1280x1024	2kflat	1998x1080
	qpal	352x288	qsxga	2560x2048	2kscope	2048x858
	sntsc	640x480	hsxga	5120x4096	4k	4096x2160
	spal	768x576	wvga	852x480	4kflat	3996x2160
	film	352x240	wxga	1366x768	4kscope	4096x1716
	ntsc-film	352x240	wsxga	1600x1024	nhd	640x360
	sqcif	128x96	wuxga	1920x1200	hqvga	240x160
	qcif	176x144	woxga	2560x1600	wqvga	400x240
	cif	352x288	wqsxga	3200x2048	fwqvga	432x240
	4cif	704x576	wquxga	3840x2400	hvga	480x320
	16cif	1408x1152	whsxga	6400x4096	qhd	960x540
	qqvga	160x120	whuxga	7680x4800	2kdci	2048x1080
	qvga	320x240	cga	320x200	4kdci	4096x2160
	vga	640x480	ega	640x350	uhd2160	3840x2160
	svga	800x600	hd480	852x480	uhd4320	7680x4320
	xga	1024x768	hd720	1280x720		

A video's horizontal dimension divided by the vertical dimension is sometimes referred to as the **aspect ratio**. This is further influenced by the dimensions of individual pixels that make up the video. (Remember that a video frame is a matrix of dots or pixels in lines and columns.) This pixel-level aspect ratio is known as the **sample aspect ratio (SAR)**.

When a video is resized, `ffmpeg` (or whichever video authoring software that is used) would have automatically adjusted the pixel dimensions (or the SAR) from square to rectangular so that the video will be played with the proper aspect ratio.

If you want a video to be played at a particular aspect ratio, you need to set the **display aspect ratio (DAR)**. This value is calculated from the width-and-height ratio multiplied by the SAR. If for some reason, the SAR value is not present in the video, it is assumed to be 1. If this makes the video distorted, set the desired DAR using the `setdar` filter and let `ffmpeg` figure out the internal SAR.

```
ffmpeg -i "distorted.mpg" \
        -vf setdar=dar=4/3 \
        restored.mpg
```

   You will learn more about filters in Chapter 7.

Figure 6-1. *The distortion in the background video was fixed using a filter that changed the DAR (display aspect ratio)*

These ratios may seem similar but there are subtle differences, as presented in Table 6-2.

Table 6-2. *Terms related to video dimensions*

Term	Description
Aspect ratio	= video width ÷ video height
	Standard definition ratio is 4:3. For widescreen, it is 16:9
Sample aspect ratio (SAR) a.k.a **pixel aspect ratio**	= pixel width ÷ pixel height
	For square pixels, it is 1. For rectangular pixels, it will be a fraction
Display aspect ratio (DAR)	= (video width ÷ video height) × sample aspect ratio or = video aspect ratio × sample aspect ratio

Editing Options

Some often used video- and audio-editing options are listed in Table 6-3.

Table 6-3. *More ffmpeg options for editing*

Option	For
-t	Duration (in hh:mm:ss[.xxx] format or in seconds) of the output file
-ss	Timestamp of playback location (in hh:mm:ss[.xxx] format or in seconds) from which processing needs to be performed
-c:v, -c:a, -c:s	Use specified encoder (not codec) for specific type of stream
	If you use the value copy as in -c copy, ffmpeg will not use an encoder and just copy the stream(s)

Cut a Portion of a Video

If the video segment that you want to remove is the beginning, then use the -ss option to specify the timestamp from which the content needs to be copied.

```
ffmpeg -ss 00:01:00 -i sponsored-video.mp4 \
       the-video.mp4
```

☞   Use the -ss option before the -i option so that ffmpeg can quickly jump to the location of the specified timestamp. If you place it after the input file and before the output file, there will be a delay as ffmpeg decodes all the data from the beginning to the timestamp and then discards it (as it is not wanted)!

The timestamp values can be specified in the format hh:mm:ss.ms. Parts that are zero in the beginning can be omitted, as shown in Table 6-4.

Table 6-4. *Examples of time or duration values*

Usage	Implication
20	20 seconds
1:20	One minute and 20 seconds
02:01:20	Two hours, 1 minute, and 20 seconds
02:01:20.220	Two hours, 1 minute, 20 seconds, and 220 milliseconds
20.020	20 seconds and 20 milliseconds

☞   Before the milliseconds value, there needs to be a dot, not a colon.

If the video segment that you want to remove is the ending, then use -t option to specify the duration of the content that needs to be copied from the beginning.

```
ffmpeg -i long-tail.mp4 \
    -t 00:01:00 \
    no-monkey.mp4
```

If you want to cut from the middle, then you need to use both options.

```
ffmpeg -ss 00:01:00 -i side-burns.mp4 \
    -t 00:1:10 \
    clean-shaved.mp4
```

In this case, ffmpeg starts cutting -t duration of content from the timestamp specified by the -ss option, not from the beginning.

All of these commands will re-encode the video. Because the (raw) source video (from which the input video was created) is not being used, the output video will have lesser quality and have freshly introduced blemishes and artifacts.

You may encounter another problem here. When you do not specify conversion settings, then FFmpeg will use its own default encoder settings. If your uncut video had better quality than encoder defaults, then you may end up with lesser quality. If the input file had lower quality, then the encoder defaults may result in increased file size.

To avoid such problems, run ffprobe on the input file and use similar conversion settings with ffmpeg.

```
~/Desktop
$ ffprobe lucas.mp4
Input #0, mov,mp4,m4a,3gp,3g2,mj2, from 'lucas.mp4':
  Duration: 00:00:20.02, start: 0.000000, bitrate: 575 kb/s
    Stream #0:0(und): Video: h264 (Constrained Baseline) (avc1 / 0x3163
661), yuv420p, 640x360 [SAR 1:1 DAR 16:9] 472 kb/s, 29.97 fps, 29.97 t
r, 30k tbn, 59.94 tbc
    Metadata:
      handler_name    : VideoHandler
    Stream #0:1(eng): Audio: aac (mp4a / 0x6134706D), 44100 Hz, stereo,
fltp, 96 kb/s
    Metadata:
      handler_name    : SoundHandler

~/Desktop
$ ffmpeg -i lucas.mp4 \
>         -vcodec libx264 -b:v 472k -r:v 30 \
>         -acodec libfaac -b:a 96k \
>         -t 0:0:10 \
>         lucas-cut.mp4
```

Figure 6-2. *The ffprobe output shows settings that you can use for the next ffmpeg task*

Cut Without Re-encoding

Apart from losing quality, re-encoding takes time. Cutting without re-encoding does not have these disadvantages. Use the option `-codec copy` to ensure there is no re-encoding and the original quality is retained.

```
ffmpeg -ss 00:01:00 -i dog-eared.mp4 \
       -t 00:1:10 \
       -codec copy \
       clean-cut.mp4
```

There are disadvantages with this option too. The entirety of the audio and video information may not be present at the timestamps you have specified for FFmpeg to make a clean cut. A few seconds of the video may have to be sacrificed or go out of sync. Out-of-sync audio by one or two seconds is not really a problem in videos where the speaker remains in the background.

Use `-codec copy` only when the container of the output file supports the existing codec of the input stream you are trying to copy. You cannot copy streams from an OGV file to a MP4 file, but you can do that with an MKV output file. First, check whether input codecs are among the default codecs listed by the muxer of the output container.

```
ffmpeg -help muxer=matroska | head -5 ; \
ffmpeg -help muxer=ogv | head -5; \
ffmpeg -help muxer=avi | head -5 ; \
ffmpeg -help muxer=mp4 | head -5
```

These commands list the default extensions and codecs used by some popular containers.

```
Muxer matroska [Matroska]:
    Common extensions: mkv.
    Mime type: video/x-matroska.
    Default video codec: h264.
    Default audio codec: vorbis.
Muxer ogv [Ogg Video]:
    Common extensions: ogv.
    Mime type: video/ogg.
    Default video codec: theora.
    Default audio codec: vorbis.
Muxer avi [AVI (Audio Video Interleaved)]:
    Common extensions: avi.
    Mime type: video/x-msvideo.
    Default video codec: mpeg4.
    Default audio codec: mp3.
Muxer mp4 [MP4 (MPEG-4 Part 14)]:
    Common extensions: mp4.
    Mime type: video/mp4.
    Default video codec: h264.
    Default audio codec: aac.
```

Append Videos (Concatenate)

If you need to put together several videos to create one big video containing all of them, then you can use the `concat` demuxer. To use it, you need to first create a text file containing file names or full pathnames of the input videos. The file details should be formatted like this:

- One line should be used for each input file.

- The relative or absolute pathname of a file should be wrapped in quotation marks and preceded by the word "file."

```
file '/tmp/video.mp4'
file '/home/yourname/Desktop/video1.mp4'
file '/media/USB1/DCIM/DS00002.mp4'
```

Ideally, the file locations should be relative to the current directory and have simple file names. Because these files do not satisfy that condition, I have used the option `-safe 0` in this `ffmpeg` command. The next command will re-encode the preceding input files using the specified MP4 settings.

```
ffmpeg -f concat \
       -safe 0 \
       -i list.txt \
       -c:v libx264 -r 24 -b:v 266k -s qvga \
       -c:a libmp3lame -r:a 44000 -b:a 64k -ac 2 \
       mixology.mp4
```

☞   The default for the `-safe` option is 1. In production environments, it prevents rogue users from using files that would otherwise crash FFmpeg-based software systems.

☞   Use the `-f concat` option setting before the `-i` option.

I advise against the use `-f concat` demuxer. The output files have a tendency to confuse and crash media players. If input videos are not of the same type, the concatenation will fail or the output file will not be playable. The same thing can happen if some of the input files are `-codec copy` veterans. You are lucky if conversion starts at all. If you are forced to use the `concat` demuxer, then read about it in the official documentation. The text file supports other directives (not just `file`) to make it more informative to the demuxer.

For more resilient concatenations, use the `concat` filter as described in Chapter 7.

```
ffmpeg -i engine.mp4 -i coach.mp4 \
    -filter_complex \
    "[0:v:0][0:a:0][1:v:0][1:a:0]concat=n=2:v=1:a=1[v][a]" \
    -map '[v]' -map '[a]' \
    -c:v libx264 -r 24 -b:v 266k -s qvga \
    -c:a libmp3lame -b:a 64k -ac 2 \
    -f mp4 \
    train.mp4
```

Whether you use -codec copy or the concat filter, all the input files should be of the same type (same dimensions, codecs, frame rates, etc.).

Don't Knock `-codec copy`

After spending considerable time with FFmpeg, you will realize that a lot of multimedia software generate audio/video files that seem to play fine but have a lot of internal encoding errors. Strangely enough, FFmpeg's notorious `-codec copy` option fixes a good many of these container errors.

```
ffmpeg -i smugly.mp4 -codec copy smooth.mp4
```

Summary

FFmpeg provides some very neat options to edit multimedia files from the command line. With some files, you may be able to `-codec copy` the streams. With others, you will have to re-encode them. Both methods have advantages and disadvantages.

In the next chapter, you will finally learn about the `ffmpeg` filters that I have been all along teasing you with.

CHAPTER 7

Using FFmpeg Filters

In the previous chapters, you would have encountered several filters. A great deal of FFmpeg functionality is hidden in them. Most users avoid filters or use them sparingly because the online examples of filters tend to be cryptic. There is a method to the madness. You can crack it. In this chapter, you will learn what filters are and how to use them.

Filter Construction

In an `ffmpeg` command, a filter is used to perform advanced processing on the multimedia and metadata data decoded from the input file(s). A **simple filter** consumes an input stream, processes it, and generates an output stream. The input and output will be of the same type. An **audio filter** (used with the option `-filter:a` or `-af`) consumes an audio stream and outputs an audio stream. A **video filter** (specified by a `filter:v` or `-vf` option) consumes a video stream and outputs a video stream.

You can daisy-chain multiple simple filters to create a **filter chain**. In such a filter chain, the output of one filter is consumed by a subsequent filter. Thus, as a whole, the filter chain will also have one input and one output.

When such a linear filter chain is not possible, you need to use a **complex filtergraph** (with the option `-filter_complex`). A complex filtergraph can contain several filters or filter chains. The constituent filters can have zero to several inputs. They can consume streams of different types and output streams of different types. The number of inputs need not match the number of outputs. It is not necessary for a filter to consume the output of the previous filter.

© V. Subhash 2023
V. Subhash, *Quick Start Guide to FFmpeg*, https://doi.org/10.1007/978-1-4842-8701-9_7

Some filters known as **source filters** do not have inputs. There are also **sink filters** that do not generate any outputs.

In an ffmpeg command, you specify a filter in this fashion:

```
[input label1][input label2]...[input_labelN]filter=
key1=value1:key2=value2...keyN=valueN[output label1]
[output label2]...[output labelN];
```

You need to follow these rules when using filters:

- When a filter is expected to create an output stream, label it with a name in square brackets ([ ]).

- Use these labeled output streams as inputs for other filters or use them in -map options. ffmpeg automatically names the unlabeled input of the first filter as [in] and the unlabeled output of the last filter as [out].

- Between two filters that are part of a linear filter chain (when you daisy-chain them), use a comma (,) as a delimiter. This implies that the output of the first filter is to be consumed as input by the second filter.

- Between two filters that are part of a nonlinear complex filtergraph, use a semicolon (;) as a delimiter. Specify the inputs and outputs using stream identifiers or labels for each filter. If you do not specify input streams, ffmpeg will select streams using an internal logic. (Read the official FFmpeg documentation about it.) If the selected input stream cannot be used by the filter, ffmpeg will encounter an error. Similarly, when you do not label the output streams, ffmpeg will attempt to dump them in the next output file. If the container of the next output file does not support those output streams, ffmpeg will encounter an error.

- Specify filter-specific options as key-value pairs. You
  need to use a colon (:) as a delimiter between them.
  You can omit the option names (keys) and only
  use values if you specify them in the same order as
  specified in the official FFmpeg documentation or help
  output. This cryptic style is error-prone, difficult to
  understand, and therefore not recommended.

☞   There are lots of filters and you need to pore over pages of
documentation to find the one that will work for you.

Filter Errors

Sometimes, you will encounter a "No such filter" error. This is probably
because (out of habit) you placed a semicolon after the last filter. Some
filters have an exact number of inputs or outputs. If you fail to identify one
of them, `ffmpeg` will throw an error. Other common filter errors are caused
when a labeled input or output is not consumed. If you use an output label
more than once, you will get an 'Invalid stream specifier' error. An output
stream can only be labelled once and used once. If you want to use a filter
output stream as input for more than one filter, use the `split` or `asplit`
filters to duplicate the stream.

Filter-Based Timeline Editing

Many filters support a generic `enable` option. It can be used to specify the
start and end timestamps when the filter should be applied. For example,
the option `enable='between(t, 6, 12)'` would ensure that the filter is
applied on the video between 6th and 12th seconds of the audio or video.

☞   In the output for `ffmpeg -filters` command, the filters with the flag "T" support timeline editing.

Expressions in FFmpeg Filter Definitions

In the values of some filter options, you can specify algebraic expressions that combine explicit numbers, functions, and some *constants*. (The last two are listed in Table 7-1.) The section *Expression Evaluation* in the documentation describes several functions that can be used in the expressions. FFmpeg defines three *constants* that can be used in any filter.

Table 7-1. *Functions and constants used in ffmpeg filter expressions*

Functions			
abs(x)	floor(expr)	log(x)	sin(x)
acos(x)	gauss(x)	lt(x, y)	sinh(x)
asin(x)	gcd(x, y)	lte(x, y)	sqrt(expr)
atan(x)	gt(x, y)	max(x, y)	squish(x)
atan2(x, y)	gte(x, y)	min(x, y)	st(var, expr)
between(x, min, max)	hypot(x, y)	mod(x, y)	tan(x)
bitand(x, y)	if(x, y)	not(expr)	tanh(x)
bitor(x, y)	if(x, y, z)	pow(x, y)	taylor(expr, x)
ceil(expr)	ifnot(x, y)	print(t)	taylor(expr, x, id)
clip(x, min, max)	ifnot(x, y, z)	print(t, l)	time(0)
cos(x)	isinf(x)	random(x)	trunc(expr)
cosh(x)	isnan(x)	root(expr, max)	while(cond, expr)
eq(x, y)	ld(var)	round(expr)	
exp(x)	lerp(x, y, z)	sgn(x)	
Constants			
PI	E	PHI	QP2LAMBDA
(22/7)	(Euler's number or exp(1) ~ 2.718)	(golden ratio or (1+sqrt(5))/2 ~ 1.618)	118

Several filters define their own *constants*. These are actually real-time variables whose values can change depending on the input files, the processing options, or even time. You need to look at the documentation for each filter to see what these filter constants represent.

☞   You should try to become proficient in the use of filter expressions. They are force multipliers.

☞   When you specify a filter within double quotes (" "), the commas separating the parameters of a function will have to be escaped as `\,` to prevent `ffmpeg` from interpreting them as delimiters used to separate two filters.

Inset Video (Picture-in-Picture Overlay)

Sometimes, people in news media need to use a sign-language inset video. The following `ffmpeg` command scales down a video containing the sign-language track and positions it over the right corner of a news report.

```
ffmpeg -y -i Delphine.mp4 -i accessibility.mp4  \
  -filter_complex \
    "[1:v]scale=w=150:h=150[inset];
    [0:v][inset]overlay=x=W-w-20:y=20[v]" \
  -map '[v]' -map 0:a:0 \
  Delphine-with-accessibility.mp4
```

This command may also be written without the names and only the values of the filter options.

```
ffmpeg -y -i Delphine.mp4 -i accessibility.mp4  \
  -filter_complex \
    "[1:v]scale=150:150[inset];
    [0:v][inset]overlay=W-w-20:20[v]" \
  -map '[v]' -map 0:a:0 \
  Delphine-with-accessibility.mp4
```

☞   If you encounter such commands, they will seem very cryptic. You will have to look up the filter in the official documentation or the help output (`ffmpeg -help filter=scale`) and ascertain the order of the used filter options.

Figure 7-1. *The* `overlay` *filter has been used to place the sign-language video track in the top-right corner of a news report video*

The `scale` filter specifies actual width and height values (`150:150`) to which the inset video needs to be resized. The `overlay` filter specifies x- and y-coordinates of the top-left corner of the inset video on the news report video. The x-coordinate uses a *filter expression* (`W-w-20`) with *filter constants* `W` (width of the background video) and `w` (width of the inset video) to correctly inset the video 20 pixels away from the right edge of the background video. The y-coordinate is specified with the actual value, that is, 20 pixels from the top edge.

89

The input for the scale filter is the inset video ([1:v] or the video stream of the second input file). Its output is labeled [inset]. The inputs for the overlay filter are the news report ([0:v] or the video stream of the first file) and the output of the scale filter labeled previously as [inset]. The overlay filter has one output and it is labeled [v]. This overlaid video and the original audio of the news report (0:a:0) are then mapped into the output file.

To construct a *filter expression* with useful *filter constants*, you need to refer to the documentation of the filter. If these expressions try to hurt your brain (they will initially), you can specify explicit values. The preceding command can be rewritten as follows:

```
ffmpeg -y -i Delphine.mp4 -i accessibility.mp4  \
  -filter_complex \
     "[1:v]scale=150:150[inset];
      [0:v][inset]overlay=370:20[v]" \
  -map '[v]' -map 0:a:0 \
  Delphine-with-accessibility.mp4
```

Split Video (Side-by-Side Overlay)

When you place two videos side-by-side, their heights should be the same. If you place them one above the other, their widths should be the same. Else, there will be some empty space in the final video.

The sign-language video in the previous section is a 332×332-pixel video. It is smaller than the news report video. If we want them placed side-by-side, the news report video's height needs to be reduced to the height of the sign-language video.

This scale filter in this ffmpeg command does that. To maintain the same aspect ratio (width ÷ height) of the scaled video, the new width is specified using the filter expression 332*iw/ih. (The value -2 would have worked as well. As to how it would, **R**efer **T**he **F**ine **M**anual. ☺) This multiplies the aspect ratio with the new height. (`iw` and `ih` represent filter constants for the width and height of the input video.)

```
ffmpeg -y -i Delphine.mp4 -i accessibility.mp4 \
        -filter_complex "[0:v]scale=332*iw/ih:332[sv];
                         [sv]pad=(iw+332):332:0:0[frame];
                         [frame][1:v]overlay=W-w:0[v]" \
        -map '[v]' -map 0:a:0 \
        Delphine-et-accessibility.mp4
```

Figure 7-2. *The* scale *filter was used to reduce the height of the first video. The pad filter has been used to expand the frame of the scaled video. The* overlay *filter has been used to place the second video in the empty area of the expanded frame*

☞   Because the second video is a sign-language video, I discarded its audio. If it were needed, I would have mixed the two audio streams or assigned them to the left and right speaker channels, as described in Chapter 8.

After the `scale` filter, the frame size of the scaled video is expanded sideways so that the second video can be placed in the new empty area. The `pad` filter uses the expression `iw+332` to arrive at the new expanded size of the frame. It then places the scaled video at the top-left corner (`0:0`) of the new frame. That is, the scaled video will be on the left side of the expanded frame.

In the empty area on the right side of the expanded frame (`[frame]`), we place the second input file (`[1:v]`) using the `overlay` filter.

Without using filter expression, the last `ffmpeg` command can be rewritten with actual values as follows:

```
ffmpeg -y -i Delphine.mp4 -i accessibility.mp4 \
       -filter_complex "[0:v]scale=498:332[sv];
                        [sv]pad=830:332:0:0[frame];
                        [frame][1:v]overlay=498:0[v]" \
       -map '[v]' -map 0:a:0 \
       Delphine-et-accessibility.mp4
```

☞   When you want to use the same command on another set of files with different dimensions, you will have to recalculate and re-specify the values. Filter expressions can eliminate a lot of this hassle so use them when you can.

If you do not want the news video to be downscaled, then you could put some white space... (in this case) yellow space around the second video. In the next command, filter expressions and actual values have been used to correctly position the second video in the middle of the expanded frame.

```
ffmpeg -y -i Delphine.mp4 -i accessibility.mp4 \
  -filter_complex
    "[0:v:0]pad=w=(iw+360):h=ih:x=0:y=0:color=yellow[frame];
    [frame][1:v:0]overlay=x=W-360+(360-w)/2:y=(H-h)/2[v]" \
  -map '[v]' -map 0:a:0 \
  -t 0:0:12 -pix_fmt yuv420p \
  Delphine-et-accessibility-et-margin.mp4
```

☞ It is much more easier and faster to use the filters `hstack` and `vstack`. However, these filters require the input videos to have the same pixel format (data encoding scheme of pixel color) and the same dimensions (height for `hstack` and width for `vstack`.)

Figure 7-3. *The pad filter was used to expand the width of original frame by 360 pixels while maintaining the same height. The expanded area was given a yellow background that was 360×360 pixels. Using filter expressions with the* overlay *filter, the 332×332-pixel second video was placed right in the middle of the yellow background*

Append Videos Using a Filter

In Chapter 6, you learned to concatenate several videos using the `concat` demuxer. The `concat` filter provides more control if you have only a few input files.

```
ffmpeg -i engine.mp4 -i coach.mp4 \
  -filter_complex \
    '[0:v:0][0:a:0][1:v:0][1:a:0]concat=n=2:v=1:a=1[vo][ao]' \
  -map '[vo]' -map '[ao]' \
  -c:v libx264 -r 24 -b:v 266k -s qvga \
  -f mp4 train.mp4
```

☞   This will re-encode the input files, as will any other filter.

Specify the video and audio streams of the input clips or segments in the order that they need to be appended by the filter. `[0:v:0][0:a:0]` refers to the video and audio streams of the first input clip. `[1:v:0]` `[1:a:0]` refers to the video and audio streams of the second clip. The filter option n refers to the number of input clips. v refers to the number of output video streams, and a refers to the number of output audio streams. The concatenated video and audio streams are the filter outputs labeled as `[vo]` and `[ao]`. These labeled outputs are then mapped to the output file.

Delete a Portion of a Video in the Middle

Sometimes, you need to delete part of a video. For that, you can use the `trim`, `atrim`, and `concat` filters. In this command, the second scene (between seconds 16 and 36) is deleted by eliminating it using `trim` and `atrim` filters.

```
ffmpeg -y -i barbara.mp4 \
  -filter_complex \
    "[0:v:0]trim=start=0:end=16, setpts=PTS-STARTPTS[lv];
     [0:v:0]trim=start=36:end=44, setpts=PTS-STARTPTS[rv];
     [0:a:0]atrim=start=0:end=16, asetpts=PTS-STARTPTS[la];
     [0:a:0]atrim=start=36:end=44, asetpts=PTS-STARTPTS[ra];
     [lv][rv]concat=n=2:v=1:a=0[v];
     [la][ra]concat=n=2:v=0:a=1[a]" \
  -map '[v]' -map '[a]' barb-cut.mp4
```

☞   I have used seconds instead of timestamps because the "hh:mm:ss" format requires a lot of nonintuitive escaping.

The concat filter is prone to timestamp errors. The setpts and asetpts filters may be able to fix them. A filter setting with asetpts=N/SAMPLE_RATE/TB will generate new timestamps by counting actual samples in the processed audio segments, but it can be used only with constant frame rate videos. A better value is to use PTS-STARTPTS (similar to the video filter), as it will also remove empty regions in the audio.

Rotate a Video

Some videos that people take from a mobile phone are rotated by 90 or 180 degrees from normal. You can manually fix them by specifying a transpose filter.

```
# Rotate to right
ffmpeg -i slt.mp4 \
        -filter:v "transpose=1" \
        slt-rotated-1.mp4
```

```
# Rotate to left
ffmpeg -i slt.mp4 \
        -filter:v "transpose=2" \
        slt-rotated-2.mp4

# Rotate to left and flip vertically
ffmpeg -i slt.mp4 \
        -filter:v "transpose=0" \
        slt-rotated-0.mp4

# Rotate to right and flip vertically
ffmpeg -i slt.mp4 \
        -filter:v "transpose=3" \
        slt-rotated-3.mp4
```

For the `transpose` filter option `dir`, a value of 1 or 2 turns the video 90 degrees **right or left**. Values 0 and 3 turn the video **left or right** and also vertically flip them. Mobile phone users should stick with the first two values.

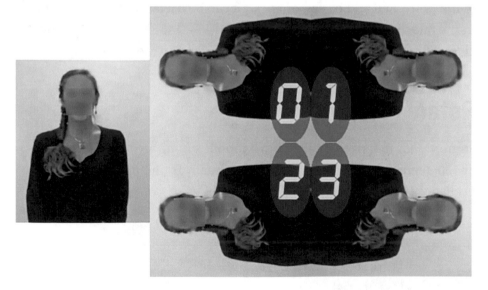

Figure 7-4. *These still images show* `dir` *values that can be used with the* `transpose` *filter*

The `transpose` filter option `passthrough` can have values none, portrait, and `landscape`. The value none is default. One of the last two values will be particularly useful in automated scripts to prevent unnecessary rotation, that is, when the video is already in the orientation specified by the `passthrough` filter option. It will also prevent `ffmpeg` from autorotating a video and then applying your transpose setting (causing further rotation).

You can rotate videos by more discrete levels than multiples of 90 degrees. The `rotate` filter accepts values in radians rather than degrees. The following `ffmpeg` command rotates a video by 16 degrees.

```
ffmpeg -y -i malampuzha-lake.mp4 \
        -filter_complex \
            "rotate=angle=16*PI/180:fillcolor=brown" \
        malampuzha-lake-tilt-16-chopped.mp4
# Rotates video but corners get cut off
```

☞   If the video becomes distorted, correct it using `setdar` filter.

☞   To convert degrees to radians, it has to be multiplied with $\pi/180$.

To prevent the corners from getting chopped off, the frame dimensions need to be increased. You can use the `rotw` and `roth` functions for determining these new dimensions. The two functions use these formulas internally.

$$\text{rotw}(\theta) = \text{Height} \times \text{Sine}(\theta) + \text{Width} \times \text{Cosine}(\theta)$$
$$\text{roth}(\theta) = \text{Width} \times \text{Sine}(\theta) + \text{Height} \times \text{Cosine}(\theta)$$

```
# Rotate video and enlarge the frame to prevent
# corners from getting cut off
ffmpeg -y -i malampuzha-lake.mp4 \
       -filter_complex \
           "rotate=angle=16*PI/180:
           ow=trunc(rotw(16*PI/180)/2)*2:
           oh=trunc(roth(16*PI/180)/2)*2:
           fillcolor=brown" \
       malampuzha-lake-tilt-16.mp4
```

As FFmpeg requires that the new width and height be even numbers, that is, divisible by 2, the calculated dimensions are first divided by 2, truncated off, and then multiplied by 2.

Figure 7-5. *The first video has the original dimensions, but the rotated content has chopped-off corners. The second video has bigger dimensions to accommodate the extruding corners*

Flip a Video

Some videos are flipped for some reason. Use `vflip` or `hflip` to set them right.

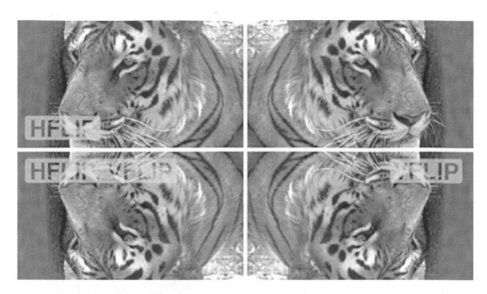

Figure 7-6. *These still images show which filter to us for what effect*

```
ffmpeg -i exhibit.mp4 \
      -filter:v "vflip" \
      exhibit-upside-down.mp4

ffmpeg -i exhibit.mp4 \
      -filter:v "hflip" \
      exhibit-half-crazy.mp4

ffmpeg -i exhibit.mp4 \
      -filter:v "hflip,vflip" \
      exhibit-totally-flipped.mp4
```

Brighten a Video (Adjust Contrast)

It is inevitable that some of your videos are dark, even when they were captured in broad daylight. You can use the eq filter to adjust the brightness. However, adjusting the brightness requires a subsequent adjustment of the contrast. The ranges for the options of this filter are listed in Table 7-2.

Figure 7-7. *After cumulative applications of brightness, saturation, and contrast filters, more detail of the green barbet is visible. Forget the background*

First, I decided to do a side-by-side comparison.

```
ffmpeg -y -i barbet.mp4 \
  -filter_complex \
    "[0:v]pad=(iw*2):ih:0:0[frame];
    [0:v]eq=brightness=0.2[bright];
    [bright]eq=saturation=3[color];
    [color]eq=contrast=2[dark];
    [frame][dark]overlay=W/2:0[out]" \
  -map '[out]' -map 0:a \
  barbet-test.mp4
```

Table 7-2. *Options for filter eq*

Filter option	Lowest	Highest	Default
Brightness	-1	1.0	0
Contrast	-1000	1000	1
Saturation	0	3	1
Gamma	0.1	10	1

After some trial-and-error attempts, I applied the filters to the original video.

```
ffmpeg -y -i barbet.mp4 \
  -filter_complex \
    "[0:v]eq=brightness=0.2[bright];
    [bright]eq=saturation=3[color];
    [color]eq=contrast=2[dark]" \
  -map '[dark]' -map 0:a \
  barbet-bright.mp4
```

Generate a Test Video

In the good old days, when there was just one TV channel in India, the transmission began in the evening with a 30-minute video test – something like this!

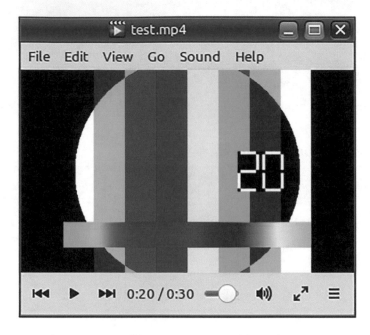

Figure 7-8. *The* `testsrc` *filter is a source filter that generates a test video stream*

The test video has a color pattern, a scrolling gradient, and a changing timestamp. The audio is a low white noise. I do not know who needs this video, but if it floats your boat, then here is the command to create it.

```
ffmpeg -f lavfi \
       -i "testsrc=size=320x260[out0];
          anoisesrc=amplitude=0.06:color=white[out1]" \
       -t 0:0:30 -pix_fmt yuv420p \
       test.mp4
```

☞   This command uses a set of filters as a pseudo file source (`-f lavfi`). It requires that the filter outputs be labeled `out0`, `out1`, `out2`,....

☞   Filters whose name end in "`src`" are *source filters*. They do not require an input stream.

Remove Logo

In 2019, a newspaper in New York published an opinion alleging bias against women in government experiments. NASA's Apollo Space Program was then celebrating its 50th anniversary.

```
ffmpeg -i apollo-program.mp4 \
       -filter:v "delogo=x=520:y=10:w=100:h=50" \
       apollo-program-you-are-dead.mp4
```

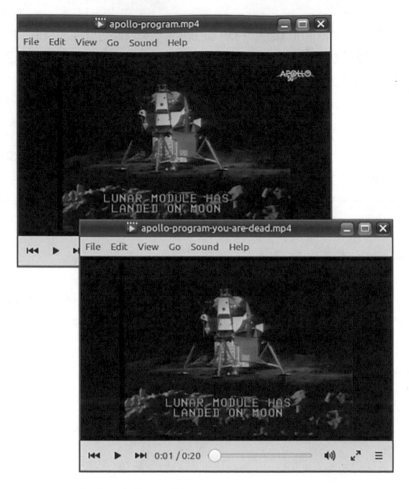

Figure 7-9. *With the* delogo *filter, it is very easy to remove an unwanted logo from a video*

☞   After applying the filter, the logo has disappeared from the top-right corner.

☞   This video is only a simulation.

Fade into Another Video (And in Audio Too)

In order to prove aliens do not exist and have fun while doing that, I took videos from two authoritative US government agencies – NASA and IRS. The videos are in public domain, as the agencies are taxpayer-funded. The NASA video clearly states that there are no aliens, but I am not interested in their explanation. The IRS video is a tax advisory for noncitizens, also known as aliens. That is the fun part. In the output video, the first video plays fine until six seconds after which it fades out in three seconds. As the first video fades away, the second video starts fading in for three seconds. After that, it plays for six seconds.

Figure 7-10. *These screenshots show the crossfade sequence involving the two input videos*

Mixing these two videos can be done with one command, but for clarity, I have split it into four commands. (You should combine the filters to avoid multiple re-encoding.) The crossfade effect is performed by the `fade` filter for video and the `afade` filter for audio. The `trim` and `atrim` filters are used to divide the video and audio tracks into two parts – one where the stream plays normally and another where the fade filters take effect. I used `overlay` and `amix` filters to mix the second parts. After that, the `concat` filter was used to put three segments together – normal playback from the first file, crossfade effect from both files, and then normal playback from the second file.

```
# Make the second video same size as the first
ffmpeg -y -i irs-tax-advice-for-alien-mates.mp4 \
  -filter:v "pad=w=640:h=ih:x=(ow-iw)/2:y=0:color=yellow,
            fps=24" \
  -t 0:0:20 -pix_fmt yuv420p \
  irs-tax-advice-for-alien-mates2.mp4

# Create the fade-in-fade-out video
ffmpeg -y -i Do-Aliens-Exist-We-Asked-a-NASA-Scientist.mp4 \
  -i irs-tax-advice-for-alien-mates2.mp4 \
  -filter_complex \
  "[0:v:0]trim=start=0:end=6, setpts=PTS-STARTPTS, fps=24[v1];
   [1:v:0]trim=start=3:end=9, setpts=PTS-STARTPTS, fps=24[v2];
   [0:v:0]trim=start=6:end=9, setpts=PTS-STARTPTS, fps=24[v3];
   [1:v:0]trim=start=0:end=3, setpts=PTS-STARTPTS, fps=24[v4];
   [v3]fade=t=out:d=3:alpha=1, setpts=PTS-STARTPTS,
     fps=24[nasafade];
   [v4]fade=t=in:d=3:alpha=1, setpts=PTS-STARTPTS,
     fps=24[irsfade];
   [nasafade][irsfade]overlay, setpts=PTS-STARTPTS,
     fps=24[fading];
```

```
  [v1][fading][v2]concat=n=3:v=1:a=0[v]" \
 -map '[v]' -pix_fmt yuv420p \
 aliens-r-us-v.mp4

# Create the fade-in-fade-out audio
ffmpeg -y -i Do-Aliens-Exist-We-Asked-a-NASA-Scientist.mp4 \
    -i irs-tax-advice-for-alien-mates2.mp4 \
    -vn \
    -filter_complex \
     "[0:a:0]atrim=start=0:end=9, asetpts=PTS-STARTPTS[a1];
      [1:a:0]atrim=start=0:end=9, asetpts=PTS-STARTPTS[a2];
      [a1][a2]acrossfade=duration=3" \
     aliens-r-us-a.m4a

# Mix the video and audio
ffmpeg -i aliens-r-us-v.mp4 -i aliens-r-us-a.m4a \
       -codec copy \
       aliens-r-us.mp4
```

Crop a Video

For some screenshots in the beginning of this chapter, I needed a public-domain video of a sign-language translator. I found one but it was too big. I grabbed a still image from the video using a media player and edited it in GIMP.

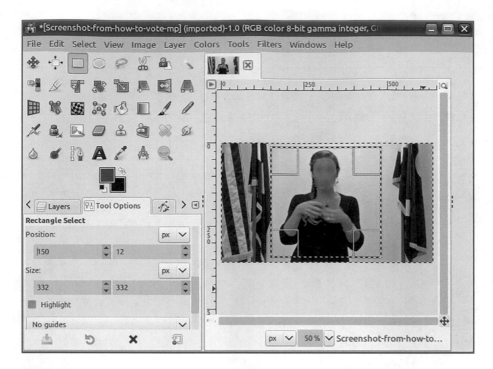

Figure 7-11. *First, take a screengrab from the video. Then, use an image-editing program to identify the location (150,12) and dimensions (332,332) of the region you want to cut out*

I then selected the region that I wanted cut into. I noted down the coordinates and dimensions of the region from GIMP's *Tool Options* panel. I used the details from GIMP in the options for a `crop` filter that I used on the video.

```
ffmpeg -i how-to-vote.mp4 \
       -filter:v "crop=332:332:150:12" \
       accessibility.mp4
```

Figure 7-12. *The* crop *filter cut into a portion of a video*

Blur or Sharpen a Video

When this video was shot, there was a lot of camera refocusing and the action was blurry. The smartblur filter almost fixes this when it is set to *sharpen* the video.

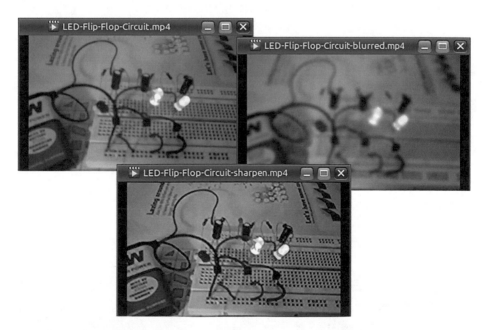

Figure 7-13. *With the* smartblur *filter, you can blur or sharpen a video*

```
ffmpeg -i LED-Flip-Flop-Circuit.mp4 \
       -filter:v
         "smartblur=luma_radius=5:luma_strength=1.0:
          luma_threshold=30" \
       LED-Flip-Flop-Circuit-blurred.mp4

ffmpeg -i LED-Flip-Flop-Circuit.mp4 \
       -filter:v
         "smartblur=luma_radius=5.0:luma_strength=-1.0:
          luma_threshold=30" \
       LED-Flip-Flop-Circuit-sharpen.mp4
```

The smartblur filter can blur or sharpen videos *without affecting the outlines*. It works on the brightness of the pixels. The luma_radius (0.1 to 5) represents the variance of the Gaussian blur filter. luma_strength (-1 to 1) varies between sharpness to blurring. luma_threshold (-30 to 30) varies the focus of the filter from the edges to interior flatter areas.

Blur a Portion of a Video

Sometimes, you need to protect the identity of some people (e.g., bystanders) who are not really the focus of a video. Use the boxblur filter. This command tries to blur two regions in a video where human faces appear.

```
ffmpeg -y -i stilt.mp4 \
  -filter_complex \
    "[0:v]crop=260:80:400:550[c1];
     [0:v]crop=100:60:1:550[c2];
     [c1]boxblur=6:6[b1];
     [c2]boxblur=6:6[b2];
     [0:v][b1]overlay=400:550[v1];
```

```
    [v1][b2]overlay=1:550[v]" \
   -map '[v]' -map 0:a -c:a copy \
  stilt-masked.mp4
```

Unlike `smartblur`, it does not respect object outlines. And, contrary to its name, `boxblur` does not blur inside the box or a part of the video. It affects the whole frame of the input video stream.

Figure 7-14. *With the* `boxblur` *filter, you can blur content without discrimination of any outlines*

☞   To avoid any doubt or confusion, I would like to state that I have masked faces of private individuals (even in public-domain content) in several screenshots using an image-editing program. In this screenshot, however, the effect was achieved using the `ffmpeg` filter `boxblur`.

111

Draw Text

To draw text on video, you need to use the `drawtext` filter and also specify the location of the font file. When you are drawing several pieces of text, it is better to daisy-chain your texts (using commas, not semicolons).

```
ffmpeg -y -i color-test.mp4 \
  -filter_complex \
    "[0:v:0]drawtext=x=(w-tw)/2:y=10:fontcolor=white: \
        shadowx=1:shadowy=1:text='Detonation Sequence': \
        fontsize=25: fontfile=AllertaStencil.ttf, \
    drawtext=x=(w-tw)/2:y=60:fontcolor=white: \
        shadowx=1:shadowy=1: \
        text='This TV will self-destruct in t seconds.': \
        fontsize=15:fontfile=Exo-Black.ttf[v]" \
  -map '[v]' -map 0:a:0 -pix_fmt yuv420p \
  idiot-box-1.mp4
```

Figure 7-15. *With the* drawtext *filter, you can draw text formatted with fonts, styles, shadows, transparencies, etc. on video*

Draw a Box

You can use the drawbox filter to render all kinds of boxes, filled or bound, with all sorts of colors and transparencies.

```
ffmpeg -y -i color-test.mp4 \
  -filter_complex \
    "[0:v:0]drawbox=x=20:y=3:w=280:h=36:color=tomato@0.4:
    t=fill, \
    drawbox=x=11:y=49:w=294:h=40:color=lime:t=1, \
    drawtext=x=(w-tw)/2:y=10:fontcolor=white: \
        shadowx=1:shadowy=1:text='Detonation Sequence': \
```

```
        fontsize=25: fontfile=AllertaStencil.ttf, \
    drawtext=x=(w-tw)/2:y=60:fontcolor=white: \
        shadowx=1:shadowy=1: \
        text='This TV will self-destruct in t seconds.': \
        fontsize=15:fontfile=Exo-Black.ttf[v]" \
  -map '[v]' -map 0:a:0 -pix_fmt yuv420p \
  idiot-box-2.mp4
```

The part of the color value after the @ symbol refers to the transparency level. It ranges from 0 (fully transparent) to 1 (opaque). If you specify the value `fill` for the filter option `t` or `thickness`, then the box will be filled with that color. Otherwise, it applies to the border.

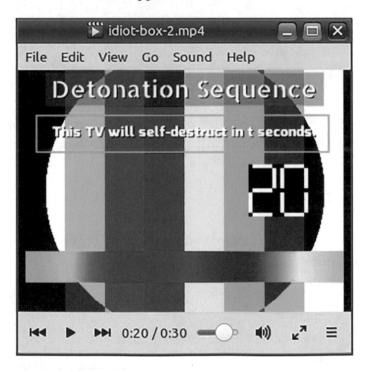

Figure 7-16. *With the* drawbox *filter, two rectangles around the text. (See original video in previous section.) The first rectangle is filled with red. The second rectangle is bordered green*

Speed Up a Video

When you increase the playback speed of a video, its duration decreases. When you slow down a video, its duration increases. There is no one filter that changes the speed of both the audio and the video. You need to use two different filters – one for video and one for audio. The two filters do not work in the same way. The two need to be calibrated correctly so that the same effect is achieved on both the audio and the video.

For the video, you need to set the `setpts` video filter to a fraction of the PTS filter constant. If you want to double the speed of the video, divide PTS by 2. If you want the video to be four times fast, then divide PTS by 4. For the audio, you need to use the `atempo` filter. The range of this filter is from half the speed to 100 times. The following command fast-forwards a video by four times (4x).

```
ffmpeg -y -i barb.mp4 \
  -filter_complex \
    "[0:v]setpts=PTS/4[v];
    [0:a]atempo=4[a]" \
  -map '[v]' -map '[a]' \
  barb-speed.mp4
```

☞   In older versions of FFmpeg, the maximum limit of the `atempo` filter was just 2. To go beyond that limit, multiple filters had to be daisy-chained: `atempo=2, atempo=2`

Slow Down a Video

In the *Tom & Jerry* film *Baby Puss*, one of the alley cats tries to dance with a seemingly innocuous doll. In the middle of it, I thought, the doll had become possessed and slammed the cat down on the floor! I slowed the video down with Ffmpeg, and my suspicions were confirmed.

To slow down a video, you need to use the same filters as in the previous section, but the multipliers will have to be different.

This command slows down the video and the audio to one-fourth.

```
ffmpeg -y -i tom.mp4 \
  -filter_complex \
    "[0:v]setpts=PTS*4[v];
     [0:a]atempo=0.5, atempo=0.5[a]" \
  -map '[v]' -map '[a]' \
  possessed-doll.mp4
```

☞   Note the different multiples used for video and audio to achieve the same effect. The audio filter has been used twice because of the limitation in its range.

☞   Read previous section for more information on these two filters.

Laurie Lennon, from the Lennon Sisters family, has published a tribute video for the *Merrie Melodies* number "Oh, Wolfie!". When I saw it for the first time some years ago, I felt the tempo was too high. I slowed the audio down in Audacity. (I have all songs featuring *Lou* as MP3 files, complete with Wolfie's and Droopy's crazy antics.) For my 2020 book, I tried to do the same using FFmpeg and apply the change to the video as well. My calculation became easier when I used seconds. The original video was 114 seconds, and my slowed-down audio was 128 seconds.

```
# 128/114 and 114/128
ffmpeg -y -i Laurie-Lennon-Original.mp4 \
    -filter_complex \
    "[0:v]setpts-PTS*(128/114)[v];
     [0:a]atempo=(114/128)[a]" \
    -map '[v]' -map '[a]' \
    Laurie-Lennon-Slow.mp4
```

The links to these videos and those used in other examples in this book are available online:

```
www.vsubhash.in/ffmpeg-book.html
```

Summary

The examples in this chapter would have amply demonstrated that a lot of useful and powerful multimedia-processing abilities are hidden in the filters functionality. You need to read the relevant documentation to make full use of a filter. *Filter expressions* using built-in real-time variables (*filter constants*) and functions provide a lot of versatility and extensibility to command-line users that would have otherwise been limited to programmers who use the `libav` *libraries*.

In this book, the teaching portion about FFmpeg functionality ends here. The subsequent chapters are topic-specific for those who want quick answers to a particular type of problem and do not want to read through dense explanatory text before finding the answer. You will find some information repeated or not mentioned at all.

## CHAPTER 8

All About Audio

In this chapter, you will learn to perform several tasks related to audio content. While it is convenient to have a separate chapter just for audio, you will find some information repeated from other chapters. If there is no explanation, then it must be self-explanatory.

Most audio-related tasks can be performed using audio filters. If any of the filters used in this chapter seem too complicated, find out what the official FFmpeg documentation has to say on them. If you are unfamiliar with using filters, read Chapter 7.

Convert from One Audio Format to Another

```
ffmpeg -i alarm.ogg \
       -c:a libmp3lame \
       -ac 2 \
       -b:a 128K \
       alarm.mp3            # Ogg to MP3
```

Extract Audio from a Video

```
ffmpeg -i music-video.mp4 \
       -c:a libmp3lame \
       -ac 2 \
       -b:a 128K \
       music-video.mp3      # Audio saved as MP3
```

© V. Subhash 2023
V. Subhash, *Quick Start Guide to FFmpeg*, https://doi.org/10.1007/978-1-4842-8701-9_8

Convert a MIDI File to MP3 or Ogg

You may have noted that there are no codecs for MIDI. That is because MIDI files are quite different from ordinary sound files. Ordinary sound files contain the wave form encoded in a predefined format. In contrast, MIDI files are merely a collection of references to a common sound bank.

Timidity is the Linux way of playing MIDI files. You can use Timidity to playback MIDI files in WAVE format and write it to its *standard output*. Simultaneously, FFmpeg can be made to consume the wave output as its input file (from its *standard input* over a pipe) and convert it as a regular sound file.

```
timidity yamaha.midi -Ow -o - | ffmpeg -i - -b:a 128k
yamaha.ogg
```

The -Ow makes Timidity to output the playback in WAVE format. Its -o option is used to specify the output file. Instead of an output file, we use - to make it write to the *standard output*. The Timidity output is then piped over to an FFmpeg command, where it is captured from the *standard input* with yet another - (hyphen).

Change Volume

FFmpeg can increase the loudness of an audio file using its volume filter. The filter accepts a multiple either as a number (scalar) or in decibels (logarithmic).

```
ffmpeg -i sarah.mp3 -af 'volume=3' sarah-more.mp3
```

I had an audio file that continued to have low volume, even after trebling the levels. I opened it in Audacity and found the reason.

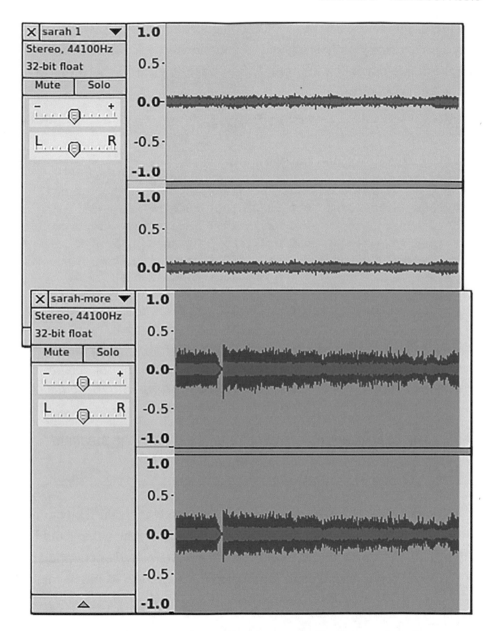

Figure 8-1. *Audacity confirms that irrationally increasing the volume is not making much of a difference*

Increasing sound like this is based on guesswork. It might work. It may also damage your hearing and/or your speaker system. The correct approach is to normalize the sound after observing the decibel levels in the current waveform.

```
ffmpeg -i sarah.mp3 -af "volumedetect" -f null -
```

```
~/Desktop
$ ffmpeg -i sarah.mp3 -af "volumedetect" -f null /dev/null
[Parsed_volumedetect_0 @ 0x226c100] mean_volume: -32.4 dB
[Parsed_volumedetect_0 @ 0x226c100] max_volume: -17.3 dB
[Parsed_volumedetect_0 @ 0x226c100] histogram_17db: 6
[Parsed_volumedetect_0 @ 0x226c100] histogram_18db: 15
[Parsed_volumedetect_0 @ 0x226c100] histogram_19db: 56
[Parsed_volumedetect_0 @ 0x226c100] histogram_20db: 452
[Parsed_volumedetect_0 @ 0x226c100] histogram_21db: 1676
```

Figure 8-2. *Run the* volumedetect *filter before increasing the volume. It helps you in determining the highest number of decibels to which the volume can be increased without cutting into the waveform*

☞   The volumedetect filter outputs text data to the *standard output*. It does not create an audio stream.

The volumedetect filter shows that we can safely increase the volume to 16db. If we raised the volume to 17dB or higher, normalization would cut into the waveform, and the peaks would get attenuated or chopped off. At 17dB, six sound samples (the loudest) in the waveform would be lost.

```
ffmpeg -i sarah.mp3 \
       -af 'volume=16dB' -f ogg \
       sarah-normalized.ogg
```

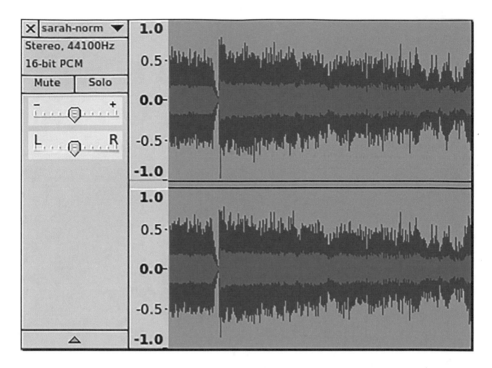

Figure 8-3. *Audacity confirms that the volume has been increased without cutting into the waveform*

This is fine. Now, how do you decrease the volume? Well, choose a fraction between 0 and 1 for the volume filter. For example, to decrease the volume by two-thirds, you should set the multiple at 0.33. (You know ⅓ = 0.33?)

```
ffmpeg -i sarah-normalized.ogg -af 'volume=0.33' sarah-less.mp3
```

Change Volume in a Video File

Say, to irrationally increase the volume by three times,

```
ffmpeg -i sarah.mp4 \
      -c:v copy \
      -af 'volume=3' \
      -c:a libmp3lame -b:a 128k \
      sarah-more.mp4
```

To safely and intelligently increase the volume in a video file,

```
ffmpeg -i sarah.mp4 \
      -af 'volumedetect' \
      -vn \
      -f null \
      /dev/null
# Displays that the loudest samples are at 17dB

# Increase the volume to 16dB (to safely normalize the audio)
ffmpeg -i sarah.mp4 \
      -c:v copy \
      -af 'volume=16dB' \
      -c:a libmp3lame -b:a 128k \
      sarah-normalized.mp4
```

To decrease volume by two-thirds in a video file, you need to use fractions:

```
# Reduces volume by two-thirds (or to one-thirds)
ffmpeg -i sarah-normalized.mp4 \
        -c:v copy \
        -af 'volume=0.33' \
        -c:a libmp3lame -b:a 128k \
        sarah-less.mp4
```

Dynamic Range Compression/Normalization

Sometimes, normalization does not make any difference. The volume seems to be unchanged. Examining the audio in Audacity can show you the problem. There are volume spikes in some locations while much of the file is at low volume. (These spikes usually occur when the mic is shaken or bumped while it is recording.) Normalization cannot proceed as long as the spikes remain. The solution is to identify the low-volume regions and expand the waveform. This more selective normalization is known as Dynamic Range Normalization. Alternatively, you could bring down the high-volume regions to the level of the rest of the audio. This selective compression of the waveform is known as Dynamic Range Compression (DRC).

Both techniques make irreversible changes to the waveform, so do not use them indiscriminately. DRC is the bane of popular music today and makes it very boring.

In Carl Orff's composition of *O Fortuna* or Ryuichi Sakamoto's score for the end credits of the movie *Femme Fatale*, the music starts on a low note, building slowly in a steady crescendo and abruptly drops off a high cliff. Applying DRC on such an audio would ruin the composer's intent. However, a recording of a teleconferencing session where multiple participants are heard speaking at different volumes would be an ideal candidate for DRC.

The dynaudnorm filter can perform both functions, but the default is normalization. When the guasssize option is set at the lower end of 3, it behaves like a typical compressor. At the other end of 300, it becomes a traditional normalizer.

```
ffmpeg -y -i train-trip-low.mp3 \
       -filter:a dynaudnorm=gausssize=3 \
       train-trip-low-dynaudnormalized.mp3
```

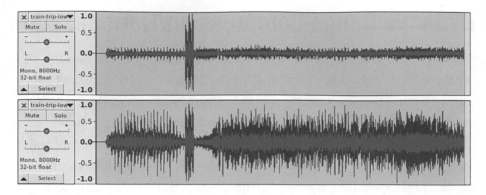

Figure 8-4. *A few unexplained spikes in volume can prevent normalization from happening on the rest of the waveform. Dynamic Range Compression and Dynamic Range Normalization are not affected by these spikes and change the entire waveform*

Channels

An audio stream can have one or more channels. A *channel* is an independent sequence of audio. All channels in an audio stream are of the same length, and they are played back simultaneously. The idea of having a separate channel is to have a different choice of musical instruments or sounds to play in different speakers. Audio content creators may move back and forth sounds between different channels at different volume levels. This can be useful in creating a 2D or 3D effect to the sound. Typically, each channel in an audio stream is assigned to a particular speaker. This composition of channels in a multichannel stream is known as its *channel layout*. When the number of speakers is less than the number of channels, then that particular channel may not be heard, or the device may *downmix* the channels so that the excess channels will be heard on the existing speakers.

Monaural audio has only one channel. Stereo music has two channels – left and right. Movies can have two, six, seven, eight, or more channels.

When working with channels, you will need to use filters such as `amerge`, `channelmap`, `channelsplit`, and `pan`. These filters make use of certain IDs for channels and channel layouts. Table 8-1 and Table 8-2 list these IDs.

126

Table 8-1. *Channels*

ID	Channel
FL	Front left
FR	Front right
FC	Front center
LFE	Low frequency
BL	Back left
BR	Back right
FLC	Front left-of-center
FRC	Front right-of-center
BC	Back center
SL	Side left
SR	Side right
TC	Top center
TFL	Top front left
TFC	Top front center
TFR	Top front right
TBL	Top back left
TBC	Top back center
TBR	Top back right
DL	Downmix left
DR	Downmix right
WL	Wide left
WR	Wide right
SDL	Surround direct left
SDR	Surround direct right
LFE2	Low frequency 2

Table 8-2. *Channel layouts*

ID	Layout composition
Mono	FC
Stereo	FL+FR
2.1	FL+FR+LFE
3.0	FL+FR+FC
3.0(back)	FL+FR+BC
4.0	FL+FR+FC+BC
Quad	FL+FR+BL+BR
Quad(side)	FL+FR+SL+SR
3.1	FL+FR+FC+LFE
5.0	FL+FR+FC+BL+BR
5.0(side)	FL+FR+FC+SL+SR
4.1	FL+FR+FC+LFE+BC
5.1	FL+FR+FC+LFE+BL+BR
5.1(side)	FL+FR+FC+LFE+SL+SR
6.0	FL+FR+FC+BC+SL+SR
6.0(front)	FL+FR+FLC+FRC+SL+SR
Hexagonal	FL+FR+FC+BL+BR+BC
6.1	FL+FR+FC+LFE+BC+SL+SR
6.1	FL+FR+FC+LFE+BL+BR+BC
6.1(front)	FL+FR+LFE+FLC+FRC+SL+SR
7.0	FL+FR+FC+BL+BR+SL+SR
7.0(front)	FL+FR+FC+FLC+FRC+SL+SR
7.1	FL+FR+FC+LFE+BL+BR+SL+SR
7.1(wide)	FL+FR+FC+LFE+BL+BR+FLC+FRC
7.1(wide-side)	FL+FR+FC+LFE+FLC+FRC+SL+SR
Octagonal	FL+FR+FC+BL+BR+BC+SL+SR
Hexadecagonal	FL+FR+FC+BL+BR+BC+SL+SR+WL+WR+TBL+TBR+TBC+TFC+TFL+TFR
Downmix	DL+DR
22.2	FL+FR+FC+LFE+BL+BR+FLC+FRC+BC+SL+SR+TC+TFL+TFC+TFR+TBL+TBC+TBR+LFE2+TSL+TSR+BFC+BFL+BFR

127

Swap Left and Right Channels

In some videos, sounds from the left side of the video are heard on the right channel and those from the right side are on the left channel. In such a case, you can do a switcheroo.

```
# Switch right and left channels of stereo audio
ffmpeg -i wrong-channels.mp4 \
        -c:v copy \
        -filter_complex "channelmap=map=FR-FL|FL-FR" \
        fine-channels.mp4
```

You can specify the channel settings using the map filter option in this format:

```
        input_channel_id-output_channel_id|input_channel↵
        _id-output_channel_id|...
```

This filter also has a channel_layout option.

Turn Off a Channel

In some video files, the narration or commentary is on one channel, and the ambient noise or background music is on the other. If what you want is on the left, you can turn the right channel off by setting its gain to zero (0).

```
# Silence right channel
ffmpeg -i moosic.mp3  \
        -c:v copy \
        -filter_complex "pan=stereo|FL=FL|FR=0" \
        moosic4lefty.mp3
```

☞   Changing the audio to mono (single-channel audio) is not an option because mono audio is played on both front and left speakers.

You can specify the channel settings in this format:

```
l|output_channel_id=gain*input_channel_id|output⏎
_channel_id=gain*input_channel_id...
```

The filter option l is used to specify the channel layout. After that, you have to specify how much of what channel (in the input stream) you need for each channel in the output audio stream. For specifying that proportion or the gain, you can specify a multiple or a fraction. If you omit the gain, it implies that you want that channel as is or that the gain is equal to 1 (one). If you use 0 (zero), it means that you want that channel totally attenuated.

Move Channel to a Separate Audio Track

In some videos, the left and right audio channels are independent tracks. What these content creators do is place the original audio on one channel and the most annoying royalty-free music on the other. Instead of deleting the offending channel, you could move each channel to a separate audio stream while preserving the original stereo stream in a third stream.

The channelsplit filter has a channel_layout filter option which by default assumes the input audio stream is stereo. Because of that, this command splits the left and right channels of the audio stream in the video to two mono streams, which I have labeled as L and R.

```
# Split channels to separate audio streams
# and also preserve existing audio stream
ffmpeg -y -ss 0:0:20 -t 0:0:20 -i zombie.mp4 \
        -c:v copy \
        -filter_complex "channelsplit[L][R]" \
```

129

```
-map 0:v:0  -map '[L]' -map '[R]' -map 0:a:0 \
-c:a:0 aac -ac:a:0 1 \
-c:a:1 aac -ac:a:1 1 \
-c:a:2 copy \
zombie-tracks.mp4
```

Because the first two of the mapped output audio streams need to be freshly encoded as mono streams and the last mapped audio stream just needs to be copied without re-encoding, encoder (-c) and channel count (-ac) need to be specified on a *per-stream* basis.

☞   The -c and -ac options are limited to the streams specified by the -map options specified before them.

Fix Out-of-Phase Audio Channels

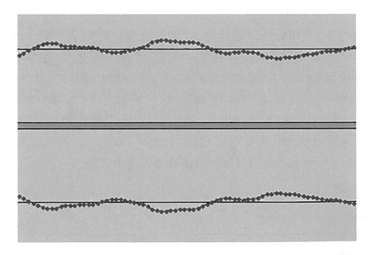

Figure 8-5. *This zoomed-in waveform shows out-of-phase left and right channels*

Rarely, when you downmix to mono sound, out-of-phase audio in the channels may cancel each other out. The audio will sound muted. You can fix it by saving either the left or the right channel in the input file as the only (mono) channel in the output file. (Monaural audio is played the same on both sides.)

Change Stereo to Mono

Stereo audio has two channels – left and right. Most of the time, both channels have the same audio. However, in many cases, the left channel will have some sounds that are not available in the right channel. The loudness of certain sounds may also differ. This difference will be lost when you convert to mono. Remember this before converting to mono. Mono audio cannot be converted back to stereo. It can only be made to look like stereo. You can convert stereo to mono either by downmixing both left and right channels to a mono channel or dropping one of the channels.

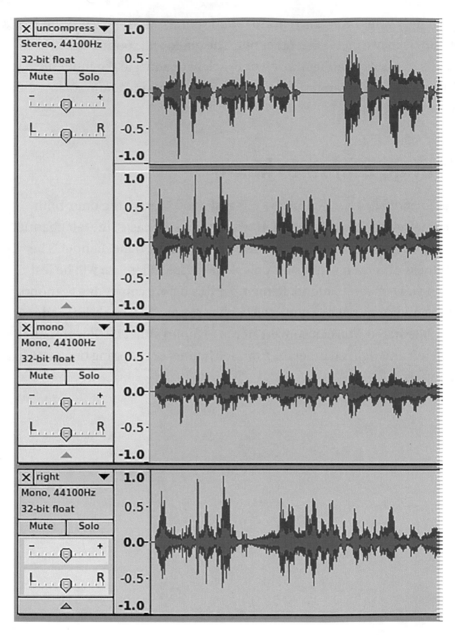

Figure 8-6. _To convert from stereo to mono, you can downmix_
left and right channels to a single mono channel or drop one of the
channels. In either case, if the two channels are different, there will be
some irreversible loss of the waveform

```
# Downmix to mono
ffmpeg -i uncompressed-stereo.wav \
       -ac 1 \
       mono.mp3

# Drop left channel
ffmpeg -i uncompressed-stereo.wav \
       -filter channelmap=FR-FC:mono \
       right.mp3
```

Convert Mono to Stereo

Mono audio has only one channel. On a stereo audio output device, the same channel will anyway be played on the left and right speakers. Hence, it does not make any difference to convert mono to stereo. If at all this needs to be done, then the audio can be split with a second channel.

```
ffmpeg -i mono.mp3 \
       -ac 2 \
       stereo-kind-of.mp3
```

Make Audio Comfortable for Headphone Listening

When wearing headphones, the sounds feel like they are arising inside your head and between your ears. The earwax filter makes the sound feel like it is outside and in front of your head.

```
ffmpeg -i in-head.flac -filter "earwax" out-head.mp3

ffmpeg -i tl.mp4 -filter:a "earwax" -c:v copy tl-head.mp4
```

Downmix 5.1 Audio to Stereo

Using the `-ac` (audio channels) option with the necessary number of channels is enough for most downmixing operations.

```
ffmpeg -i AAC-LC-Channel-ID.mp4 \
    -ac 2 \
    stereo.mp3
```

Downmix Two Stereo Inputs to One Stereo Output

When you place two videos side-by-side each other, you need to do something about their two audio streams.

```
ffmpeg -y -i beto.mp4 -i fallon.mp4  \
  -filter_complex \
    "[0:v]pad=1280:360:0:0 [frame];
    [frame][1:v]overlay=640:0 [overlaid];
    [0:a]channelsplit=channel_layout=mono[beto];
    [1:a]channelsplit=channel_layout=mono[fallon];
    [beto][fallon]join=inputs=2:channel_layout=stereo[audio]" \
  -map '[overlaid]' -map '[audio]' \
  fallon-aces-beto.mp4

ffmpeg -y -i beto.mp4 -i fallon.mp4  \
  -filter_complex \
    "[0:v]pad=1280:360:0:0 [frame];
    [frame][1:v]overlay=640:0 [overlaid];
    [0:a][1:a]amerge=inputs=2[audio]" \
  -map '[overlaid]' -map '[audio]' \
  -ac 2 \
  fallon-aces-beto2.mp4
```

The first command uses `channelsplit` filter to convert stereo audio from the two input files to mono streams. It then uses the `join` filter to use the two mono streams to create a stereo stream where the mono audio from the first file is the left channel and the mono audio from the second file becomes the right channel.

The second command uses `amerge` filter to create a four-channel audio stream from the two input stereo (two-channel) streams. The `-ac 2` conversion setting downmixes the four-channel audio to a two-channel stereo output.

In the first command, the input audio streams are assumed to be of equal length. If they are not of equal length, then the `apad` filter needs to be used to add silence to last till the end of the video stream.

For the Laurie Lennon video mentioned in an earlier chapter, I had also created a video with both the original version and the slowed-down version side-by-side for comparison. The slowed-down video was of greater duration. Without adding the extra silence, FFmpeg would continue adding duplicate data at the end of the shorter stream. The process would never complete, and my computer would have run out of space.

```
// Slow MP4 was 128 seconds. The original was 114 seconds.
ffmpeg -i Laurie-Lennon-Slow.mp4 \
       -i Laurie-Lennon-Original.mp4 \
       -loop 1 -i bg.png \
    -filter_complex \
    "[0:v:0]scale=320:180[v1];
     [1:v:0]scale=320:180[v2];
     [2:v:0][v1]overlay=320:90[v3];
     [v3][v2]overlay=0:90[v];
     [0:a:0]channelsplit=channel_layout=mono[right];
     [1:a:0]channelsplit=channel_layout=mono,apad[left];
     [left][right]join=inputs=2:channel_layout=stereo[a]" \
```

```
-map '[v]' -map '[a]' \
-t 0:2:08 \
-y laurie-lennon-comparison.mp4
```

Render a Visual Waveform of the Audio

The showwaves filter renders a visual waveform of the input audio.

```
ffmpeg -y -i dialup-modem.mp4 \
  -filter_complex \
    "[0:a]showwaves=s=160x90:mode=line[waves];
    [0:v]drawbox=x=(iw-20-w):y=(ih-20-h):w=160:h=90:
         color=yellow@0.6:t=fill[bg];
    [bg][waves]overlay=x=(W-20-w):y=(H-20-h)[over]" \
  -map '[over]' -map 0:1 \
  dialup-modem-handshake.mp4
```

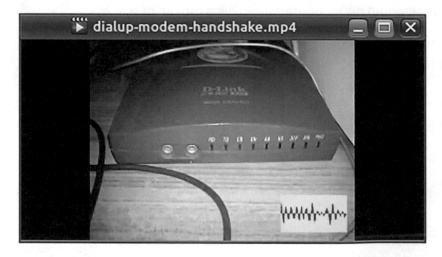

Figure 8-7. *This command draws a waveform of the dialup modem handshake tones on the video. To make the waveform easily visible, the command has drawn a translucent yellow box behind it*

In 2021, I wrote a book on electronics. In that, I described how to create the most annoying-sounding alarm noise using a blinking LED. I wanted to publish an online video of the alarm but felt queasy about posting a video of the ceiling where the alarm was installed. FFmpeg to the rescue! I used the `showfreqs` filter to generate the "power spectrum" of the audio recording.

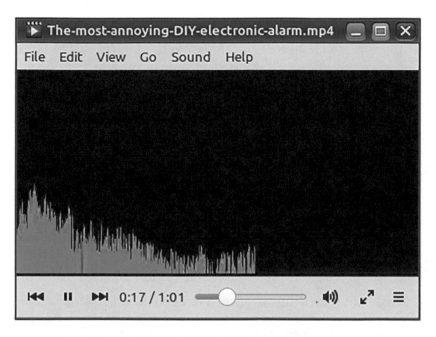

Figure 8-8. *The* showfreqs *filter shows how energy in an audio signal is spread across the range of frequencies that are audible to the human ear*

```
ffmpeg -i The-most-annoying-DIY-electronic-alarm.mp3 \
      -filter_complex \
        "showfreqs=s=640x320:mode=bar[v]" \
      -map '[v]' -map 0:a:0 \
      -c:v mpeg4 -b:v 466k -r 24 \
      The-most-annoying-DIY-electronic-alarm.mp4
```

There are a few other filters similar to this one. Check the documentation. These filters are very interesting.

Detect Silence

I have a shell script for censoring movies. (It uses FFmpeg, of course.) I use it to protect kids from foul dialog and unsuitable scenes. It asks for timestamps where the audio needs to be silenced and the video needs to be blacked out. After it does the job, I need to double-check these locations before the grand première on the TV. I use this command:

```
ffmpeg -i edited-movie.mp4 \
    -filter:a "silencedetect" \
    -vn -f null -
```

This command outputs timestamps wherever silence is detected. This helps me to directly skip to the censored locations using my media player on my computer.

Silence the Video

Heck, you do not want sound at all! Just remove the audio stream.

```
ffmpeg -i music-video.mp4 \
    -an \
    -c:v copy \
    sound-of-silence.mp4
```

Convert Text to Speech

If your `ffmpeg` executable has been built-in with support for the `libflite` text-to-speech synthesizer library, then you can convert text content to spoken words.

```
ffmpeg -f lavfi \
        -i "flite=textfile=speech.txt:voice=slt" \
        speech.mp3
```

This library has an option for a female voice, but I like the male-only espeak better. You can find other options for the flite filter option voice by typing the following:

```
ffprobe -f lavfi "flite=list_voices=1"
```

On my computer, this command lists awb, kal, kal16, rms, and slt as voices that are supported.

Apply a Low-Pass Filter

In an earlier chapter, I mentioned that I used Audacity to apply a *low-pass filter*. A low-pass filter makes all frequencies above a certain level to steeply drop to a zero while not disturbing all frequencies below that level. There is also a *high-pass filter* which does the opposite and attenuates frequencies below a certain level.

The audio recording in my example had a lot of noise typical of old gramophone recordings. When the low-pass filter was applied, the noise disappeared. At that time, I did not know much about FFmpeg filters. If I did, I could have fixed the audio in just one step.

```
ffmpeg -i Stopmotion-hot-wheels.mp4 \
        -filter:a "lowpass=frequency=1000" \
        -codec:v copy \
        Stopmotion-hot-wheels-audio-passed-low.mp4
```

The default option in Audacity was 1000 Hz for the frequency and 6 dB per octave for the roll-off. The roll-off specifies how steeply the frequencies are attenuated. The `lowpass` filter can apply a 3 dB roll-off if you set its `poles` option to 1. The default 2 applies a 6 dB roll-off, and I did not have to explicitly specify it in the above command.

Summary

In this chapter, you learned how to perform several tasks with audio content. You may find it helpful to initially use Audacity to understand audio problems. As you get more familiar with what ails audio content, you can rely on FFmpeg entirely. FFmpeg has a ton of audio filters, and this chapter used just a few of them. Check the FFmpeg documentation on audio filters, and you will find more exciting things you can do with audio.

CHAPTER 9

All About Subtitles

In this chapter, you will learn to perform several tasks related to subtitles. Subtitles are dialogs that are displayed as text on a video. The subtitles may be burned into the video or be available as a separate content stream in the multimedia file. In case of the former, the subtitles cannot be turned off as they have become part of the video. In case of the latter, the subtitles can be turned on or off using a remote button or by selecting an onscreen menu option.

Videos on streaming media, optical media, and broadcast TV can have subtitles in multiple languages. Some websites maintain a crowd-sourced library of subtitles (in multiple languages) of a wide variety of movies, popular and obscure. Several video-hosting sites also display subtitles. They do not let you download subtitles separate from the video. However, there are some other websites that will fetch the subtitles if you give them the address where the original video is hosted.

Subtitles are available in many formats. Subrip (.srt) files are the most popular. Advanced Substation Alpha (.ass or .ssa) is very versatile. WebVTT (Web Video Text Tracks Format) is used by browsers for online videos. TTML is used by the broadcast industry and online applications. DVDs use `.dvdsub` files.

I prefer SSA because I can specify a custom display font with it. For use with FFmpeg, subtitles should be a stream in a media file or an external text file. Subtitles that are already burned into a video (not as a separate stream) cannot be processed by FFmpeg (or rather not covered by this book). However, FFmpeg can be used to burn subtitles permanently on a video.

© V. Subhash 2023
V. Subhash, *Quick Start Guide to FFmpeg*, https://doi.org/10.1007/978-1-4842-8701-9_9

Add Subtitles to a Video as an Extra Stream

To add a subtitle file to a video, you need to use a subtitle format that is compatible with the video file's container. Or, you should use a suitable encoder that will convert your subtitle file in a format that is supported by the container. The subtitle format for MP4, MOV, and 3GPP containers is known as "MPEG4 Timed Text." You will have to encode your SRT or SSA subtitle files with the encoder `mov_text` for these containers. For the versatile Matroska (MKV) format, you can straightaway use SRT and SSA subtitle files.

Suppose that you have a DVD without subtitles in your favorite language and the DVD seller released a new updated collector's edition DVD that has subtitles in that language. If you were able to download the new subtitles as an SRT file from somewhere, then you can add it to your DVD backup file as an extra stream. If you are saving the DVD as an MKV file, convert the SRT file beforehand to the Substation Alpha (SSA) format to take advantage of the ability of the latter to use a custom font.

```
ffmpeg -i dvd-movie.srt dvd-movie.ass

# Edit the SSA file in some subtitle editor
# and add your custom styles and fonts

ffmpeg -i dvd-movie.ogv -i dvd-movie.ass \
    -map 0:v -map 0:a -map 1:s \
    -c:s mov_text \
    -metadata:s:s:0 language=eng \
    dvd-movie-subtitled.mp4 \
     \
    -map 0:v -map 0:a -map 1:s \
    -codec copy \
    -metadata:s:s:0 language=eng \
    dvd-movie-subtitled.mkv
```

☞   When you add subtitles as an additional stream like this, the viewer can turn them on/off with the device remote or a screen menu option.

Did you notice something else with the above command? I subtitled the movie in two formats (MP4 and MKV) using one command. With the MP4, I had to encode the OGV streams because its codecs are not native to the MP4 container. With the MKV, I could use `-codec copy`. The MKV container supports a wide variety of codecs including those supported by OGV and MP4. If you are backing up DVDs for long-term storage, choose MKV. It is the best.

Permanently Burn Subtitles to a Video

When I was about to publish my first book, I wanted to upload a book-read video in which I read a few pages. I recorded the OGV video using the webcam program *Cheese*, but there were some issues with audio recording. So, I transcribed my narration using another program called *Gnome Subtitles* and saved the subtitles as a Substation Alpha (.ass) file. I did not want to upload the subtitles to the video-hosting sites because they use very tiny fonts. I wanted the subtitles to look bigger and with my own selection of the font. I then decided to use FFmpeg to permanently burn the subtitles on the video. I specified the font and subtitles location on the video in the subtitle file, NOT in the `ffmpeg` command. The SSA format let me do that. Using a filter, I drew a black box behind the subtitles so that they could be easily read against any background.

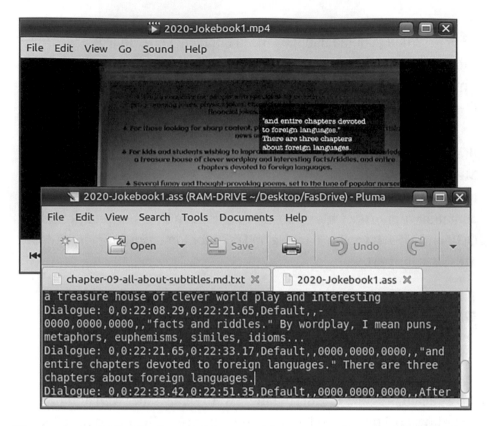

Figure 9-1. *Subtitles burned into a video cannot be turned off with the remote or a menu option*

```
ffmpeg -i 2020-Jokebook1.ogv \
    -filter_complex \
      "drawbox=w=250:h=100:x=360:y=90:color=black@0.7:t=fill,
        subtitles=2020-Jokebook1.ass" \
    -c:v libx264 -r 24 \
    2020-Jokebook1.mp4
```

☞   The `subtitles` filter has a `force_style` option to specify an SSA style for use with a subtitle format (such as SRT) that does not support styles.

☞   The black box was unnecessary. SSA has built-in support for dynamic background boxes, as you will learn later.

Add a Custom Font for Displaying Subtitles of a Video

If I wanted the subtitles in my book-read video to be optional, I could have created an MKV like this:

```
ffmpeg -i 2020-Jokebook1.ogv -i 2020-Jokebook1.ass \
       -codec copy \
       -metadata:s:s:0 language=eng \
       -attach Headline.ttf \
       -metadata:s:t:0 mimetype=application/x-truetype-font \
       2020-Jokebook1.mkv
```

☞   Font embedding increases subtitles portability and toggleability, but support is not universal.

☞   You should place the font file in the current directory or specify its full path.

145

This command adds the subtitles as an additional stream in the video. It also specifies a custom subtitle display font and embeds that font. On my PC, Totem and VLC display the subtitles with that font. However, my *WDTV HD* media player box, which I used for many years, always played the subtitles with its own built-in font.

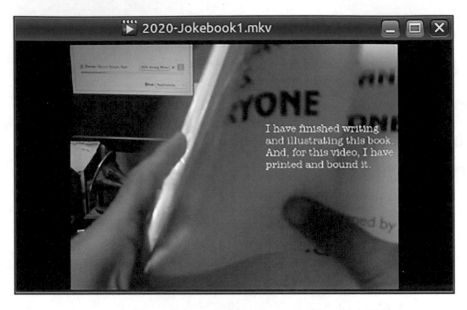

Figure 9-2. *When subtitles are added as a stream, the viewer can turn them on/off using the remote or with a menu option*

About the Substation Alpha (SSA/ASS) Subtitle Format

Although SRT is the popular subtitle format, I prefer the Substation Alpha (.ass or .ssa) because it supports fonts and several other cool features. You can convert SRT to SSA using `ffmpeg`.

```
ffmpeg -i dvd-movie.srt dvd-movie.ass
```

However, I prefer not to do that. I download the SRT file, let it open in a GUI program called *Gnome Subtitles,* and save it as a SSA file. After this, I run a BASH script on the .ass file to change its style statement. The style statement generated by `ffmpeg` and Gnome Subtitles refers to Windows fonts. These fonts are not available in Linux and the resultant subtitles do not look cool. My script uses a better style statement with a font I already have installed in Linux.

`ffmpeg` version:

```
Style: Default,Arial,16,&Hffffff,&Hffffff,&H0,&H0,↵
0,0,0,0,100,100,0,0,1,1,0,2,10,10,10,0
```

Gnome Subtitles version:

```
Style: Default,Tahoma,24,&H00FFFFFF,&H00FFFFFF,↵
&H00FFFFFF,&H00C0C0C0,-1,0,0,0,100,100,0,0.00,↵
1,2,3,2,20,20,20,1
```

My version:

```
Style: Default,Headline,20,&H00FFFFFF,&H006666EE,↵
&H00000000,&HAA00EEEE,-1,-1,0,0,100,100,0,0.00,↵
1,4,0,2,20,20,20,1
```

When I used this style in the book-read video, the subtitles...

```
ffmpeg -y -i 2020-Jokebook1.ogv \
        -i 2020-Jokebook1-shadows.ass \
        -map 0:v -map 0:a -map 1:s \
        -c:v copy -c:a copy -c:s ass \
        -metadata:s:s:0 language=eng \
        -attach Headline.ttf \
        -metadata:s:3 mimetype=application/x-truetype-font \
        2020-Jokebook1-shadows.mkv
```

... look like this:

Figure 9-3. *In this video, the subtitles have a text outline. (This eliminated the need to render a black box behind the subtitles using an FFmpeg filter. SSA subtitles support multiple such styles in the same file.) The subtitle shadow has been zeroed*

The specification of the wonderfully useful but screwed-up SSA format is available on the matroska.org website (*Technical Info » Subtitles » SSA*). However, I will risk a description here for the style statement.

```
Style: Name, Fontname, Fontsize, PrimaryColour,
SecondaryColour, OutlineColour, BackColour, Bold,
Italic, Underline, StrikeOut, ScaleX, ScaleY, Spacing,
Angle, BorderStyle, Outline, Shadow, Alignment,
MarginL, MarginR, MarginV, Encoding
```

Name refers to a subtitle display style. You can define and use many different styles, not just the Default. The colors are in hexadecimal AABBGGRR format. (*Ese*, are they *loco*? No. It is allegedly to help with video-to-text conversion.) PrimaryColour is the color of the subtitle text. OutlineColour is for the outline of the text. BackColour is the color of the shadow behind the text. SecondaryColour and OutlineColour will be automatically used when timestamps collide. Bold, italic, et al. are -1 for true and 0 for false. (Yeah, I know. The bash shell does the same.) ScaleX and ScaleY specify magnification (1-100). Spacing is additional pixel space between letters. Angle is about rotation (0-360) and controlled by Alignment. BorderStyle uses 1 (outlined and drop-shadowed text), 3 (outline box and shadow box), and 4 (outlined text and drop-shadow box). Outline represents the border width (1-4) of the outline or the padding around the text in the outline box. Shadow represents the offset (1-4) of the shadow from the text or the space around the text in the shadow box. Alignment takes 1 (left), 2 (center), and 3 (right). If you add 4 to them, the subtitle appears at the top of the screen. If you add 8, it goes to the middle. Then, we have margin from the left, right, and bottom edges of the screen. Encoding is 0 for ANSI Latin and 1 for Unicode (I think).

To really go bonkers with subtitles, I say we render subtitles with a miasma of colors, location, and tilt.

```
Style: Default,Headline,22,&H6600FFFF,&H006666EE,
&H660000FF,&H220066EE,-1,-1,0,0,100,100,0,25.00,
3,4,4,2,20,20,120,1
```

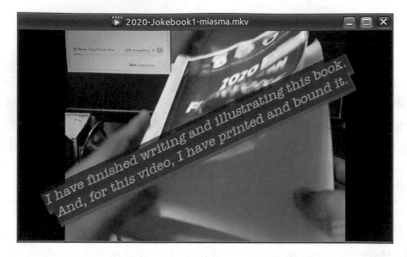

Figure 9-4. *This is truly subtitles gone wild. SSA subtitle format offers the most control and options. There is a yellow shadow to the red outline. Because the colors are translucent, their intersection appears orange*

Add Subtitle Files in Different Languages

When adding multiple subtitles, it is obligatory on your part to specify metadata identifying the language of each output subtitle stream.

Let us pretend that I am trying to corner the French jokebook market and have a French transcript ready as well:

```
# Multi-language subtitled MP4
ffmpeg -i 2020-Jokebook1.ogv \
       -i 2020-Jokebook1-en.ass  -i 2020-Jokebook1-fr.ass \
       -map 0:v -map 0:a -map 1:s -map 2:s \
       -c:s mov_text \
       -metadata:s:s:0 language=eng \
       -metadata:s:s:1 language=fre \
       2020-Jokebook1-subtitled-en-fr.mp4
```

```
# Multi-language subtitled MKV
ffmpeg -i 2020-Jokebook1.ogv \
        -i 2020-Jokebook1-en.ass  -i 2020-Jokebook1-fr.ass \
        -map 0:v -map 0:a -map 1:s -map 2:s \
        -c:v copy -c:a copy -c:s copy \
        -metadata:s:s:0 language=eng \
        -metadata:s:s:1 language=fre \
        2020-Jokebook1-subtitled-en-fr.mkv
```

Figure 9-5. *Do not forget to specify metadata for the subtitles*

☞   The codes that you can use for setting the language are further described in Chapter 10.

Extract Subtitles from a Video

Use ffprobe to check if a video file has a subtitle stream.

```
ffprobe 2020-Jokebook1-subtitled-en-fr.mkv
```

```
$ ffprobe 2020-Jokebook1-subtitled-en-fr.mkv
Input #0, matroska,webm, from '2020-Jokebook1-subtitled-en-fr.mkv':
  Metadata:
  Duration: 00:23:53.26, start: 0.000000, bitrate: 489 kb/s
    Stream #0:0: Video: theora, yuv420p, 640x360 [SAR 1:1 DAR 16:9], 2
    Metadata:
      DURATION        : 00:23:53.253000000
    Stream #0:1: Audio: vorbis, 44100 Hz, stereo, fltp (default)
    Metadata:
      DURATION        : 00:23:53.259000000
    Stream #0:2(eng): Subtitle: ass (default)
    Metadata:
      DURATION        : 00:23:53.263000000
    Stream #0:3(fre): Subtitle: ass (default)
    Metadata:
      DURATION        : 00:23:53.263000000
```

Figure 9-6. *Use ffprobe output to identify the subtitle formats and any metadata they might have. und stands for "undetermined"*

If the file has only one subtitle stream, you can extract it using FFmpeg just by specifying the correct extension.

```
ffmpeg -i dvd-movie-subtitled.mp4 \
       dvd-movie-subtitle-default.ass
```

If the video has multiple subtitle streams, you need to specify mapping. The next command saves the second subtitle stream in the input file as an SSA file.

```
ffmpeg -i 2020-Jokebook1-subtitled-en-fr.mkv \
       -map 0:s:1 \
       2020-Jokebook1-subtitle-fr.ass
```

Extract Subtitles from a DVD

The files in a DVD are usually encrypted or obfuscated to prevent bootlegging. There are several free DVD-ripping applications that will decrypt the VOB files and quickly extract subtitle files. Forcing ffprobe to find subtitle streams on big VOB files is not worth the trouble.

Summary

Subtitles are available in several formats including SRT, Substation Alpha, and MPEG4 Timed Text. The Substation Alpha is the most versatile subtitle format, and MKV seems to be the best container for it. The style specification for the Substation Alpha format may seem intimidating at first but will be accommodative in customizing subtitles for a variety of use cases.

CHAPTER 10

All About Metadata

In this chapter, you will learn to perform several tasks related to metadata. Metadata means to data about data. Multimedia metadata refers to information such as title, artist, album, subject, genre, year, copyright, producer, software creator, comments, lyrics, and even album art images that are used to describe the video and/or audio content.

An audio or video file can have global metadata (i.e., at the file level) and stream-specific metadata too. You can use ffprobe and ffmpeg -i commands to display metadata that a file already has. You use the -metadata option to add new metadata.

Add Album Art to MP3

You can add several pieces of album art to an MP3 file. However, each image will need to have a unique title and comment metadata. There can be one for front cover, another for the back, and yet another for the inlay art. FFmpeg will treat all album art images as video streams, as if they were single-frame videos.

```
ffmpeg -y \
  -i Uthralikavu-Pooram.mp3 \
  -i Uthralikavu-Pooram-festival-fireworks.png \
  -i Uthralikavu-Pooram-festival-crowds.png \
```

© V. Subhash 2023
V. Subhash, *Quick Start Guide to FFmpeg*, https://doi.org/10.1007/978-1-4842-8701-9_10

```
-map 0 -map 1 -map 2 \
-metadata:s:1 title="pooram-fireworks.png" \
-metadata:s:1 comment="Cover (front)" \
-metadata:s:2 title="pooram-crowds.png" \
-metadata:s:2 comment="Cover (back)" \
-codec copy \
-f mp3 \
Uthralikavu-Pooram-festival-fireworks.mp3
```

☞   Album art are added as single-frame video streams, not
metadata. The metadata you add for album art will apply to the video
streams of those images.

There are several options for the `comment` key, as defined in the ID3 tag
specification.

```
https://id3.org/id3v2.3.0
```

There is no uniform implementation among media players. When
there are more than one album art images, `ffplay` chooses the first cover
image that is mapped. Some other players follow a different pecking order.

Figure 10-1. *The album art displayed by different media players for the same MP3 file can be different*

Set MP3 Tags

How do I add metadata to an MP3 file?

```
ffmpeg -y -i Uthralikavu-Pooram-festival-fireworks.mp3 \
    -map 0 \
    -metadata title="Uthralikavu Pooram Festival" \
    -metadata artist="V. Subhash" \
    -metadata \
        subject="Fireworks and crowds" \
    -metadata album="Pooram festival fireworks" \
    -metadata date="2013-12-26" \
    -metadata genre="Event" \
```

```
-metadata comment="Best outdoor event I ever attended" \
-metadata \
    copyright="© 2013 V. Subhash. All rights reserved" \
-id3v2_version 3 \
-codec copy \
Kerala-Uthralikavu-Pooram-festival-fireworks.mp3
```

☞   MP3 tags metadata get added at the global level. They are not stream-specific.

Figure 10-2. *Media player support for MP3 tags may be buggy or not 100%. Do not break your head just because some tags do not get displayed by a media player*

Export Metadata

You can export metadata to a text file using the `-f ffmetadata` option.

```
ffmpeg -i Kerala-Uthralikavu-Pooram-festival-fireworks.mp3 \
    -f ffmetadata \
    mp3-meta.txt
```

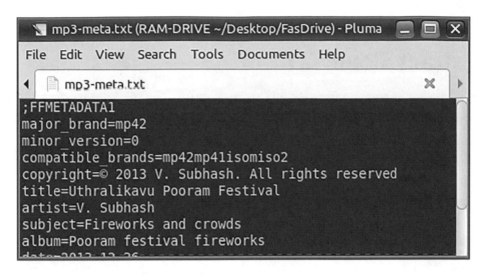

Figure 10-3. ffmpeg *exported this text file containing name-value pairs representing the metadata of an MP3 file*

Import Metadata

Let us imagine that I modified the metadata in the text file (from the previous section) using a text editor. Now, I want the updated metadata to be imported back into the audio file. How can I do it?

```
ffmpeg -y \
  -i Kerala-Uthralikavu-Pooram-festival-fireworks.mp3 \
  -i mp3-meta-modified.txt \
  -codec copy \
  -map_metadata 1 \
  Kerala-Uthralikavu-Pooram.mp3
```

Here, `-map_metadata 1` refers to the second input file, that is, the modified metadata file. (`-map_metadata 0` would have simply copied the metadata from the first input file, that is, the MP3 file. We did not want that.)

Extract Album Art

You downloaded an MP3 and you like the album art? If the audio file has only one album art, you can extract the image easily.

```
ffmpeg -i Blobfish.mp3 blobfish-album-art.png
```

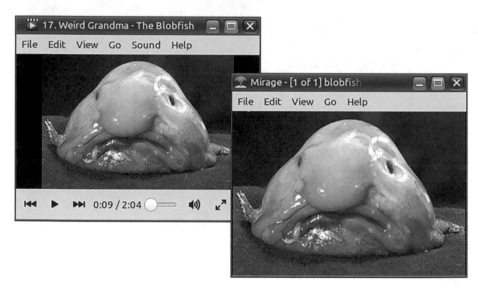

Figure 10-4. *An MP3 audio file and the album art extracted from it*

If there are more than one album art, you need to check the ffprobe output and then extract the album art using a map.

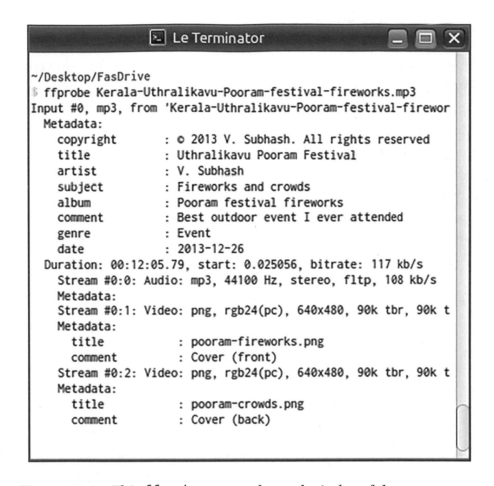

Figure 10-5. *This ffprobe output shows the index of the streams containing the album art images*

The crowds image is identified as a video stream with index `0:2` (third among all streams). To extract it, I should use the map `0:2`. To be safer, I refer to it as `0:v:1` (second video stream).

```
ffmpeg -i Kerala-Uthralikavu-Pooram-festival-fireworks.mp3 \
        -map 0:v:1 \
        crowds.png
```

Remove All Metadata

When working on an earlier chapter, I found that the Mate Screenshot app was unable to work with the video of the sign-language translator. The app names its screenshot after the title of the subject window. I noted that this video had a URL displayed in the title of the video player window. The URL came from the title metadata of the video. Because the Linux file system does not allow a file name to include a URL (because of the backslash and other illegal characters), the screenshot app may have been unable to save the image to file. When I removed the metadata, I realized that my hunch was right and I was able to take the screenshots from the metadata-free video.

To remove the metadata, I pretended to import metadata from a nonexistent input file (with index -1).

```
ffmpeg -i "Sign_Language_-_How_To_Vote.mp4" \
       -codec copy \
       -map_metadata -1 \
       how-to-vote.mp4
```

I have had portable media players that do not play MP3 files if they have album art. Album art cannot be removed as metadata because they are encoded as video streams. So, I use -codec copy and specify a -map for the audio stream. By omitting video streams, the output file will not have any album art.

```
ffmpeg -i Kerala-Uthralikavu-Pooram.mp3 \
       -map 0:a \
       -codec copy \
       pooram.mp3
# You can also use -vn instead of the -map option
```

Set Language Metadata for Audio Streams

Let us imagine that I created audio instructions in English, Malayalam, and Tamil for this DIY electronics video. While media players could switch between the language tracks, they would have assigned generic or confusing names to them.

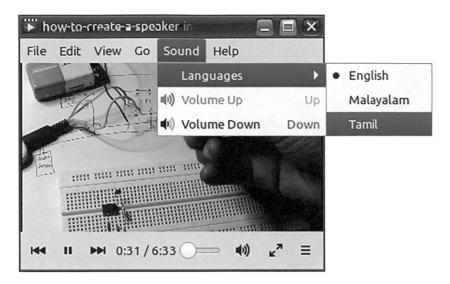

Figure 10-6. *This video has audio tracks in three languages. The metadata for the audio streams helps identify the languages*

The following command sets the language names using ISO codes and makes the menus a lot more informative.

```
ffmpeg -i how-to-create-a-speaker-instructions.mp4 \
       -map 0 \
       -metadata:s:a:0 language=eng \
       -metadata:s:a:1 language=mal \
       -metadata:s:a:2 language=tam \
       -codec copy \
       how-to-create-a-speaker-instructions-multilang.mp4
```

`map 0` includes all streams in the first input file (#0), that is, including the video stream and the three audio streams. (If not used, there will be just one video stream and one audio stream in the output file.) `-metadata:s:` is used to set metadata for a stream, not a subtitle.

☞   Apart from `s` identifier for streams, FFmpeg uses identifiers `p` and `c` for DVD programs and chapters of the VOB file container. These are not covered by this book.

`-metadata:s:a` is used to set metadata for an audio stream specified by its index. `language` is the metadata key, and what follows after the = sign is the value in the metadata key-value pair. `-codec copy` ensures that the streams are not re-encoded – only the metadata is added.

The three-letter language codes (such as `eng, mal,` and `tam`) are specified in the **ISO 639-2** standard. Although the standard allows codes for exceptional situations (`mis` for "uncoded languages," `mul` for "multiple languages," `qaa-qtz` for "reserved for local use," `und` for "undetermined," and `zxx` for "no linguistic content" or "not applicable"), many software and hardware remain ignorant of them.

`www.loc.gov/standards/iso639-2/php/code_list.php`

Summary

In this chapter, you learned to use ffmpeg to easily add, examine, edit, export, import, and remove metadata. Metadata can be specified at the container level (global) and for individual streams. This information can greatly enrich the experience with media players. In their absence, media players will try to make guesses and/or frustrate you with generic or wrong interface choices. Media formats and software/hardware applications may be picky and choosy about the kind of metadata they support.

With the end of this chapter, all that remains is a set of tips and tricks that could not be accommodated anywhere else.

CHAPTER 11

FFmpeg Tips and Tricks

I like tips and tricks, and I cannot lie. I have written an entire book titled *Linux Command-Line Tips and Tricks*. The tips and tricks in this chapter are mostly about FFmpeg. If you spend a lot of time with FFmpeg, these tips will be useful. Some advanced FFmpeg solutions, which could not be accommodated elsewhere, are also included.

Customize the Terminal

FFmpeg commands tend to be very long. Modify the `~/.bashrc` file to ensure that you have enough real estate at the prompt.

```
PS1="\a\n\n\[\e[31;1m\]\u@\h on \d at \@\n\[\e[33;1m\]↵
\w\[\e[0m\]\n\[\e[32;1m\]\$ \[\e[0m\]"
```

© V. Subhash 2023
V. Subhash, *Quick Start Guide to FFmpeg*, https://doi.org/10.1007/978-1-4842-8701-9_11

Figure 11-1. *This is a very informative terminal prompt with almost the entire length of the window available for your epic ffmpeg commands*

☞   For this prompt to work effectively, you need to change the background of the terminal to black.

For a minimal style of the prompt, use the following:

```
PS1="\a\n\n\[\e[31;1m\]\w\n\[\e[33;1m\]\$ \[\e[0m\]"
```

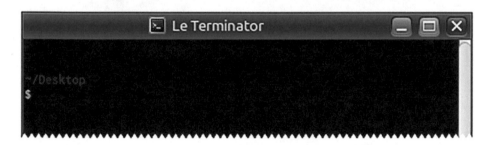

Figure 11-2. *Same as in the previous screenshot but with less information overload*

File Manager Automation

The first rule of software development is "Give what the user wants." This rule implies another thing – "Do not give what the user does not want." But, it was not to be... When the Chrome browser was released, it lacked options to change important settings. Apologists claimed that most users did not need them or know how to use them. This was no accident. For several years, there had been a shift away from "More power to users" objective to "The user is stupid" mantra. In the open source community, Gnome 3 desktop environment project became plagued with this attitude. The project decided that users of their glorious touch-me-not desktop should not be allowed to customize or personalize anything. (*Linus Torvalds finds GNOME 3.4 to be a "total user experience design failure"*; 2012; ZDnet.com) Customization and changing default settings were compared to the tragedy that was known as Myspace personal pages. They claimed that users did not need extra features. Windows 8 developers also justified the destruction of their desktop in similar terms. They removed features and claimed it was an improvement. All kinds of snake oil was used to sell this deprivation of usability – "This is the new way of doing things," "Don't be stuck in old ways," "You are unwilling to change," "Embrace change," and the dreaded "Change is goooooooood."

Fortunately, not all developers succumbed to this impairment of judging faculties. Some of them developed the Mate (pronounced "mah-tay") desktop environment that continued support for the intuitive and user-friendly Gnome 2.

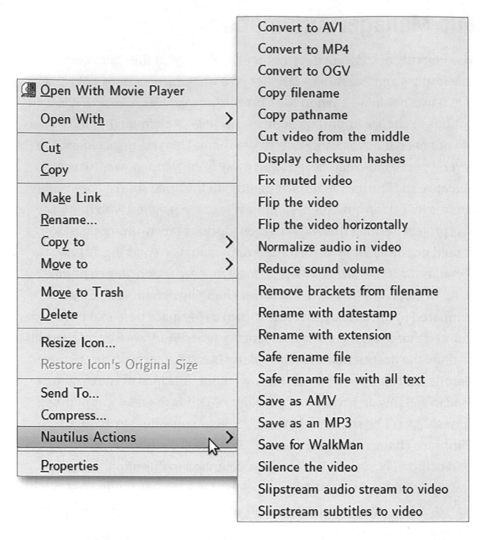

Figure 11-3. *In the year 2020, the context menu options in the file manager of my desktop became so heavy with FFmpeg automation scripts that I decided to write this book*

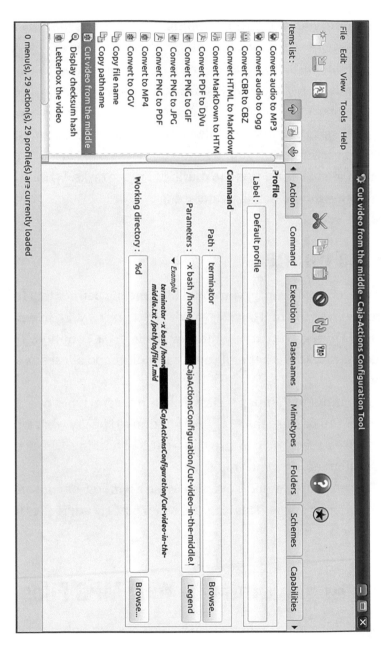

Figure 11-4. *In the Mate desktop, the file manager is called Caja. You can use the app Caja Actions Configuration to add your own custom context-sensitive menu options inside Caja*

In Gnome 2, you could install *Nautilus Actions Configuration* to add custom context menu options to *Nautilus*, the default file and desktop manager. In Gnome 3, Nautilus lost most of its features and became frustratingly useless. Thankfully, however, the *Mate desktop project* continued support for Nautilus and forked it as Caja. Caja has a fork of the Nautilus Actions Configuration called *Caja Actions Configuration*.

Now, stop fighting with your desktop and switch to Mate. Write your own context menus and automate routine FFmpeg tasks. Writing long FFmpeg poems should be for greater things.

Hide the Banner

In older versions of FFmpeg, you could hide the big banner that it displays by redirecting it to the null device (`2> /dev/null` or `2> NUL`). In new versions of FFmpeg, you can use the new `-hide_banner` option. Typing this option is a hassle, so it is better if you create command aliases as described in Chapter 2.

The log output of FFmpeg is classified into several types of information. You can use the `-loglevel` option to specify what types you would like to see. You can also choose to see nothing. Check the documentation for what you would like.

`ffplay` can be prevented from displaying a window or console output using the option `-nodisp`. This is useful when playing audio files in shell scripts.

Add an espeak Intro to Your MP3 Files

I have lots of vintage radio shows as MP3 files. My DIY boombox does not display any tags or filenames - only file numbers.

Figure 11-5. *I built this boombox. The MP3 player module's display is limited to song numbers*

I use a script that iterates through the MP3 files in a directory and adds an espeak intro to the files. If a file is named "Fibber-n-Molly-Fibber-Makes-His-Own-Chili-Sauce.mp3," then espeak intelligently reads it out as "Fibber n Molly Fibber Makes His Own Chili Sauce." This audio is first saved to a wave file and then concatenated to the MP3 file.

```
cd "$1"     # Moves to a directory with MP3 files
if [ ! -d AnnD ]; then
  mkdir AnnD
fi

for sFile in *.mp3
do
  sFileName=${sFile%.*}
  espeak -w "${sFileName}.wav" "$sFileName"
  echo "Processing ${sFile}..."
  ffmpeg -i "${sFileName}.wav" -i "$sFile" \
         -filter_complex \
             "[0:a:0][1:a:0]concat=n=2:v=0:a=1[outa]" \
```

```
            -map_metadata 1 -id3v2_version 3 \
            -map "[outa]" \
            -c:a libmp3lame  \
            "AnnD/${sFileName}-AnnD.mp3" 2> /dev/null
    echo -e "\tsaved to AnnD/${sFileName}-AnnD.mp3"
    rm "${sFileName}.wav"
done
```

Although FFmpeg can be used to tag MP3 files, I prefer to use *EasyTAG* instead. It has sophisticated options to mass-rename files and set MP3 tags. (I am not an FFmpeg fanatic and neither should you be one.) After I neatly tag and name the MP3 files, I let this FFmpeg script do its thing.

```
~/Desktop/FasDrive
$ bash add-intro-to-mp3s.txt ./vintage-radio-shows
Processing Duffy's-Tavern-Fred-Allen-Hosts-A-Pig-Roast.mp3...
        saved to AnnD/Duffy's-Tavern-Fred-Allen-Hosts-A-Pig-Roast-AnnD.mp3
Processing Duffy's-Tavern-The-Raffle-Joan-Bennet.mp3...
        saved to AnnD/Duffy's-Tavern-The-Raffle-Joan-Bennet-AnnD.mp3
Processing Fibber-n-Molly-Ceramics.mp3...
        saved to AnnD/Fibber-n-Molly-Ceramics-AnnD.mp3
Processing Fibber-n-Molly-Fibber-Get-His-Draft-Notice.mp3...
        saved to AnnD/Fibber-n-Molly-Fibber-Get-His-Draft-Notice-AnnD.mp3
Processing Fibber-n-Molly-Fibber-Makes-His-Own-Chili-Sauce.mp3...
        saved to AnnD/Fibber-n-Molly-Fibber-Makes-His-Own-Chili-Sauce-AnnD.

~/Desktop/FasDrive
$
```

Figure 11-6. *If an MP3 file is informatively named, then this script can add a useful spoken introduction to it*

I prefer espeak to libflite. However, unlike espeak, libflite has a female voice option.

```
ffmpeg -f lavfi -i "flite=textfile=speech.txt:voice=slt" \
       speech.mp3
```

Best MP3 (MPEG 2 Audio Layer 3) Conversion Settings

MP3 is a lossy compression scheme for audio. When the bitrate is higher, the loss is minimized. This applies only when the source is of high quality. However, most people are unable to discern the difference between a song encoded at 64kbps and the same encoded at 320kbps. (It also depends on the equipment used to play the music.)

There are two popular methods of encoding MP3s - VBR (variable bitrate) and CBR (constant bitrate). With VBR, the bitrate rate changes over the length of playback and file size is optimized. CBR maintains the same bitrate throughout the length of the audio. When the same amount of data is used to encode data that is not much different, file size may be on the higher side.

MP3 processing (decoding and encoding) is a mature technology now and does not require a lot of processing power. There is no reason to use CBR. VBR is better because it focuses on quality.

To create a VBR MP3 file, use the `-qscale:a` option with the Lame MP3 encoder. The option's range is 0 to 9. For close resemblance to the original, use a value from 0 to 3. For most people, however, a `-qscale:a` value of 4 is good enough.

```
ffmpeg -i uncompressed.wav \
     -c:a libmp3lame \
     -qscale:a 4 \
     good.mp3
```

To create an old-school CBR MP3 file, use the `b:a` (bitrate) option.

```
ffmpeg -i uncompressed.wav \
     -c:a libmp3lame \
     -b:a 128k \
     goot.mp3
```

173

Colors in Hexadecimal

Any color can be represented as a combination of three color channels - red (R), green (G), and blue (B). Sometimes, a fourth value called alpha or transparency is also specified. When alpha is present, the colors can range from totally transparent to totally opaque. When alpha is not present, the color can range from black to the full color.

Colors are often represented in hexadecimal. This is a numbering system with a base of 16. It uses the numerals 0 to 9 and A to F.

- When one hexadecimal digit is used, the values can range from 0 to 15.

- With two digits (00 to FF), the range is 0 to 255.

Using these digit combinations,

- Red can be represented as F00 (RGB), F00F (RGBA), FF0000 (RRGGBB), and FF0000FF (RRGGBBAA).

- Blue can be represented as 00F, 00FF, 0000FF, and 0000FFFF.

- Black is represented as 000, 000F, 000000, and 000000FF.

- White is represented as FFF, FFFF, FFFFFF, and FFFFFFFF.

- Half-transparent red can be represented as F007 or FF000077.

The alpha channel affects all the other three channels. It needs to be at its maximum value (F, FF) for a color to be totally opaque. If it is any less, the entire color will have some transparency, and any object below the color will show through it. If there are not more than one layer of colors, then alpha value has no relevance and will be ignored.

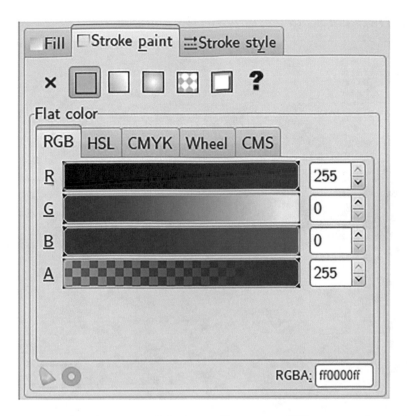

Figure 11-7. *Any image-editing application will have a color palette. This one is from Inkscape*

For ffmpeg, colors are specified in the form of 0xRRGGBBAA. The AA part, standing for the alpha channel, is optional.

Colors in Literal

While you can specify colors in hexadecimal, FFmpeg also supports some literal names, as listed in Table 11-1. These are the same nonstandard color names that Microsoft introduced into Internet Explorer and forced Firefox to adopt them to maintain compatibility. In addition to these color names, you can also use the literal random and let FFmpeg choose a color by random.

Table 11-1. *Color names supported by FFmpeg*

AliceBlue 0xF0F8FF	AntiqueWhite 0xFAEBD7	Aqua 0x00FFFF	Aquamarine 0x7FFFD4
Azure 0xF0FFFF	Beige 0xF5F5DC	Bisque 0xFFE4C4	Black 0x000000
BlanchedAlmond 0xFFEBCD	Blue 0x0000FF	BlueViolet 0x8A2BE2	Brown 0xA52A2A
BurlyWood 0xDEB887	CadetBlue 0x5F9EA0	Chartreuse 0x7FFF00	Chocolate 0xD2691E
Coral 0xFF7F50	CornflowerBlue 0x6495ED	Cornsilk 0xFFF8DC	Crimson 0xDC143C
Cyan 0x00FFFF	DarkBlue 0x00008B	DarkCyan 0x008B8B	DarkGoldenRod 0xB8860B
DarkGray 0xA9A9A9	DarkGreen 0x006400	DarkKhaki 0xBDB76B	DarkMagenta 0x8B008B
DarkOliveGreen 0x556B2F	Darkorange 0xFF8C00	DarkOrchid 0x9932CC	DarkRed 0x8B0000
DarkSalmon 0xE9967A	DarkSeaGreen 0x8FBC8F	DarkSlateBlue 0x483D8B	DarkSlateGray 0x2F4F4F
DarkTurquoise 0x00CED1	DarkViolet 0x9400D3	DeepPink 0xFF1493	DeepSkyBlue 0x00BFFF
DimGray 0x696969	DodgerBlue 0x1E90FF	FireBrick 0xB22222	FloralWhite 0xFFFAF0
ForestGreen 0x228B22	Fuchsia 0xFF00FF	Gainsboro 0xDCDCDC	GhostWhite 0xF8F8FF
Gold 0xFFD700	GoldenRod 0xDAA520	Gray 0x808080	Green 0x008000
GreenYellow 0xADFF2F	HoneyDew 0xF0FFF0	HotPink 0xFF69B4	IndianRed 0xCD5C5C
Indigo 0x4B0082	Ivory 0xFFFFF0	Khaki 0xF0E68C	Lavender 0xE6E6FA
LavenderBlush 0xFFF0F5	LawnGreen 0x7CFC00	LemonChiffon 0xFFFACD	LightBlue 0xADD8E6
LightCoral 0xF08080	LightCyan 0xE0FFFF	LightGoldenRodYellow .0xFAFAD2	LightGreen 0x90EE90
LightGrey 0xD3D3D3	LightPink 0xFFB6C1	LightSalmon 0xFFA07A	LightSeaGreen 0x20B2AA
LightSkyBlue 0x87CEFA	LightSlateGray 0x778899	LightSteelBlue 0xB0C4DE	LightYellow 0xFFFFE0
Lime 0x00FF00	LimeGreen 0x32CD32	Linen 0xFAF0E6	Magenta 0xFF00FF
Maroon 0x800000	MediumAquaMarine 0x66CDAA	MediumBlue 0x0000CD	MediumOrchid 0xBA55D3

(continued)

Table 11-1. (*continued*)

MediumPurple 0x9370D8	MediumSeaGreen 0x3CB371	MediumSlateBlue 0x7B68EE	MediumSpringGreen 0x00FA9A
MediumTurquoise 0x48D1CC	MediumVioletRed 0xC71585	MidnightBlue 0x191970	MintCream 0xF5FFFA
MistyRose 0xFFE4E1	Moccasin 0xFFE4B5	NavajoWhite 0xFFDEAD	Navy 0x000080
OldLace 0xFDF5E6	Olive 0x808000	OliveDrab 0x6B8E23	Orange 0xFFA500
OrangeRed 0xFF4500	Orchid 0xDA70D6	PaleGoldenRod 0xEEE8AA	PaleGreen 0x98FB98
PaleTurquoise 0xAFEEEE	PaleVioletRed 0xD87093	PapayaWhip 0xFFEFD5	PeachPuff 0xFFDAB9
Peru 0xCD853F	Pink 0xFFC0CB	Plum 0xDDA0DD	PowderBlue 0xB0E0E6
Purple 0x800080	Red 0xFF0000	RosyBrown 0xBC8F8F	RoyalBlue 0x4169E1
SaddleBrown 0x8B4513	Salmon 0xFA8072	SandyBrown 0xF4A460	SeaGreen 0x2E8B57
SeaShell 0xFFF5EE	Sienna 0xA0522D	Silver 0xC0C0C0	SkyBlue 0x87CEEB
SlateBlue 0x6A5ACD	SlateGray 0x708090	Snow 0xFFFAFA	SpringGreen 0x00FF7F
SteelBlue 0x4682B4	Tan 0xD2B48C	Teal 0x008080	Thistle 0xD8BFD8
Tomato 0xFF6347	Turquoise 0x40E0D0	Violet 0xEE82EE	Wheat 0xF5DEB3
White 0xFFFFFF	WhiteSmoke 0xF5F5F5	Yellow 0xFFFF00	YellowGreen 0x9ACD32

Streams Information from `ffprobe`

`ffprobe` can display precise and structured information about a media file that can be filtered by your shell scripts or software programs for further processing.

```
ffprobe -show_streams -i somefile.mp4
```

The output of the preceding command is as printed in the following.

```
[STREAM]
index=0
codec_name=h264
codec_long_name=H.264 / AVC / MPEG-4 AVC / MPEG-4 part 10
profile=High
codec_type=video
codec_tag_string=avc1
codec_tag=0x31637661
width=640
height=480
coded_width=640
coded_height=480
closed_captions=0
film_grain=0
has_b_frames=2
sample_aspect_ratio=4:3
display_aspect_ratio=16:9
pix_fmt=yuv420p
level=30
color_range=unknown
color_space=unknown
color_transfer=unknown
color_primaries=unknown
chroma_location=left
field_order=progressive
refs=1
is_avc=true
nal_length_size=4
id=0x1
r_frame_rate=90000/2999
```

```
avg_frame_rate=90000/2999
time_basc=1/90000
start_pts=0
start_time=0.000000
duration_ts=1802399
duration=20.026656
bit_rate=488521
max_bit_rate=N/A
bits_per_raw_sample=8
nb_frames=601
nb_read_frames=N/A
nb_read_packets=N/A
extradata_size=40
DISPOSITION:default=1
DISPOSITION:dub=0
DISPOSITION:original=0
DISPOSITION:comment=0
DISPOSITION:lyrics=0
DISPOSITION:karaoke=0
DISPOSITION:forced=0
DISPOSITION:hearing_impaired=0
DISPOSITION:visual_impaired=0
DISPOSITION:clean_effects=0
DISPOSITION:attached_pic=0
DISPOSITION:timed_thumbnails=0
DISPOSITION:captions=0
DISPOSITION:descriptions=0
DISPOSITION:metadata=0
DISPOSITION:dependent=0
DISPOSITION:still_image=0
TAG:language=eng
```

```
TAG:handler_name=VideoHandle
TAG:vendor_id=[0][0][0][0]
[/STREAM]
[STREAM]
index=1
codec_name=aac
codec_long_name=AAC (Advanced Audio Coding)
profile=LC
codec_type=audio
codec_tag_string=mp4a
codec_tag=0x6134706d
sample_fmt=fltp
sample_rate=48000
channels=2
channel_layout=stereo
bits_per_sample=0
id=0x2
r_frame_rate=0/0
avg_frame_rate=0/0
time_base=1/48000
start_pts=0        .
start_time=0.000000
duration_ts=960000
duration=20.000000
bit_rate=129267
max_bit_rate=N/A
bits_per_raw_sample=N/A
nb_frames=939
nb_read_frames=N/A
nb_read_packets=N/A
extradata_size=5
```

```
DISPOSITION:default=1
DISPOSITION:dub=0
DISPOSITION:original=0
DISPOSITION:comment=0
DISPOSITION:lyrics=0
DISPOSITION:karaoke=0
DISPOSITION:forced=0
DISPOSITION:hearing_impaired=0
DISPOSITION:visual_impaired=0
DISPOSITION:clean_effects=0
DISPOSITION:attached_pic=0
DISPOSITION:timed_thumbnails=0
DISPOSITION:captions=0
DISPOSITION:descriptions=0
DISPOSITION:metadata=0
DISPOSITION:dependent=0
DISPOSITION:still_image=0
TAG:language=eng
TAG:handler_name=SoundHandle
TAG:vendor_id=[0][0][0][0]
[/STREAM]
```

This output can be narrowed down to a particular stream using the
`select_streams` option.

```
ffprobe -show_streams -select_streams v:0 \
        -i somefile.mp4 2> /dev/null
```

This option can also be output in several other formats such as ini and
CSV. For more information, check the documentation that came with your
version of FFmpeg.

```
ffprobe -show_streams -select_streams v:0 \
    -print_format csv \
    -i somefile.mp4 > somefile-videostream-info.csv
```

With the -sections option, you can find out how the streams information is organized.

```
ffprobe -sections
```

This is the output:

```
Sections:
W.. = Section is a wrapper (contains other sections,⏎
no local entries)
.A. = Section contains an array of elements of the⏎
same type
..V = Section may contain a variable number of fields⏎
with variable keys
FLAGS NAME/UNIQUE_NAME
---
W..    root
.A.        chapters
...            chapter
..V                tags/chapter_tags
...        format
..V            tags/format_tags
.A.        frames
...            frame
..V                tags/frame_tags
.A.                side_data_list/frame_side_data_list
...                    side_data/frame_side_data
.A.                        timecodes
...                            timecode
.A.                        components
```

```
...                        component
.A.                         pieces
...                           section
.A.         logs
...            log
...       subtitle
.A.    programs
...       program
..V          tags/program_tags
.A.          streams/program_streams
...            stream/program_stream
...              disposition/program_stream_
                 disposition
..V              tags/program_stream_tags
.A.    streams
...       stream
...          disposition/stream_disposition
..V          tags/stream_tags
.A.          side_data_list/stream_side_data_list
...            side_data/stream_side_data
.A.    packets
...       packet
..V          tags/packet_tags
.A.          side_data_list/packet_side_data_list
...            side_data/packet_side_data
...    error
...    program_version
.A.    library_versions
...       library_version
.A.    pixel_formats
...       pixel_format
```

```
...                    flags/pixel_format_flags
.A.                    components/pixel_format_components
...                       component
```

To display a particular key, say "duration," I can use the `-show_entries` option.

```
ffprobe -select_streams v:0  \
        -show_entries "stream=duration" \
        -i somefile.mp4 2> /dev/null
```

```
        [STREAM]
        duration=20.026656
        [/STREAM]
```

To eliminate section headers and key name, I use the `-print_format` option.

```
ffprobe -select_streams v:0  \
        -show_entries "stream=duration" \
        -print_format "default=nokey=1:noprint_wrappers=1" \
        -i somefile.mp4 2> /dev/null
```

Cue heavenly music!

```
        20.026656
```

Now, the command output contains just the duration value. Similarly, other details about an input file can be atomized. Your shell script or some other program can capture these values for further processing.

```
~/Desktop/FasDrive
$ w=$(ffprobe -select_streams v:0 \
>               -show_entries "stream=width:" \
>               -print_format "default=nokey=1:noprint_wrappers=1" \
>               -i festival-fireworks.avi 2> /dev/null)


~/Desktop/FasDrive
$ h=$(ffprobe -select_streams v:0 \
>               -show_entries "stream=height" \
>               -print_format "default=nokey=1:noprint_wrappers=1" \
>               -i festival-fireworks.avi 2> /dev/null)


~/Desktop/FasDrive
$ echo "$w × $h"
1280 × 720
```

Figure 11-8. *ffprobe output can be filtered for obtaining precise information about a multimedia file. This information can be stored in memory variables for further use in shell scripts*

Extract Non-pixelated Images from a Video

When a video undergoes lossy compression, there are bound to be some artifacts in any still images that you extract from it. If the bitrate is low or there is a lot of fast-paced action, the artifacts can be impossible to ignore. You have a better chance at obtaining high-quality stills if you extract only the *I frames* in the video. I frames or key frames in a video stream have all the data to form a full image. There are other frames, known as *P frames*, that are immediately before and after an *I frame* that do not have all the data. Their data is limited to those regions of the frame that are different from the nearest I frame. When you extract still images, FFmpeg tries to recreate a full frame using data from several frames. As not all of them are likely to be I frames, there may be some inevitable pixelation.

```
ffmpeg -y -i train.mp4 \
       -r 1 \
       -f image2 \
       nofilter-still%02d.jpg

ffmpeg -y -skip_frame nokey -i train.mp4 \
        -r 1 \
       -f image2 \
         filter-still%02d.jpg
```

The preceding first command tries to extract frames as usual without any discrimination. The second command picks only I frames, which are most likely to be without much pixelation.

Figure 11-9. *The source video was taken from a moving train. The first command took still images at regular intervals without consideration for image quality. The second command only took the I frames with maximal detail and less pixelation*

If you want a good-quality still from a particular timestamp, try something like this:

```
ffmpeg -y -ss 0:0:20 -skip_frame nokey -i aero-india.mp4 \
        -frames:v 1 -f image2 \
            still20.jpg
```

This command takes a still after the 20-second mark. When there is a lot of action at that timestamp, `ffmpeg` may not be able to find an I frame there, and this may result in some inevitable pixelation.

Create a Thumbnail Gallery for a Video

This shell script creates a 3x3 tiled gallery of thumbnails at one-third of the dimensions of the original video.

```
#!/bin/bash
# BASH script to create a 3x3 thumbnail gallery for a video
# Accepts the pathname of the video as argument ($1)

###########################################################
# Floating point number functions by Mitch Frazier
# Adapted from
# https://www.linuxjournal.com/content/floating-point-math-bash
###########################################################

# Default scale used by float functions
float_scale=2

# Evaluate a floating point number expression.
function float_eval() {
  local stat=0
  local result=0.0
  if [[ $# -gt 0 ]]; then
```

```
    result=$(echo "scale=$float_scale; $*" | bc -q 2>/dev/null)
    stat=$?
    if [[ $stat -eq 0  &&  -z "$result" ]]; then
      stat=1
    fi
  fi
  echo $result
  return $stat
}

# Evaluate a floating point number conditional expression.
function float_cond() {
  local cond=0
  if [[ $# -gt 0 ]]; then
    cond=$(echo "$*" | bc -q 2>/dev/null)
    if [[ -z "$cond" ]]; then
      cond=0
    fi
    if [[ "$cond" != 0  &&  "$cond" != 1 ]]; then
      cond=0
    fi
  fi
  local stat=$(((cond == 0)))
  return $stat
}
###############################################################
# Floating point number functions end

# Prefix for images
FILE_NAME=${1%.*}
#echo $FILE_NAME

NUMBER_OF_THUMBNAILS=9
```

```
MOVIE="$1"
COUNTER=0

# Number of seconds
MOVIE_DURATION=$(ffprobe \
                  -show_entries "format=duration" \
                  -of "default=nokey=1:noprint_wrappers=1" \
                  -i $MOVIE 2> /dev/null)
#echo $MOVIE_DURATION

MOVIE_WIDTH=$(ffprobe -select_streams v:0 \
              -show_entries "stream=width:" \
              -print_format \
                "default=nokey=1:noprint_wrappers=1" \
              -i $MOVIE 2> /dev/null)
MOVIE_HEIGHT=$(ffprobe -select_streams v:0 \
              -show_entries "stream=height" \
              -print_format \
                "default=nokey=1:noprint_wrappers=1" \
              -i $MOVIE 2> /dev/null)
#echo "$MOVIE_WIDTH x $MOVIE_HEIGHT"

TW=$(float_eval "$MOVIE_WIDTH/3")
TH=$(float_eval "$MOVIE_HEIGHT/3")
THUMB_WIDTH=${TW%.*}
THUMB_HEIGHT=${TH%.*}
#echo "$THUMB_WIDTH x $THUMB_HEIGHT"

for i in $(seq $NUMBER_OF_THUMBNAILS)
do
  let COUNTER=COUNTER+1
  #echo $COUNTER
  LOCATION_FLOAT=$(float_eval \
```

```
                "($i-0.5)*$MOVIE_DURATION/$NUMBER_OF_THUMBNAILS")
#echo $LOCATION_FLOAT
LOCATION_INT=${LOCATION_FLOAT%.*}
#echo $LOCATION_INT

# Create the thumbnails
ffmpeg -y -skip_frame nokey -ss $LOCATION_INT -i $MOVIE \
        -frames:v 1 \
        -s ${THUMB_WIDTH}x${THUMB_HEIGHT} \
        "${FILE_NAME}_${COUNTER}.jpg"
done

# Create the gallery
montage -density 96 -tile 3x3 -geometry +4+4 \
        -border 1 "${FILE_NAME}*.jpg" \
        "${FILE_NAME}-thumbnail.jpg"
```

☞   This script is my implementation of a pseudocode found at
https://superuser.com/a/821680.

The last command in the shell script uses *ImageMagick*, which is a powerful open source program for processing images.

This script can be easily modified for greater grid sizes. It is also very fast, as it quickly skips to different locations in the file to take the thumbnail snapshots. It does not parse through the entire file.

The script only picks I-frame images from the file. Totem media player creates a thumbnail gallery similar to this. It is very fast but its thumbnails are just equidistant in time. They are not necessarily high-quality images.

When you run this script on a video file, pass its pathname as the first argument:

```
bash create-thumbnail-gallery.txt festival-fireworks.avi
```

Figure 11-10. *The Totem media player creates a thumbnail gallery much faster than this script. However, it does not find I frames like this script does. With I frames, you get more detail*

Record from Microphone

A PC may have more than one sound device - built-in sound card, the webcam, HDMI output audio, and sometimes even a USB microphone. In Linux, these sound cards are identified as `hw:0`, `hw:1`.... You have to find which one you are using or what can record audio through its microphone. **Check your desktop sound configuration utility, and ensure that it is responding to noises in your room.** After this,

- Type `alsamixer` in Terminal.

- Press F6 key to display the list of cards. Make a note of the number of the card, as you will need it later.

- After selecting the card, press the F2 to display the list of devices on that card. Select `/proc/sound/devices` to check if you have an *audio capture* device on that card.

- Exit `alsamixer` by pressing the Esc key.

- If you are then able to record from the device using the number of the card with this command, then you are all set to record from the microphone.

```
ffmpeg -f alsa -i hw:1 -t 10 microphone-test.mp3
```

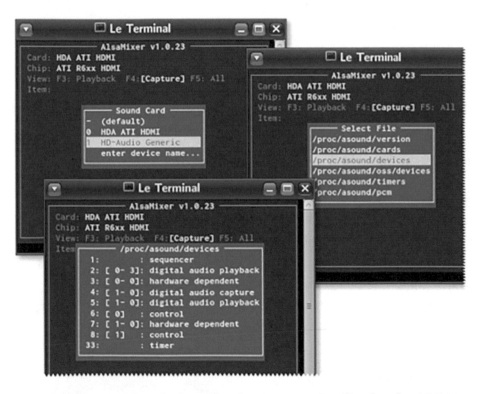

Figure 11-11. *A console-based volume control utility for the ALSA sound system*

If you are still unable to record, then audio capture may have been disabled.

- Type the command `amixer -c` followed by the number of the sound card.

- Note the name of the device for the microphone. Usually, it is named `Mic` or `Internal Mic`.

- Type a command like `amixer -c 1 sset Mic,0 mute cap`. This ensures that the sound captured from the second sound card (1) is not played back (`mute`) but is available for recording (`cap`).

If you have made changes to your audio configuration, it is best if you restart the OS and try again. If nothing works, then try the PulseAudio (`-i pulse`) hack.

```
ffmpeg -f alsa -i pulse -t 10 microphone-pulse-test.mp3
```

Record from Webcam

Recording from a webcam or grabbing the screen output in Windows is not easy. There is a FOSS tool called *CamStudio* that internally uses FFmpeg. If you are able to use it, then follow the FFmpeg Wiki on the topic.

In Linux, things are very easy. Even then, install *Cheese* or a similar webcam application before you use `ffmpeg`. Ensure that the device is working properly. Check the preferences and leave it at the best settings. Then, close it and try this `ffmpeg` command:

```
ffmpeg -y -f v4l2 \
       -i /dev/video0 \
       -s vga -r 12 -b:v 466k \
       -t 0:0:10 \
       webcam.ogv
```

☞   Where did I get this `/dev/video0` thingy? Install `v4l-ctl` or `v4l-utils` and type the command `v4l2-ctl --list-devices`.

☞   To tell you the truth, I do not use webcams anymore. This command was tested on an ancient Logitech cam that still works fine. Check the settings supported by your hi-res Hasselblad, and update the size and bitrate options accordingly.

You can simultaneously capture from your webcam and microphone.

```
ffmpeg -f v4l2 -r 12 -s qvga -i /dev/video0 \
       -f alsa -i hw:1 \
       -t 0:0:6 \
       webcam2.ogv
```

On my old laptop (with a new OS), this command struggles to record the audio. With the PulseAudio hack, it magically starts working fine.

```
ffmpeg -f v4l2 -r 12 -s qvga -i /dev/video0 \
       -f alsa -i pulse \
       -t 0:0:6 \
       webcam3.ogv
```

Screen Capture

The `-f x11grab` format option can be used to capture the video display (`-i :0.0`, known as *X* in Linux). You need to specify the capture settings in the order given here, that is, `-f`, `-s`, `-i`, and `-b`. The frame rate can be 12 at the minimum. Otherwise, the output capture file will be very big.

```
ffmpeg -y -f x11grab -s 1366x768 -r 12 \
       -i :0.0 \
       -b:v 1024k \
       -t 0:0:10 \
       screen.ogv
```

☞   Replace the value for the `-s` option with the pixel resolution of the screen you are trying to grab.

While screen capturing, use a high bitrate so that as much data is captured. The capture will be lag-free if the CPU is not tied up with real-time compression (encoding). You can compress the file to your heart's content after the capture but not during it.

To capture a part of the screen, add the x- and y-offsets of the region in the `-i` option.

```
# Records a 600x600 region at 100,100 pixels
# from the top-left corner.
ffmpeg -y -f x11grab -s 600x600 -r 12 \
       -i :0.0+100,100 \
       -b:v 1024k \
       -t 0:0:10 \
       screen-region.ogv
```

You can capture sound playing on the speakers while you grab the screen. The input to capture (sound mixer) is not easy to nail down on my computer, so this command uses the PulseAudio hack (`-i pulse`) again.

```
ffmpeg -f x11grab -s 1366x768 -r 12 -i :0.0 \
       -f alsa -i pulse \
       -b:v 2024K -b:a 128K \
```

```
-ac 2 \
-t 0:0:10 \
-y screen2.ogv
```

Render an Animated GIF on a Video

Humble as it is, an animated GIF can be more dramatic than a static JPEG or PNG. For this example, I rendered a GIF animation that I use on my website over a demo video that I created for my Android browser.

```
ffmpeg -y -i subhash-browser-rss-demo.mp4  \
    -ignore_loop 0 -i animation-download.gif \
    -filter_complex \
    "[0:v:0]overlay=(W-w-10):(H-h)/2:shortest=1[v]" \
    -map '[v]' -map 0:a:0  \
    -c:v libx264 -c:a copy \
    subhash-browser-rss-demo-with-download-button.mp4
```

If I were to upload this demo to a video-hosting site, I could add an interactive download link to the region where the animated GIF is playing on the video. When I used the overlay filter with a GIF on a video, the animation played once and then stopped. I found a solution to this problem, that is, -ignore_loop 0, hidden in the help output of the GIF demuxer (ffmpeg -h demuxer=gif). This however had a limitation in that the looping is limited to whatever value the GIF image is set to. This could be infinite or 1 to 65535 times. If it was set to a finite number, then the looping would have stopped eventually.

A better approach is to use the -stream_loop option so that you can specify the looping instead of the GIF image. You can set this option to the number of loops, 0 for no looping or -1 for indefinite looping.

```
ffmpeg -y -i subhash-browser-rss-demo.mp4  \
       -stream_loop -1 -i animation-download.gif \
       -filter_complex \
        "[0:v:0]overlay=(W-w-10):(H-h)/2:shortest=1[v]" \
       -map '[v]' -map 0:a:0  \
       -c:v libx264 -c:a copy \
        subhash-browser-rss-demo-with-download-button.mp4
```

The -shortest option in the overlay filter ensures that the filter processing ends when the output from the video file has been completed. Otherwise, the endlessly looping GIF animation will continue the processing forever.

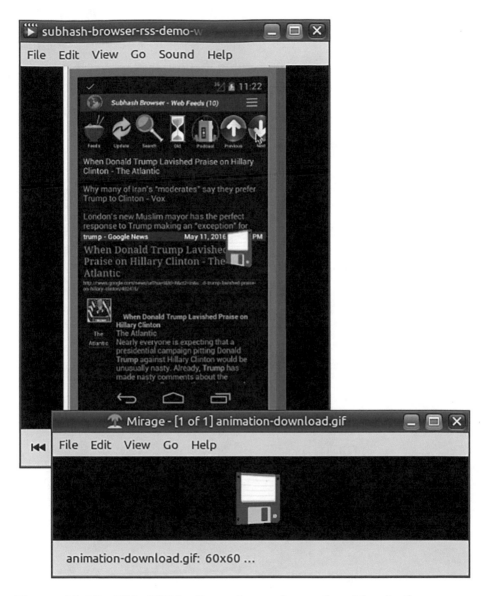

Figure 11-12. *This GIF is also animated over the video in the background window*

Show a Timer on the Video

The drawtext filter has a timecode option that can be used in place of
the text option. To ensure that the timer is accurate, the timecode_rate
should be the same as the frame rate of the video. (Use ffprobe for
obtaining the exact value.)

```
ffmpeg -y -i rollcage-video.mp4 \
        -filter:v \
           "drawtext=:x=100:y=h-lh-100:
                shadowcolor=FFFFFF66:shadowx=1:shadowy=2:
                fontfile=Time.ttf:fontcolor=00000066:fontsize=70:
                timecode=\'00\:00\:00\:00\':timecode_
rate=29.91" \
           race-timer.mp4
```

Figure 11-13. *This command uses an option of the* drawtext *filter to render a timer on the video*

Create a Silent Ringtone

Some mobile phones do not have a silent ringtone. This can prevent you from silencing certain obnoxious contacts. You can use the anullsrc filter to create a silent ringtone.

```
ffmpeg -f lavfi \
      -i anullsrc \
      -vn -t 0:0:12 -b:a 128k -c:a libmp3lame \
      silent.mp3
```

This command uses the filter as a virtual input file. The `anullsrc` filter does not require an input file. By default, it generates a 44100 Hz wave as output. This one will have no sound though.

Create a Countdown Beep Audio

Television quiz shows usually play a timer-countdown audio with a beep every second. Can you create it using FFmpeg?

```
ffplay -f lavfi \
       -i "sine=frequency=220:beep_factor=3:duration=20"

ffmpeg -f lavfi \
       -i "sine=frequency=220:beep_factor=3:duration=20" \
       sine.wav
```

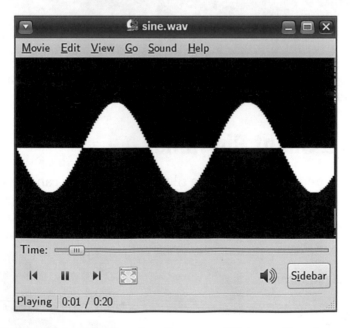

Figure 11-14. *The visualization feature of this media player confirms that the audio is a sine wave*

For more customized waveforms, the `aevalsrc` filter can be used.

```
ffmpeg -f lavfi \
       -i aevalsrc='sin(1000*PI*t*lt(t-trunc(t)\,0.1))' \
       -t 0:0:20 sine.wav
```

Generate Noise of a Certain "Color"

FFmpeg can generate noise in several "colors" - white, pink, brown, blue, violet, and velvet.

```
ffplay -f lavfi -showmode 0 -i 'anoisesrc=color=brown'
```

The "brown" noise is closer to the sound that a TV generates when its CATV signal cable is unplugged.

```
ffmpeg -y -i barbara.mp4 \
  -filter_complex \
    "[0:v:0]noise=alls=100:allf=a+t:enable='between(t,6,12)'[v];
    [0:a:0]atrim=start=0:end=6, asetpts=N/SAMPLE_RATE/TB[fa];
    anoisesrc=color=brown:d=6[ma];
    [0:a:0]atrim=start=12:end=20, asetpts=N/SAMPLE_RATE/TB[la];
    [fa][ma][la]concat=n=3:v=0:a=1[a]" \
  -map "[v]" -map "[a]" \
  -t 0:0:20 \
  barb-intermission.mp4
```

This command uses a video noise filter between seconds 6 and 12. In the same interval, the aforementioned brown noise is used in place of the original audio.

Create a Bleep Audio

A few months ago, I created a video where I needed to bleep out some segments of a speaker's audio. I did not have an audio file containing the bleep sound. I then found that there were several programs including FFmpeg that could be used to create the bleep sound. This example uses a 1000 Hz wave of a continuous bleep sound instead of the original audio for seconds 6 and 7.

```
ffmpeg -y -i barbara.mp4 \
  -filter_complex \
    "[0:a:0]atrim=start=0:end=5, asetpts=N/SAMPLE_RATE/TB[a1];
    sine=frequency=1000:duration=2[a2];
    [0:a:0]atrim=start=7:end=10, asetpts=N/SAMPLE_RATE/TB[a3];
    [a1][a2][a3]concat=n=3:v=0:a=1[a]" \
  -map 0:v:0 -map '[a]' \
  -t 0:0:10 \
  barb-bleep.mp4
```

Add an Echo to Part of a Video

This command adds a six-second echo in the middle of playback using the aecho filter.

```
ffmpeg -y -i barbara.mp4 \
  -filter_complex \
    "[0:a:0]atrim=start=0:end=5, asetpts=N/SR/TB[a1];
    [0:a:0]atrim=start=6:end=12, asetpts=N/SR/TB,
      aecho=0.8:0.9:1000:0.3[a2];
    [0:a:0]atrim=start=13:end=16, asetpts=N/SR/TB[a3];
    [a1][a2][a3]concat=n=3:v=0:a=1[a]" \
```

```
-map 0:v:0 -map '[a]' \
-t 0:0:16 \
barb-echo.mp4
```

☞   The `atrim` and `concat` filters were used because `aecho` does not support timeline editing.

Reverse a Video

In some of his movies, Jim Carrey does a live rewind of a shot. Does he sound intelligible if you rewind that footage?

☞   This routine is actually copied from another movie (whose name I forget), and it involves a mentally disturbed prisoner who thinks he is trapped in a film camera!

```
ffmpeg -y -i ace-ventura-reverse.mp4 \
  -filter_complex \
    "[0:v:0]reverse[v]; [0:a:0]areverse[a]" \
  -map '[v]' -map '[a]' \
  ace-ventura-reverse-reversed.mp4

# Place the videos side-by-side
ffmpeg -y -i ace-ventura-reverse.mp4 \
      -i ace-ventura-reverse-reversed.mp4 \
  -filter_complex  \
    "[0:v:0]pad=1280:360:0:0[frame];
    [frame][1:v:0]overlay=640:0[fullvideo];
    [fullvideo]drawtext=x=30:y=60:fontcolor=yellow:
```

```
    text='Original audio on left speaker':fontsize=30:
    fontfile=Florentia.ttf[lefttext];
 [lefttext]drawtext=x=670:y=60:fontcolor=yellow:
    text='Reversed audio on right speaker':
    fontsize=30:fontfile=Florentia.ttf[v];
 [0:a:0]channelsplit=channel_layout=mono[leftaudio];
 [1:a:0]channelsplit=channel_layout=mono[rightaudio];
 [leftaudio][rightaudio]join=inputs=2: \
    channel_layout=stereo[a]" \
-map '[v]' -map '[a]' ace-ventura-reversal-truth.mp4
```

The documentation warns that the reverse filter consumes a lot of memory, so use small clips.

Fade into Another Video Using a Transition Effect

The xfade filter can be used to transition between two video files. By default, it starts at the beginning of the file, so you need to offset it to the end of the first video. Check the documentation for the different kinds of transitions that are supported. The audio filter acrossfade works as expected at the end of the first file. You just need to set it to the same duration as the xfade video filter.

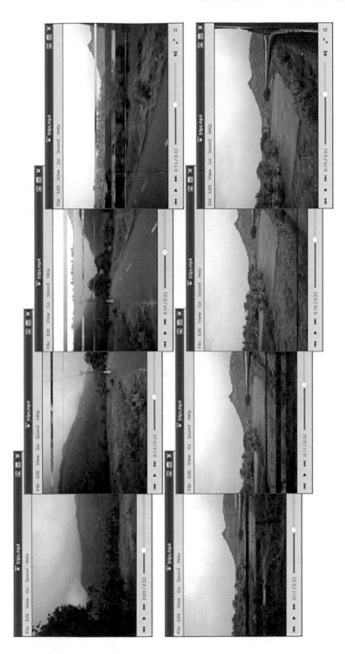

Figure 11-15. *Use* xfade *filter transition from one video to another.*
Use crossfade *to do the same for audio*

```
ffmpeg -y -i bike-trip.mp4 -i train-trip.mp4 \
 -filter_complex \
  "[0:v:0][1:v:0]xfade=transition=vdslice:
                  duration=8:offset=12[v];
   [0:a:0][1:a:0]acrossfade=d=8[a]" \
 -c:v libx264 -crf 21 -tune film -pix_fmt yuv420p \
 -map '[v]' -map '[a]' \
 trips.mp4
```

If you get any time base or frame rate errors because of differences in the videos, try this instead:

```
ffmpeg -y -i bike-trip.mp4 -i train-trip.mp4 \
 -filter_complex \
   "[0:v:0]settb=AVTB, framerate=24[v1];
    [1:v:0]settb=AVTB, framerate=24[v2];
    [v1][v2]xfade=transition=vdslice:duration=8:offset=12[v];
    [0:a:0][1:a:0]acrossfade=d=8[a]" \
 -c:v libx264 -crf 21 -tune film -pix_fmt yuv420p \
 -map '[v]' -map '[a]' \
 trips.mp4
```

Create Waveform Video of Audio

In an earlier section, you learned how to create a sine wave tone. In my old OS, the media player's visualization confirmed that it is indeed a sine wave. In my new OS, the media player has no audio visualization support. How do I know that it is indeed a sine wave? Use the `showwaves` filter! This filter can read an audio stream and generate a video stream containing visual waveform data.

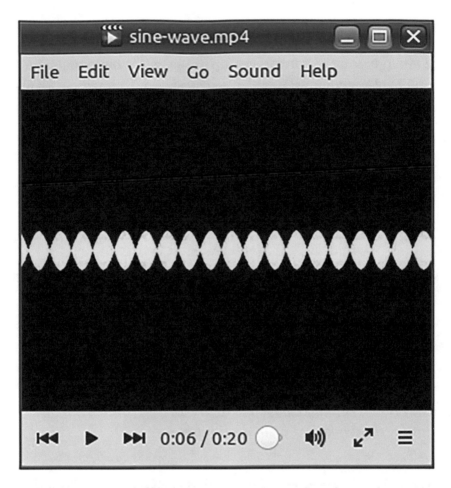

Figure 11-16. *The showwaves filter confirms that the audio is a sine wave*

```
ffmpeg -i sine.wav \
    -filter_complex \
      "showwaves=s=vga:mode=cline:draw=full:
      colors=yellow[v]" \
    -map '[v]' -map 0:a:0 \
    -c:v mpeg4 -b:v 300K -r 24 \
    sine-wave.mp4
```

Create a Waveform Image of Audio

Some audio-hosting sites use waveform images as the background for their audio player controls. How can you create similar images? Use the showwavespic filter.

```
ffmpeg -y -i ace-ventura-reverse.mp4 \
       -lavfi "showwavespic=s=600x120:split_channels=1:
                          colors=yellow|red:scale=sqrt" \
       ace-waveform.png
```

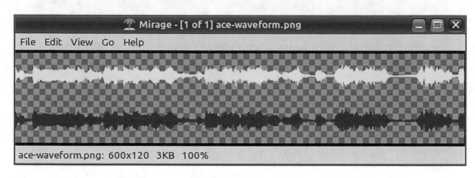

Figure 11-17. *The* showwavespic *filter can generate an image containing the waveform of an audio stream*

Forensic Examination of Audio (Not Really)

Browsing through the FFmpeg documentation, I found several filters that generate visual waveform data from audio streams. I used them on the audio stream of a music recording and then rendered the generated visuals on the input video stream.

```
ffmpeg -y -i chenda-music.mp4 \
  -filter_complex \
    "[0:a:0]showfreqs=s=250x100:mode=bar:cmode=separate:
```

```
    colors=orange|red[chartf];
    [0:a:0]showvolume=w=250:h=50:p=0.6:dm=2:dmc=red[chartv];
    [0:a:0]showwaves=s=250x100:mode=cline:draw=full:
    colors=yellow|orange:split_channels=1[chartw];
    color=color=black@0:size=vga[bg];
    [bg][chartf]overlay=x=20:y=20[v1];
    [v1][chartv]overlay=x=20:y=150[v2];
    [v2][chartw]overlay=x=20:y=280[v3];
    [0:v:0][v3]overlay[v]" \
    -map '[v]' -map 0:a:0 -shortest \
chenda-music-sound-levels.mp4
```

Figure 11-18. *Several filters were used to generate visual waveform data from the audio stream and render it on the video stream*

Replace a Green-Screen Background with Another Video

Do you have a green-screen video? Do you wish to place some other video in place of the green background? The `colorkey` filter is your friend. It replaces a color of your choice with transparency.

```
ffmpeg -y -i festival-fireworks.avi -i van-damme.mp4  \
       -filter_complex \
         "[1:v]colorkey=0x008000:0.2:0.2[v1];
         [0:v:0][v1]overlay=(W-w)/2:(H-h)[v];
         [0:a:0][1:a:0]amerge=inputs=2[a]" \
       -map "[v]" -map '[a]' \
       -s nhd -ac 2 -t 0:2:0 \
       green-screen-eliminated.mp4
```

The `colorkey` filter requires three keys - the color, how strictly shades of colors closer to the one specified are also made transparent, and by how much the transparent pixels should blend with the background.

Figure 11-19. *The green-screen video has been rendered on the fireworks video*

☞   Jean-Claude Van Damme produced and donated this green-screen video to the public.

Turn All Colors Gray Except One

How do some commercials and music videos eliminate all colors except a few? With the `colorhold` filter!

```
ffmpeg -i color-test.mp4 \
       -filter:v "colorhold=yellow:similarity=0.2" \
       hold-yellow.mp4
```

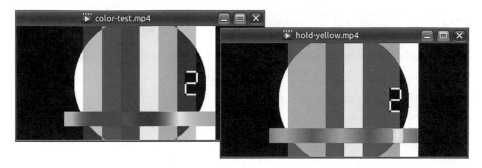

Figure 11-20. *Using the* `colorhold` *filter, all colors in the original video have been removed except yellow*

How to Pan Across a Video

Can you create the effect of a camera panning from top-left corner across to a particular region on the video? The next command tries to pan to a region that is 332x332 with the top-left coordinates at 150,12. The effect starts from the 20th second and lasts just 5 seconds. After the panning effect, this video continues with the rest of the cropped video without any panning.

```
ffmpeg -y -ss 20 -i how-to-vote.mp4 \
  -filter_complex \
      "[0:v:0]crop=w=332:h=332:
      x=(150*min(t\,5)/5):y=(12*min(t\,5)/5)" \
  -codec:a copy \
  how-to-vote-panned.mp4
```

213

In this command, the filter constant `t` representing the seconds is used to move the x-y coordinates of the crop region to its ultimate location at 150,12. For this, the coordinate is multiplied by `t` and divided by the total duration of the effect (five seconds). The `min` function expires the offsets of the crop filter after it has reached the destination at the end of five seconds.

Using FFmpeg with Timeline-Based Video-Editing Software

This tip comes from Apress author Seth Kenlon who mentioned it in his podcast some years ago. A lot of content creators record their videos in high definition. Editing these videos is quite a hassle in timeline-based video editing software. His trick was to downsize the video to say qvga (320x240) and then import that smaller video into his video-editing software. Because the video was so small, the editing software was more responsive, and he could finish the editing quickly. After he saved the project, he would close the editor. He would then manually overwrite the smaller video file with the original video. He would then start the editor again, open the project file, and only render (export) the video.

Your video editor must have built-in support for this kind of proxy editing. If not, it is likely to suffer from synchronization and scaling issues. Alternatively, you could reduce the frame rate to 12. This can make quite a difference if the source was recorded at say 60.

Make `ffmpeg -version` More Meaningful

If you had installed the pre-built ffmpeg executable and checked the `-version` option, `ffmpeg` displays the version like any other command-line program. If you build from source, then `ffmpeg` will display the label of the source code snapshot on the FFmpeg `git` repository.

```
~/Desktop
$ ffmpeg -version | head -1
ffmpeg version N-107964-g7de9c0e9d7 Copyright (c) 2000-2022
the FFmpeg developers
```

Figure 11-21. *This* git *label is likely to be meaningless to most users. Is* ffmpeg *trying to be anonymous?*

I studied the build script and made a few changes to one of the files extracted from the tarball (the downloaded compressed source code).

```
# Backup the file containing the git label
cp VERSION VERSION.bak

# Suffix the current date and release version number to
# the label
echo  -e \
  "$(cat VERSION.bak) [$(date +%Y-%m-%d)] [$(cat RELEASE)] " \
  > VERSION
```

Then, I ran the make and make install commands to build the binaries. Now, the version number is more meaningful. If I have to deal with multiple ffmpeg binaries sometime in the future, this information will be useful.

```
~/ffmpeg_sources/ffmpeg
$ ~/bin/ffmpeg -version | head -1
ffmpeg version N-108219-g129cbbd7be [2022-09-20] [5.1.git]
Copyright (c) 2000-2022 the FFmpeg developers
```

Figure 11-22. *The* -version *option displays the* git *label for whatever it is worth, YOUR build date, and the number of the last release version*

This of course assumes that you will build the binaries on the same day you downloaded the source.

Hardware Acceleration

Computer video cards have encoders and decoders of some popular codecs in their chips. These hardware encoders and decoders are faster than the CPU running software-based encoders and decoders. You can offload the encoding and decoding operations of supported codecs from the processor (CPU) on your computer's motherboard to the processor chip (GPU) on your graphics card. (AMD calls 'em GPUs as APUs.)

What the heck is all that? Well, instead of encoding the video using your CPU with a software encoder like this,

```
ffmpeg -i raw-video.avi -codec:v libx264 compressed-video.mp4
```

… you can offload the processing to your video card like this:

```
# If you are on the red team
ffmpeg -i raw-video.avi -codec:v h264_amf compressed-video.mp4

# or

# if you are green with nv
ffmpeg -i raw-video.avi -codec:v h264_nvenc \
        compressed-video.mp4
```

Is that not cool? Well, to use such an exotic option, you need to build the FFmpeg source code forked by one of the participating video card manufacturers. You can find more information on this topic from the following:

```
        https://docs.nvidia.com/video-technologies/video-codec-
        sdk/ffmpeg-with-nvidia-gpu/

        https://trac.ffmpeg.org/wiki/HWAccelIntro
```

Beware that not all GPU models are supported. In some cases, performance may be inferior or have additional restrictions. nVidia seems to have shown more interest and openness in this field than AMD or Intel. I have AMD hardware and could not find enough documentation to build from source.

It is better if you can get statically linked builds created by someone else. For Windows users, the builds provided by the reviewer on his website (`www.gyan.dev`) had support for hardware-accelerated encoders and decoders in AMD and nVidia GPUs.

```
~/Desktop
$ wine ▮▮▮▮▮▮▮▮▮▮/ffmpeg-dos/bin/ffmpeg.exe \
>   -encoders -hide_banner | grep 'amf\|nv'
 V....D h264_amf              AMD AMF H.264 Encoder (codec h264)
 V....D h264_nvenc            NVIDIA NVENC H.264 encoder (codec h264
 V....D hevc_amf              AMD AMF HEVC encoder (codec hevc)
 V....D hevc_nvenc            NVIDIA NVENC hevc encoder (codec hevc)


~/Desktop
$ ffmpeg -encoders | grep vaapi
 V....D h264_vaapi            H.264/AVC (VAAPI) (codec h264)
 V....D hevc_vaapi            H.265/HEVC (VAAPI) (codec hevc)
 V....D mjpeg_vaapi           MJPEG (VAAPI) (codec mjpeg)
 V....D mpeg2_vaapi           MPEG-2 (VAAPI) (codec mpeg2video)
 V....D vp8_vaapi             VP8 (VAAPI) (codec vp8)
 V....D vp9_vaapi             VP9 (VAAPI) (codec vp9)
```

Figure 11-23. *Some hardware-accelerated encoders available in a Windows build and a Linux build have been listed*

☞   No, `wine` will not work. I used it only to take this screenshot of the encoder listing.

☞   The `hevc` encoders are for the newer H265 codec. Try `ffmpeg -hwaccels` to see what hardware-accelerated options you have.

☞   The `libva` library (Video Acceleration API) is supported in some Intel and AMD GPUs.

Apart from encoders and decoders, you can install some hardware-accelerated filters when you build from source.

```
~/Desktop
$ ffmpeg -filters | grep opencl
    ... avgblur_opencl      V->V       Apply average blur filter
    ... boxblur_opencl      V->V       Apply boxblur filter to in
    ... colorkey_opencl     V->V       Turns a certain color into
    ... convolution_opencl V->V        Apply convolution mask to
    ... deshake_opencl      V->V       Feature-point based video
    ... dilation_opencl     V->V       Apply dilation effect
```

Figure 11-24. *Several OpenCL-enabled filters were installed after adding the* --enable-opencl *option in the* configure *script when I built FFmpeg version 5.1 from source*

Finis

All right! What does this command do?

```
ffmpeg \
  -f image2 -loop 1 -i BG-Collage.png \
  -f mp4 -i idiot-box-2.mp4 -i chenda-music-sound-levels.mp4 \
        -i Delphine-with-accessibility.mp4 \
        -i race-timer.mp4 -i slide.mp4 \
        -i watermarked-solar.mp4 \
    -filter_complex \
      "[0:v:0]drawtext=x=(w-tw)/2:y=15:
        fontcolor=red:alpha=0.6:shadowx=1:shadowy=2:
```

```
    text='Quick Start Guide To FFmpeg by V. Subhash':
    fontsize=30:fontfile=Oswald.ttf[banner1];
  [banner1]drawtext=x=(w-tw)/2:y=270:
    fontcolor=white:alpha=0.6:shadowx=1:shadowy=2:
    text='www.Apress.com':fontsize=30:
    fontfile=Merriweather.ttf[banner];
  [1:v:0]scale=160:90[scale1];
      [banner][scale1]overlay=40:60[over1];
  [2:v:0]scale=160:90[scale2];
      [over1][scale2]overlay=240:60[over2];
  [3:v:0]scale=160:90[scale3];
      [over2][scale3]overlay=440:60[over3];
  [4:v:0]scale=160:90[scale4];
      [over3][scale4]overlay=40:170[over4];
  [5:v:0]scale=160:90[scale5];
      [over4][scale5]overlay=240:170[over5];
  [6:v:0]scale=160:90[scale6];
      [over5][scale6]overlay=440:170[video];
  [1:a:0][2:a:0][3:a:0][4:a:0][6:a:0]amerge=inputs=5[audio]" \
-map '[video]' -map '[audio]' \
-ac 2 \
-t 0:0:10 \
thank-you.mp4
```

This command creates a video that has six downscaled videos playing simultaneously on a background image. The audio from the five input files were downmixed to stereo. (The slideshow had no audio.) Even the texts on the background were rendered by ffmpeg.

Figure 11-25. *This video collage was created using several FFmpeg techniques described in this book*

This video and several others used in this book are available in an online video playlist. You can find its link on these sites:

```
www.apress.com/9781484287002

www.vsubhash.in/ffmpeg-book.html
```

What Next...

Well, you have finished the book. What else can you do?

- Check the extra resources provided for this book.

- Spend some time reading the relevant sections of the FFmpeg documentation and online wiki when you are trying out the commands.

- If you have an FFmpeg-related problem, you may be able to find answers by simply doing an online search of its error message (within quotation marks). When you post FFmpeg-related questions on a forum, post the error messages as text rather than as screenshots. The recommended forums are as follows:

  - `https://superuser.com/questions/tagged/ffmpeg`

  - `https://video.stackexchange.com/questions/tagged/ffmpeg`

- If FFmpeg made a valuable contribution to you or your organization, you could show your appreciation of the favor:

  `http://ffmpeg.org/donations.html`

- If you give this book a good rating or review online, that will also be appreciated... by me... and other current/future FFmpeg users.

- If you have any corrections or suggestions, write to info@vsubhash.com.

CHAPTER 12

Annexures

Annexure 1: Sample List of Codecs

This annexure contains sample output for the command `ffmpeg -codecs`.

```
Codecs:
 D..... = Decoding supported
 .E.... = Encoding supported
 ..V... = Video codec
 ..A... = Audio codec
 ..S... = Subtitle codec
 ..D... = Data codec
 ..T... = Attachment codec
 ...I.. = Intra frame-only codec
 ....L. = Lossy compression
 .....S = Lossless compression
 -------
 D.VI.S 012v          Uncompressed 4:2:2 10-bit
 D.V.L. 4xm           4X Movie
 D.VI.S 8bps          QuickTime 8BPS video
 .EVIL. a64_multi     Multicolor charset for Commodore 64 (encoders:
                      ↳ a64multi)
 .EVIL. a64_multi5    Multicolor charset for Commodore 64, extended with
                      ↳ 5th color (colram) (encoders: a64multi5)
 D.V..S aasc          Autodesk RLE
 D.V.L. agm           Amuse Graphics Movie
 D.VIL. aic           Apple Intermediate Codec
 DEVI.S alias_pix     Alias/Wavefront PIX image
 DEVIL. amv           AMV Video
 D.V.L. anm           Deluxe Paint Animation
 D.V.L. ansi          ASCII/ANSI art
 DEV..S apng          APNG (Animated Portable Network Graphics) image
 D.V.L. arbc          Gryphon's Anim Compressor
 D.V.L. argo          Argonaut Games Video
 DEVIL. asv1          ASUS V1
 DEVIL. asv2          ASUS V2
 D.VIL. aura          Auravision AURA
```

© V. Subhash 2023
V. Subhash, *Quick Start Guide to FFmpeg*, https://doi.org/10.1007/978-1-4842-8701-9_12

```
D.VIL. aura2              Auravision Aura 2
DEV.L. av1                Alliance for Open Media AV1 (decoders: libda v1d
                          ↳ libaom-av1 av1) (encoders: libaom-av1 libsvtav1)
D.V... avrn               Avid AVI Codec
DEVI.S avrp               Avid 1:1 10-bit RGB Packer
D.V.L. avs                AVS (Audio Video Standard) video
..V.L. avs2               AVS2-P2/IEEE1857.4
..V.L. avs3               AVS3-P2/IEEE1857.10
DEVI.S avui               Avid Meridien Uncompressed
DEVI.S ayuv               Uncompressed packed MS 4:4:4:4
D.V.L. bethsoftvid        Bethesda VID video
D.V.L. bfi                Brute Force & Ignorance
D.V.L. binkvideo          Bink video
D.VI.. bintext            Binary text
DEVI.S bitpacked          Bitpacked
DEVI.S bmp                BMP (Windows and OS/2 bitmap)
D.V..S bmv_video          Discworld II BMV video
D.VI.S brender_pix        BRender PIX image
D.V.L. c93                Interplay C93
D.V.L. cavs               Chinese AVS (Audio Video Standard) (AVS1-P2, JiZhun
                          ↳ profile)
D.V.L. cdgraphics         CD Graphics video
D.V..S cdtoons            CDToons video
D.VIL. cdxl               Commodore CDXL video
DEV.L. cfhd               GoPro CineForm HD
DEV.L. cinepak            Cinepak
D.V.L. clearvideo         Iterated Systems ClearVideo
DEVIL. cljr               Cirrus Logic AccuPak
D.VI.S cllc               Canopus Lossless Codec
D.V.L. cmv                Electronic Arts CMV video (decoders: eacmv)
D.V... cpia               CPiA video format
D.VILS cri                Cintel RAW
D.V..S cscd               CamStudio (decoders: camstudio)
D.VIL. cyuv               Creative YUV (CYUV)
..V.LS daala              Daala
D.VILS dds                DirectDraw Surface image decoder
D.V.L. dfa                Chronomaster DFA
DEV.LS dirac              Dirac (encoders: vc2)
DEVIL. dnxhd              VC3/DNxHD
DEVI.S dpx                DPX (Digital Picture Exchange) image
D.V.L. dsicinvideo        Delphine Software International CIN video
DEVIL. dvvideo            DV (Digital Video)
D.V..S dxa                Feeble Files/ScummVM DXA
D.VI.S dxtory             Dxtory
D.VIL. dxv                Resolume DXV
D.V.L. escape124          Escape 124
D.V.L. escape130          Escape 130
DEVILS exr                OpenEXR image
DEV..S ffv1               FFmpeg video codec #1
DEVI.S ffvhuff            Huffyuv FFmpeg variant
D.V.L. fic                Mirillis FIC
DEVI.S fits               FITS (Flexible Image Transport System)
DEV..S flashsv            Flash Screen Video v1
```

```
DEV.L. flashsv2              Flash Screen Video v2
D.V..S flic                  Autodesk Animator Flic video
DEV.L. flv1                  FLV / Sorenson Spark / Sorenson H.263 (Flash Video)
                             ↳ (decoders: flv) (encoders: flv)
D.V..S fmvc                  FM Screen Capture Codec
D.VI.S fraps                 Fraps
D.VI.S frwu                  Forward Uncompressed
D.V.L. g2m                   Go2Meeting
D.V.L. gdv                   Gremlin Digital Video
D.V.L. gem                   GEM Raster image
DEV..S gif                   CompuServe GIF (Graphics Interchange Format)
DEV.L. h261                  H.261
DEV.L. h263                  H.263 / H.263-1996, H.263+ / II.263-1998 / H.263
                             ↳ version 2 (decoders: h263 h263_v4l2m2m)
                             ↳ (encoders: h263 h263_v4l2m2m)
D.V.L. h263i                 Intel H.263
DEV.L. h263p                 H.263+ / H.263-1998 / H.263 version 2
DEV.LS h264                  H.264 / AVC / MPEG-4 AVC / MPEG-4 part 10
                             ↳ (decoders: h264 h264_v4l2m2m) (encoders: libx264
                             ↳ libx264rgb h264_v4l2m2m h264_vaapi)
DEVIL. hap                   Vidvox Hap
DEVIL. hdr                   HDR (Radiance RGBE format) image
DEV.L. hevc                  H.265 / HEVC (High Efficiency Video Coding)
                             ↳ (decoders: hevc hevc_v4l2m2m) (encoders:
                             ↳ libx265 hevc_v4l2m2m hevc_vaapi)
D.V.L. hnm4video             HNM 4 video
D.VIL. hq_hqa                Canopus HQ/HQA
D.VIL. hqx                   Canopus HQX
DEVI.S huffyuv               HuffYUV
D.VI.S hymt                  HuffYUV MT
D.V.L. idcin                 id Quake II CIN video (decoders: idcinvideo)
D.VI.. idf                   iCEDraw text
D.V.L. iff_ilbm              IFF ACBM/ANIM/DEEP/ILBM/PBM/RGB8/ RGBN (decoders: iff)
D.V.L. imm4                  Infinity IMM4
D.V.L. imm5                  Infinity IMM5
D.V.L. indeo2                Intel Indeo 2
D.V.L. indeo3                Intel Indeo 3
D.V.L. indeo4                Intel Indeo Video Interactive 4
D.V.L. indeo5                Intel Indeo Video Interactive 5
D.V.L. interplayvideo        Interplay MVE video
D.VIL. ipu                   IPU Video
DEVILS jpeg2000              JPEG 2000 (decoders: jpeg2000 libopenjpeg) (encoders:
                             ↳ jpeg2000 libopenjpeg)
DEVILS jpegls                JPEG-LS
DEVILS jpegxl                JPEG XL (decoders: libjxl) (encoders: libjx l)
D.VIL. jv                    Bitmap Brothers JV video
D.V.L. kgv1                  Kega Game Video
D.V.L. kmvc                  Karl Morton's video codec
D.VI.S lagarith              Lagarith lossless
.EVI.S ljpeg                 Lossless JPEG
D.VI.S loco                  LOCO
D.V.L. lscr                  LEAD Screen Capture
D.VI.S m101                  Matrox Uncompressed SD
```

```
D.V.L. mad              Electronic Arts Madcow Video (decoders: eamad)
DEVI.S magicyuv         MagicYUV video
D.VIL. mdec             Sony PlayStation MDEC (Motion DECoder)
D.V.L. mimic            Mimic
DEVIL. mjpeg            Motion JPEG (encoders: mjpeg mjpeg_vaapi)
D.VIL. mjpegb           Apple MJPEG-B
D.V.L. mmvideo          American Laser Games MM Video
D.V.L. mobiclip         MobiClip Video
D.V.L. motionpixels     Motion Pixels video
DEV.L. mpeg1video       MPEG-1 video (decoders: mpeg1video mpeg1_v4l 2m2m)
DEV.L. mpeg2video       MPEG-2 video (decoders: mpeg2video mpegvideo
                        ↳ mpeg2_v4l2m2m) (encoders: mpeg2video mpeg2_vaapi)
DEV.L. mpeg4            MPEG-4 part 2 (decoders: mpeg4 mpeg4_v4l2m2m)
                        ↳ (encoders: mpeg4 libxvid mpeg4_v4l2m2m)
D.V.L. msa1             MS ATC Screen
D.VI.S mscc             Mandsoft Screen Capture Codec
D.V.L. msmpeg4v1        MPEG-4 part 2 Microsoft variant version 1
DEV.L. msmpeg4v2        MPEG-4 part 2 Microsoft variant version 2
DEV.L. msmpeg4v3        MPEG-4 part 2 Microsoft variant version 3
                        ↳ (encoders: msmpeg4) (decoders: msmpeg4)
D.VI.S msp2             Microsoft Paint (MSP) version 2
D.V..S msrle            Microsoft RLE
D.V.L. mss1             MS Screen 1
D.VIL. mss2             MS Windows Media Video V9 Screen
DEV.L. msvideo1         Microsoft Video 1
D.VI.S mszh             LCL (LossLess Codec Library) MSZH
D.V.L. mts2             MS Expression Encoder Screen
D.V.L. mv30             MidiVid 3.0
D.VIL. mvc1             Silicon Graphics Motion Video Compressor 1
D.VIL. mvc2             Silicon Graphics Motion Video Compressor 2
D.V.L. mvdv             MidiVid VQ
D.VIL. mvha             MidiVid Archive Codec
D.V..S mwsc             MatchWare Screen Capture Codec
D.V.L. mxpeg            Mobotix MxPEG video
D.VIL. notchlc          NotchLC
D.V.L. nuv              NuppelVideo/RTJPEG
D.V.L. paf_video        Amazing Studio Packed Animation File Video
DEVI.S pam              PAM (Portable AnyMap) image
DEVI.S pbm              PBM (Portable BitMap) image
DEVI.S pcx              PC Paintbrush PCX image
DEVI.S pfm              PFM (Portable FloatMap) image
DEVI.S pgm              PGM (Portable GrayMap) image
DEVI.S pgmyuv           PGMYUV (Portable GrayMap YUV) image
D.VI.S pgx              PGX (JPEG2000 Test Format)
DEVI.S phm              PHM (Portable HalfFloatMap) image
D.V.L. photocd          Kodak Photo CD
D.VIL. pictor           Pictor/PC Paint
D.VIL. pixlet           Apple Pixlet
DEV..S png              PNG (Portable Network Graphics) image
DEVI.S ppm              PPM (Portable PixelMap) image
DEVIL. prores           Apple ProRes (iCodec Pro) (encoders: prores
                        ↳ prores_aw prores_ks)
```

```
D.VIL. prosumer              Brooktree ProSumer Video
D.VI.S psd                   Photoshop PSD file
D.VIL. ptx                   V.Flash PTX image
D.VI.S qdraw                 Apple QuickDraw
DEVI.S qoi                   QOI (Quite OK Image)
D.V.L. qpeg                  Q-team QPEG
DEV..S qtrle                 QuickTime Animation (RLE) video
DEVI.S r10k                  AJA Kona 10-bit RGB Codec
DEVI.S r210                  Uncompressed RGB 10-bit
D.V.L. rasc                  RemotelyAnywhere Screen Capture
DEVI.S rawvideo              raw video
D.VIL. rl2                   RL2 video
DEV.L. roq                   id RoQ video (decoders: roqvideo) (encoders: roqvideo)
DEV.L. rpza                  QuickTime video (RPZA)
D.V..S rscc                  innoHeim/Rsupport Screen Capture Codec
DEV.L. rv10                  RealVideo 1.0
DEV.L. rv20                  RealVideo 2.0
D.V.L. rv30                  RealVideo 3.0
D.V.L. rv40                  RealVideo 4.0
D.V.L. sanm                  LucasArts SANM/SMUSH video
D.V.LS scpr                  ScreenPressor
D.V..S screenpresso          Screenpresso
D.V.L. sga                   Digital Pictures SGA Video
DEVI.S sgi                   SGI image
D.VI.S sgirle                SGI RLE 8-bit
D.V.L. sheervideo            BitJazz SheerVideo
D.V.L. simbiosis_imx         Simbiosis Interactive IMX Video
D.V.L. smackvideo            Smacker video (decoders: smackvid)
DEV.L. smc                   QuickTime Graphics (SMC)
D.VIL. smvjpeg               Sigmatel Motion Video
DEV.LS snow                  Snow
D.VIL. sp5x                  Sunplus JPEG (SP5X)
DEVIL. speedhq               NewTek SpeedHQ
D.VI.S srgc                  Screen Recorder Gold Codec
DEVI.S sunrast               Sun Rasterfile image
..V..S svg                   Scalable Vector Graphics
DEV.L. svq1                  Sorenson Vector Quantizer 1 / Sorenson Video 1 / SVQ1
D.V.L. svq3                  Sorenson Vector Quantizer 3 / Sorenson Video 3 / SVQ3
DEVI.S targa                 Truevision Targa image
D.VI.S targa_y216            Pinnacle TARGA CineWave YUV16
D.V.L. tdsc                  TDSC
D.V.L. tgq                   Electronic Arts TGQ video (decoders: eatgq)
D.V.L. tgv                   Electronic Arts TGV video (decoders: eatgv)
DEV.L. theora                Theora (encoders: libtheora)
D.VIL. thp                   Nintendo Gamecube THP video
D.V.L. tiertexseqvideo       Tiertex Limited SEQ video
DEVI.S tiff                  TIFF image
D.VIL. tmv                   8088flex TMV
D.V.L. tqi                   Electronic Arts TQI video (decoders: eatqi)
D.V.L. truemotion1           Duck TrueMotion 1.0
D.V.L. truemotion2           Duck TrueMotion 2.0
D.VIL. truemotion2rt         Duck TrueMotion 2.0 Real Time
```

```
D.V..S tscc              TechSmith Screen Capture Codec (decoders: camtasia)
D.V.L. tscc2             TechSmith Screen Codec 2
D.VIL. txd               Renderware TXD (TeXture Dictionary) image
D.V.L. ulti              IBM UltiMotion (decoders: ultimotion)
DEVI.S utvideo           Ut Video
DEVI.S v210              Uncompressed 4:2:2 10-bit
D.VI.S v210x             Uncompressed 4:2:2 10-bit
DEVI.S v308              Uncompressed packed 4:4:4
DEVI.S v408              Uncompressed packed QT 4:4:4:4
DEVI.S v410              Uncompressed 4:4:4 10-bit
D.V.L. vb                Beam Software VB
D.VI.S vble              VBLE Lossless Codec
DEV.L. vbn               Vizrt Binary Image
D.V.L. vc1               SMPTE VC-1 (decoders: vc1 vc1_v4l2m2m)
D.V.L. vc1image          Windows Media Video 9 Image v2
D.VIL. vcr1              ATI VCR1
D.VIL. vixl              Miro VideoXL (decoders: xl)
D.V.L. vmdvideo          Sierra VMD video
D.V..S vmnc              VMware Screen Codec / VMware Video
D.V.L. vp3               On2 VP3
D.V.L. vp4               On2 VP4
D.V.L. vp5               On2 VP5
D.V.L. vp6               On2 VP6
D.V.L. vp6a              On2 VP6 (Flash version, with alpha channel)
D.V.L. vp6f              On2 VP6 (Flash version)
D.V.L. vp7               On2 VP7
DEV.L. vp8               On2 VP8 (decoders: vp8 vp8_v4l2m2m libvpx)
                         ↳ (encoders: libvpx vp8_v4l2m2m vp8_vaapi)
DEV.L. vp9               Google VP9 (decoders: vp9 vp9_v4l2m2m libvpx-vp9)
                         ↳ (encoders: libvpx-vp9 vp9 vp9_vaapi)
..V.L. vvc               H.266 / VVC (Versatile Video Coding)
DEVI.S wbmp              WBMP (Wireless Application Protocol Bitmap) image
D.V..S wcmv              WinCAM Motion Video
DEVILS webp              WebP (encoders: libwebp_animlibwebp)
DEV.L. wmv1              Windows Media Video 7
DEV.L. wmv2              Windows Media Video 8
D.V.L. wmv3              Windows Media Video 9
D.V.L. wmv3image         Windows Media Video 9 Image
D.VIL. wnv1              Winnov WNV1
DEV..S wrapped_avframe   AVFrame to AVPacket passthrough
D.V.L. ws_vqa            Westwood Studios VQA (Vector Quantized Animation) video
                         ↳ (decoders: vqavideo)
D.V.L. xan_wc3           Wing Commander III / Xan
D.V.L. xan_wc4           Wing Commander IV / Xxan
D.VI.. xbin              eXtended BINary text
DEVI.S xbm               XBM (X BitMap) image
DEVIL. xface             X-face image
D.VI.S xpm               XPM (X PixMap) image
DEVI.S xwd               XWD (X Window Dump) image
DEVI.S y41p              Uncompressed YUV 4:1:1 12-bit
D.VI.S ylc               YUY2 Lossless Codec
D.V.L. yop               Psygnosis YOP Video
DEVI.S yuv4              Uncompressed packed 4:2:0
```

```
D.V..S zerocodec         ZeroCodec Lossless Video
DEVI.S zlib              LCL (LossLess Codec Library) ZLIB
DEV..S zmbv              Zip Motion Blocks Video
..AIL. 4gv               4GV (Fourth Generation Vocoder)
D.AIL. 8svx_exp          8SVX exponential
D.AIL. 8svx_fib          8SVX fibonacci
DEAIL. aac               AAC (Advanced Audio Coding) (decoders: aac aac_fixed
                         ↳ libfdk_aac) (encoders: aac libfdk_aac)
D.AIL. aac_latm          AAC LATM (Advanced Audio Coding LATM syntax)
DEAIL. ac3               ATSC A/52A (AC-3) (decoders: ac3 ac3_fixed)
                         ↳ (encoders: ac3 ac3_fixed)
D.AIL. acelp.kelvin      Sipro ACELP.KELVIN
D.AIL. adpcm_4xm         ADPCM 4X Movie
DEAIL. adpcm_adx         SEGA CRI ADX ADPCM
D.AIL. adpcm_afc         ADPCM Nintendo Gamecube AFC
D.AIL. adpcm_agm         ADPCM AmuseGraphics Movie AGM
D.AIL. adpcm_aica        ADPCM Yamaha AICA
DEAIL. adpcm_argo        ADPCM Argonaut Games
D.AIL. adpcm_ct          ADPCM Creative Technology
D.AIL. adpcm_dtk         ADPCM Nintendo Gamecube DTK
D.AIL. adpcm_ea          ADPCM Electronic Arts
D.AIL. adpcm_ea_maxis_xa ADPCM Electronic Arts Maxis CDROM XA
D.AIL. adpcm_ea_r1       ADPCM Electronic Arts R1
D.AIL. adpcm_ea_r2       ADPCM Electronic Arts R2
D.AIL. adpcm_ea_r3       ADPCM Electronic Arts R3
D.AIL. adpcm_ea_xas      ADPCM Electronic Arts XAS
DEAIL. adpcm_g722        G.722 ADPCM (decoders: g722) (encoders: g722)
DEAIL. adpcm_g726        G.726 ADPCM (decoders: g726) (encoders: g726)
DEAIL. adpcm_g726le      G.726 ADPCM little-endian (decoders: g726le)
                         ↳ (encoders: g726le)
D.AIL. adpcm_ima_acorn   ADPCM IMA Acorn Replay
DEAIL. adpcm_ima_alp     ADPCM IMA High Voltage Software ALP
DEAIL. adpcm_ima_amv     ADPCM IMA AMV
D.AIL. adpcm_ima_apc     ADPCM IMA CRYO APC
DEAIL. adpcm_ima_apm     ADPCM IMA Ubisoft APM
D.AIL. adpcm_ima_cunning ADPCM IMA Cunning Developments
D.AIL. adpcm_ima_dat4    ADPCM IMA Eurocom DAT4
D.AIL. adpcm_ima_dk3     ADPCM IMA Duck DK3
D.AIL. adpcm_ima_dk4     ADPCM IMA Duck DK4
D.AIL. adpcm_ima_ea_eacs ADPCM IMA Electronic Arts EACS
D.AIL. adpcm_ima_ea_sead ADPCM IMA Electronic Arts SEAD
D.AIL. adpcm_ima_iss     ADPCM IMA Funcom ISS
D.AIL. adpcm_ima_moflex  ADPCM IMA MobiClip MOFLEX
D.AIL. adpcm_ima_mtf     ADPCM IMA Capcom's MT Framework
D.AIL. adpcm_ima_oki     ADPCM IMA Dialogic OKI
DEAIL. adpcm_ima_qt      ADPCM IMA QuickTime
D.AIL. adpcm_ima_rad     ADPCM IMA Radical
D.AIL. adpcm_ima_smjpeg  ADPCM IMA Loki SDL MJPEG
DEAIL. adpcm_ima_ssi     ADPCM IMA Simon & Schuster Interactive
DEAIL. adpcm_ima_wav     ADPCM IMA WAV
DEAIL. adpcm_ima_ws      ADPCM IMA Westwood
DEAIL. adpcm_ms          ADPCM Microsoft
D.AIL. adpcm_mtaf        ADPCM MTAF
```

```
D.AIL. adpcm_psx            ADPCM Playstation
D.AIL. adpcm_sbpro_2        ADPCM Sound Blaster Pro 2-bit
D.AIL. adpcm_sbpro_3        ADPCM Sound Blaster Pro 2.6-bit
D.AIL. adpcm_sbpro_4        ADPCM Sound Blaster Pro 4-bit
DEAIL. adpcm_swf            ADPCM Shockwave Flash
D.AIL. adpcm_thp            ADPCM Nintendo THP
D.AIL. adpcm_thp_le         ADPCM Nintendo THP (Little-Endian)
D.AIL. adpcm_vima           LucasArts VIMA audio
D.AIL. adpcm_xa             ADPCM CDROM XA
DEAIL. adpcm_yamaha         ADPCM Yamaha
D.AIL. adpcm_zork           ADPCM Zork
DEAI.S alac                 ALAC (Apple Lossless Audio Codec)
DEAIL. amr_nb               AMR-NB (Adaptive Multi-Rate NarrowBand) (decoders: amrnb
                            ↳ libopencore_amrnb) (encoders: libopencore_amrnb)
DEAIL. amr_wb               AMR-WB (Adaptive Multi-Rate WideBand) (decoders: amrwb
                            ↳ libopencore_amrwb) (encoders: libvo_amrwbenc)
D.AI.S ape                  Monkey's Audio
DEAIL. aptx                 aptX (Audio Processing Technology for Bluetooth)
DEAIL. aptx_hd              aptX HD (Audio Processing Technology for Bluetooth)
D.AIL. atrac1               ATRAC1 (Adaptive TRansform Acoustic Coding)
D.AIL. atrac3               ATRAC3 (Adaptive TRansform Acoustic Coding 3)
D.AI.S atrac3al             ATRAC3 AL (Adaptive TRansform Acoustic Coding 3
                            ↳ Advanced Lossless)
D.AIL. atrac3p              ATRAC3+ (Adaptive TRansform Acoustic Coding 3+)
                            ↳ (decoders: atrac3plus)
D.AI.S atrac3pal            ATRAC3+ AL (Adaptive TRansform Acoustic Coding 3+
                            ↳ Advanced Lossless) (decoders: atrac3 plusal)
D.AIL. atrac9               ATRAC9 (Adaptive TRansform Acoustic Coding 9)
D.AIL. avc                  On2 Audio for Video Codec (decoders: on2avc)
D.AIL. binkaudio_dct        Bink Audio (DCT)
D.AIL. binkaudio_rdft       Bink Audio (RDFT)
D.AIL. bmv_audio            Discworld II BMV audio
..AIL. celt                 Constrained Energy Lapped Transform (CELT)
..AIL. codec2               codec2 (very low bitrate speech codec)
DEAIL. comfortnoise         RFC 3389 Comfort Noise
D.AIL. cook                 Cook / Cooker / Gecko (RealAudio G2)
D.AIL. derf_dpcm            DPCM Xilam DERF
DEA.L. dfpwm                DFPWM (Dynamic Filter Pulse Width Modulation)
D.AIL. dolby_e              Dolby E
D.AIL. dsd_lsbf             DSD (Direct Stream Digital), least significant bit first
D.AIL. dsd_lsbf_planar      DSD (Direct Stream Digital), least significant bit
                            ↳ first, planar
D.AIL. dsd_msbf             DSD (Direct Stream Digital), most significant bit first
D.AIL. dsd_msbf_planar      DSD (Direct Stream Digital), most significant bit
                            ↳ first, planar
D.AIL. dsicinaudio          Delphine Software International CIN audio
D.AIL. dss_sp               Digital Speech Standard - Standard Play mode (DSS SP)
D.AI.S dst                  DST (Direct Stream Transfer)
DEAILS dts                  DCA (DTS Coherent Acoustics) (decoders: dca)
                            ↳ (encoders: dca)
D.AIL. dvaudio              DV audio
DEAIL. eac3                 ATSC A/52B (AC-3, E-AC-3)
D.AIL. evrc                 EVRC (Enhanced Variable Rate Codec)
```

```
D.AIL. fastaudio          MobiClip FastAudio
DEAI.S flac               FLAC (Free Lossless Audio Codec)
DEAIL. g723_1             G.723.1
D.AIL. g729               G.729
D.AIL. gremlin_dpcm       DPCM Gremlin
D.AIL. gsm                GSM
D.AIL. gsm_ms             GSM Microsoft variant
D.AIL. hca                CRI HCA
D.AIL. hcom               HCOM Audio
D.AIL. iac                IAC (Indeo Audio Coder)
D.AIL. ilbc               iLBC (Internet Low Bitrate Codec)
D.AIL. imc                IMC (Intel Music Coder)
D.AIL. interplay_dpcm     DPCM Interplay
D.AIL. interplayacm       Interplay ACM
D.AIL. mace3              MACE (Macintosh Audio Compression/Expansion) 3:1
D.AIL. mace6              MACE (Macintosh Audio Compression/Expansion) 6:1
D.AIL. metasound          Voxware MetaSound
DEA..S mlp                MLP (Meridian Lossless Packing)
D.AIL. mp1                MP1 (MPEG audio layer 1) (decoders: mp1 mp1float)
DEAIL. mp2                MP2 (MPEG audio layer 2) (decoders: mp2 mp2float)
                          ↳ (encoders: mp2 mp2fixed libtwolame)
DEAIL. mp3                MP3 (MPEG audio layer 3) (decoders: mp3float mp3)
                          ↳ (encoders: libmp3lame libshine)
D.AIL. mp3adu             ADU (Application Data Unit) MP3 (MPEG audio layer 3)
                          ↳ (decoders: mp3adufloat mp3adu)
D.AIL. mp3on4             MP3onMP4 (decoders: mp3on4float mp3on4)
D.AI.S mp4als             MPEG-4 Audio Lossless Coding (ALS) (decoders: als)
..A.L. mpegh_3d_audio     MPEG-H 3D Audio
D.AIL. msnsiren           MSN Siren
D.AIL. musepack7          Musepack SV7 (decoders: mpc7)
D.AIL. musepack8          Musepack SV8 (decoders: mpc8)
DEAIL. nellymoser         Nellymoser Asao
DEAIL. opus               Opus (Opus Interactive Audio Codec) (decoders: opus
                          ↳ libopus) (encoders: opus libopus)
D.AIL. paf_audio          Amazing Studio Packed Animation File Audio
DEAIL. pcm_alaw           PCM A-law / G.711 A-law
DEAI.S pcm_bluray         PCM signed 16|20|24-bit big-endian for Blu-ray media
DEAI.S pcm_dvd            PCM signed 20|24-bit big-endian
D.AI.S pcm_f16le          PCM 16.8 floating point little-endian
D.AI.S pcm_f24le          PCM 24.0 floating point little-endian
DEAI.S pcm_f32be          PCM 32-bit floating point big-endian
DEAI.S pcm_f32le          PCM 32-bit floating point little-endian
DEAI.S pcm_f64be          PCM 64-bit floating point big-endian
DEAI.S pcm_f64le          PCM 64-bit floating point little-endian
D.AI.S pcm_lxf            PCM signed 20-bit little-endian planar
DEAIL. pcm_mulaw          PCM mu-law / G.711 mu-law
DEAI.S pcm_s16be          PCM signed 16-bit big-endian
DEAI.S pcm_s16be_planar   PCM signed 16-bit big-endian planar
DEAI.S pcm_s16le          PCM signed 16-bit little-endian
DEAI.S pcm_s16le_planar   PCM signed 16-bit little-endian planar
DEAI.S pcm_s24be          PCM signed 24-bit big-endian
DEAI.S pcm_s24daud        PCM D-Cinema audio signed 24-bit
```

```
DEAI.S pcm_s24le              PCM signed 24-bit little-endian
DEAI.S pcm_s24le_planar       PCM signed 24-bit little-endian planar
DEAI.S pcm_s32be              PCM signed 32-bit big-endian
DEAI.S pcm_s32le              PCM signed 32-bit little-endian
DEAI.S pcm_s32le_planar       PCM signed 32-bit little-endian planar
DEAI.S pcm_s64be              PCM signed 64-bit big-endian
DEAI.S pcm_s64le              PCM signed 64-bit little-endian
DEAI.S pcm_s8                 PCM signed 8-bit
DEAI.S pcm_s8_planar          PCM signed 8-bit planar
D.AI.S pcm_sga                PCM SGA
DEAI.S pcm_u16be              PCM unsigned 16-bit big-endian
DEAI.S pcm_u16le              PCM unsigned 16-bit little-endian
DEAI.S pcm_u24be              PCM unsigned 24-bit big-endian
DEAI.S pcm_u24le              PCM unsigned 24-bit little-endian
DEAI.S pcm_u32be              PCM unsigned 32-bit big-endian
DEAI.S pcm_u32le              PCM unsigned 32-bit little-endian
DEAI.S pcm_u8                 PCM unsigned 8-bit
DEAIL. pcm_vidc               PCM Archimedes VIDC
D.AIL. qcelp                  QCELP / PureVoice
D.AIL. qdm2                   QDesign Music Codec 2
D.AIL. qdmc                   QDesign Music
DEAIL. ra_144                 RealAudio 1.0 (14.4K) (decoders: real_144)
                              ↳ (encoders: real_144)
D.AIL. ra_288                 RealAudio 2.0 (28.8K) (decoders: real_288)
D.AI.S ralf                   RealAudio Lossless
DEAIL. roq_dpcm               DPCM id RoQ
DEAI.S s302m                  SMPTE 302M
DEAIL. sbc                    SBC (low-complexity subband codec)
D.AIL. sdx2_dpcm              DPCM Squareroot-Delta-Exact
D.AI.S shorten                Shorten
D.AIL. sipr                   RealAudio SIPR / ACELP.NET
D.AIL. siren                  Siren
D.AIL. smackaudio             Smacker audio (decoders: smackaud)
..AIL. smv                    SMV (Selectable Mode Vocoder)
D.AIL. sol_dpcm               DPCM Sol
DEAI.. sonic                  Sonic
.EAI.. sonicls                Sonic lossless
DEAIL. speex                  Speex (decoders: speex libspeex) (encoders: libspeex)
D.A..S tak                    TAK (Tom's lossless Audio Kompressor)
DEA..S truehd                 TrueHD
D.AIL. truespeech             DSP Group TrueSpeech
DEAI.S tta                    TTA (True Audio)
D.AIL. twinvq                 VQF TwinVQ
D.AIL. vmdaudio               Sierra VMD audio
DEAIL. vorbis                 Vorbis (decoders: vorbis libvorbis)
                              ↳ (encoders: vorbis libvorbis)
D.AI.. wavesynth              Wave synthesis pseudo-codec
DEAILS wavpack                WavPack
D.AIL. westwood_snd1          Westwood Audio (SND1) (decoders: ws_snd1)
D.AI.S wmalossless            Windows Media Audio Lossless
D.AIL. wmapro                 Windows Media Audio 9 Professional
DEAIL. wmav1                  Windows Media Audio 1
```

```
DEAIL. wmav2               Windows Media Audio 2
D.AIL. wmavoice            Windows Media Audio Voice
D.AIL. xan_dpcm            DPCM Xan
D.AIL. xma1                Xbox Media Audio 1
D.AIL. xma2                Xbox Media Audio 2
..D... bin_data            binary data
..D... dvd_nav_packet      DVD Nav packet
..D... epg                 Electronic Program Guide
..D... klv                 SMPTE 336M Key-Length-Value (KLV) metadata
..D... mpegts              raw MPEG-TS stream
..D... otf                 OpenType font
..D... scte_35             SCTE 35 Message Queue
..D... timed_id3           timed ID3 metadata
..D... ttf                 TrueType font
..S... arib_caption        ARIB STD-B24 caption
DES... ass                 ASS (Advanced SSA) subtitle (decoders: ssa ass)
                           ↳ (encoders: ssa ass)
DES... dvb_subtitle        DVB subtitles (decoders: dvbsub) (encoders: dvbsub)
D.S... dvb_teletext        DVB teletext (decoders: libzvbi_teletextdec)
DES... dvd_subtitle        DVD subtitles (decoders: dvdsub) (encoders: dvdsub)
D.S... eia_608             EIA-608 closed captions (decoders: cc_dec)
D.S... hdmv_pgs_subtitle   HDMV Presentation Graphic Stream
                           ↳ subtitles (decoders: pgssub)
..S... hdmv_text_subtitle  HDMV Text subtitle
D.S... jacosub             JACOsub subtitle
D.S... microdvd            MicroDVD subtitle
DES... mov_text            MOV text
D.S... mpl2                MPL2 subtitle
D.S... pjs                 PJS (Phoenix Japanimation Society) subtitle
D.S... realtext            RealText subtitle
D.S... sami                SAMI subtitle
..S... srt                 SubRip subtitle with embedded timing
..S... ssa                 SSA (SubStation Alpha) subtitle
D.S... stl                 Spruce subtitle format
DES... subrip              SubRip subtitle (decoders: srt
                           ↳ subrip) (enc oders: srt subrip)
D.S... subviewer           SubViewer subtitle
D.S... subviewer1          SubViewer v1 subtitle
DES... text                raw UTF-8 text
.ES... ttml                Timed Text Markup Language
D.S... vplayer             VPlayer subtitle
DES... webvtt              WebVTT subtitle
DES... xsub                XSUB
```

Annexure 2: Sample List of Decoders

This annexure contains sample output for the command
`ffmpeg -decoders`.

```
Decoders:
V..... = Video
A..... = Audio
S..... = Subtitle
.F.... = Frame-level multithreading
..S... = Slice-level multithreading
...X.. = Codec is experimental
....B. = Supports draw_horiz_band
.....D = Supports direct rendering method 1
------
V....D 012v                Uncompressed 4:2:2 10-bit
V....D 4xm                 4X Movie
V....D 8bps                QuickTime 8BPS video
V....D aasc                Autodesk RLE
V....D agm                 Amuse Graphics Movie
VF...D aic                 Apple Intermediate Codec
V....D alias_pix           Alias/Wavefront PIX image
V....D amv                 AMV Video
V....D anm                 Deluxe Paint Animation
V....D ansi                ASCII/ANSI art
VF...D apng                APNG (Animated Portable Network Graphics) image
V....D arbc                Gryphon's Anim Compressor
V....D argo                Argonaut Games Video
V....D asv1                ASUS V1
V....D asv2                ASUS V2
V....D aura                Auravision AURA
V....D aura2               Auravision Aura 2
V..... libdav1d            dav1d AV1 decoder by VideoLAN (codec av1)
V....D libaom-av1          libaom AV1 (codec av1)
V....D av1                 Alliance for Open Media AV1
V..... av1_cuvid           Nvidia CUVID AV1 decoder (codec av1)
V....D av1_qsv             AV1 video (Intel Quick Sync Video
                           ↳ acceleration) (codec av1)
V....D avrn                Avid AVI Codec
V....D avrp                Avid 1:1 10-bit RGB Packer
V....D avs                 AVS (Audio Video Standard) video
V..... libdavs2            libdavs2 AVS2-P2/IEEE1857.4 (codec avs2)
V....D libuavs3d           libuavs3d AVS3-P2/IEEE1857.10 (codec avs3)
V....D avui                Avid Meridien Uncompressed
V....D ayuv                Uncompressed packed MS 4:4:4:4
V....D bethsoftvid         Bethesda VID video
V....D bfi                 Brute Force & Ignorance
V....D binkvideo           Bink video
V....D bintext             Binary text
VF.... bitpacked           Bitpacked
V....D bmp                 BMP (Windows and OS/2 bitmap)
```

```
V....D bmv_video          Discworld II BMV video
V....D brender_pix        BRender PIX image
V....D c93                Interplay C93
V....D cavs               Chinese AVS (Audio Video Standard)
                          ∟ (AVS1-P2, JiZhun profile)
V....D cdgraphics         CD Graphics video
V....D cdtoons            CDToons video
V....D cdxl               Commodore CDXL video
VF...D cfhd               GoPro CineForm HD
V....D cinepak            Cinepak
V....D clearvideo         Iterated Systems ClearVideo
V....D cljr               Cirrus Logic AccuPak
VF...D cllc               Canopus Lossless Codec
V....D eacmv              Electronic Arts CMV video (codec cmv)
V....D cpia               CPiA video format
VF...D cri                Cintel RAW
V....D camstudio          CamStudio (codec cscd)
V....D cyuv               Creative YUV (CYUV)
V.S..D dds                DirectDraw Surface image decoder
V....D dfa                Chronomaster DFA
V.S..D dirac              BBC Dirac VC-2
VFS..D dnxhd              VC3/DNxHD
V....D dpx                DPX (Digital Picture Exchange) image
V....D dsicinvideo        Delphine Software International CIN video
VFS..D dvvideo            DV (Digital Video)
V....D dxa                Feeble Files/ScummVM DXA
VF...D dxtory             Dxtory
VFS..D dxv                Resolume DXV
V....D escape124          Escape 124
V....D escape130          Escape 130
VFS..D exr                OpenEXR image
VFS..D ffv1               FFmpeg video codec #1
VF..BD ffvhuff            Huffyuv FFmpeg variant
V.S..D fic                Mirillis FIC
V....D fits               Flexible Image Transport System
V....D flashsv            Flash Screen Video v1
V....D flashsv2           Flash Screen Video v2
V....D flic               Autodesk Animator Flic video
V...BD flv                FLV / Sorenson Spark / Sorenson
                          ∟ H.263 (Flash Video) (codec flv1)
V....D fmvc               FM Screen Capture Codec
VF...D fraps              Fraps
V....D frwu               Forward Uncompressed
V....D g2m                Go2Meeting
V....D gdv                Gremlin Digital Video
V....D gem                GEM Raster image
V....D gif                GIF (Graphics Interchange Format)
V....D h261               H.261
V...BD h263               H.263 / H.263-1996, H.263+ /
                          ∟ H.263-1998 / H.263 version 2
V..... h263_v4l2m2m       V4L2 mem2mem H.263 decoder wrapper (codec h263)
V...BD h263i              Intel H.263
```

```
V...BD h263p              H.263 / H.263-1996, H.263+ /
                          ↳ H.263-1998 / H.263 version 2
VFS..D h264               H.264 / AVC / MPEG-4 AVC / MPEG-4 part 10
V..... h264_v4l2m2m       V4L2 mem2mem H.264 decoder wrapper (codec h264)
V....D h264_qsv           H264 video (Intel Quick Sync Video
                          ↳ acceleration) (codec h264)
V..... h264_cuvid         Nvidia CUVID H264 decoder (codec h264)
VFS..D hap                Vidvox Hap
VF...D hdr                HDR (Radiance RGBE format) image
VFS..D hevc               HEVC (High Efficiency Video Coding)
V..... hevc_v4l2m2m       V4L2 mem2mem HEVC decoder wrapper (codec hevc)
V....D hevc_qsv           HEVC video (Intel Quick Sync Video
                          ↳ acceleration) (codec hevc)
V..... hevc_cuvid         Nvidia CUVID HEVC decoder (codec hevc)
V....D hnm4video          HNM 4 video
V....D hq_hqa             Canopus HQ/HQA
VFS..D hqx                Canopus HQX
VF..BD huffyuv            Huffyuv / HuffYUV
VF..BD hymt               HuffYUV MT
V....D idcinvideo         id Quake II CIN video (codec idcin)
V....D idf                iCEDraw text
V....D iff                IFF ACBM/ANIM/DEEP/ILBM/PBM/RGB8/
                          ↳ RGBN (codeciff_ilbm)
V....D imm4               Infinity IMM4
V..... imm5               Infinity IMM5
V....D indeo2             Intel Indeo 2
V....D indeo3             Intel Indeo 3
V....D indeo4             Intel Indeo Video Interactive 4
V....D indeo5             Intel Indeo Video Interactive 5
V....D interplayvideo     Interplay MVE video
V....D ipu                IPU Video
VFS..D jpeg2000           JPEG 2000
VF...D libopenjpeg        OpenJPEG JPEG 2000 (codec jpeg2000)
V....D jpegls             JPEG-LS
V....D libjxl             libjxl JPEG XL (codec jpegxl)
V....D jv                 Bitmap Brothers JV video
V....D kgv1               Kega Game Video
V....D kmvc               Karl Morton's video codec
VF...D lagarith           Lagarith lossless
V....D loco               LOCO
V....D lscr               LEAD Screen Capture
V....D m101               Matrox Uncompressed SD
V....D eamad              Electronic Arts Madcow Video (codec mad)
VFS..D magicyuv           MagicYUV video
VF...D mdec               Sony PlayStation MDEC (Motion DECoder)
VF...D mimic              Mimic
V....D mjpeg              MJPEG (Motion JPEG)
V..... mjpeg_cuvid        Nvidia CUVID MJPEG decoder (codec mjpeg)
V....D mjpeg_qsv          MJPEG video (Intel Quick Sync Video acceleration)
                          ↳ (codec mjpeg)
V....D mjpegb             Apple MJPEG-B
V....D mmvideo            American Laser Games MM Video
V....D mobiclip           MobiClip Video
```

```
V....D motionpixels        Motion Pixels video
V.S.BD mpeg1video          MPEG-1 video
V..... mpeg1_v4l2m2m       V4L2 mem2mem MPEG1 decoder wrapper (codec mpeg1video)
V..... mpeg1_cuvid         Nvidia CUVID MPEG1VIDEO decoder (codec mpeg1video)
V.S.BD mpeg2video          MPEG-2 video
V.S.BD mpegvideo           MPEG-1 video (codec mpeg2video)
V..... mpeg2_v4l2m2m       V4L2 mem2mem MPEG2 decoder wrapper (codec mpeg2video)
V....D mpeg2_qsv           MPEG2VIDEO video (Intel Quick Sync Video acceleration)
                           ↳ (codec mpeg2video)
V..... mpeg2_cuvid         Nvidia CUVID MPEG2VIDEO decoder (codec mpeg2video)
VF..BD mpeg4               MPEG-4 part 2
V..... mpeg4_v4l2m2m       V4L2 mem2mem MPEG4 decoder wrapper (codec mpeg4)
V..... mpeg4_cuvid         Nvidia CUVID MPEG4 decoder (codec mpeg4)
V...D msa1                 MS ATC Screen
V...D mscc                 Mandsoft Screen Capture Codec
V...BD msmpeg4v1           MPEG-4 part 2 Microsoft variant version 1
V...BD msmpeg4v2           MPEG-4 part 2 Microsoft variant version 2
V...BD msmpeg4             MPEG-4 part 2 Microsoft variant version 3
                           ↳ (codec msmpeg4v3)
V....D msp2                Microsoft Paint (MSP) version 2
V....D msrle               Microsoft RLE
V....D mss1                MS Screen 1
V....D mss2                MS Windows Media Video V9 Screen
V....D msvideo1            Microsoft Video 1
VF...D mszh                LCL (LossLess Codec Library) MSZH
V....D mts2                MS Expression Encoder Screen
V....D mv30                MidiVid 3.0
V....D mvc1                Silicon Graphics Motion Video Compressor 1
V....D mvc2                Silicon Graphics Motion Video Compressor 2
V....D mvdv                MidiVid VQ
V....D mvha                MidiVid Archive Codec
V....D mwsc                MatchWare Screen Capture Codec
V....D mxpeg               Mobotix MxPEG video
VF...D notchlc             NotchLC
V....D nuv                 NuppelVideo/RTJPEG
V....D paf_video           Amazing Studio Packed Animation File Video
V....D pam                 PAM (Portable AnyMap) image
V....D pbm                 PBM (Portable BitMap) image
V....D pcx                 PC Paintbrush PCX image
V....D pfm                 PFM (Portable FloatMap) image
V....D pgm                 PGM (Portable GrayMap) image
V....D pgmyuv              PGMYUV (Portable GrayMap YUV) image
V....D pgx                 PGX (JPEG2000 Test Format)
V....D phm                 PHM (Portable HalfFloatMap) image
VF...D photocd             Kodak Photo CD
V....D pictor              Pictor/PC Paint
VF...D pixlet              Apple Pixlet
VF...D png                 PNG (Portable Network Graphics) image
V....D ppm                 PPM (Portable PixelMap) image
VFS..D prores              Apple ProRes (iCodec Pro)
V....D prosumer            Brooktree ProSumer Video
VF...D psd                 Photoshop PSD file
V....D ptx                 V.Flash PTX image
```

```
V....D qdraw                    Apple QuickDraw
VF...D qoi                      QOI (Quite OK Image format) image
V....D qpeg                     Q-team QPEG
V....D qtrle                    QuickTime Animation (RLE) video
V....D r10k                     AJA Kona 10-bit RGB Codec
V....D r210                     Uncompressed RGB 10-bit
V....D rasc                     RemotelyAnywhere Screen Capture
V..... rawvideo                 raw video
V....D rl2                      RL2 video
V....D roqvideo                 id RoQ video (codec roq)
V....D rpza                     QuickTime video (RPZA)
V....D rscc                     innoHeim/Rsupport Screen Capture Codec
V....D rv10                     RealVideo 1.0
V....D rv20                     RealVideo 2.0
VF...D rv30                     RealVideo 3.0
VF...D rv40                     RealVideo 4.0
V....D sanm                     LucasArts SANM/Smush video
V....D scpr                     ScreenPressor
V....D screenpresso             Screenpresso
V....D sga                      Digital Pictures SGA Video
V....D sgi                      SGI image
V....D sgirle                   Silicon Graphics RLE 8-bit video
VF...D sheervideo               BitJazz SheerVideo
V....D simbiosis_imx            Simbiosis Interactive IMX Video
V....D smackvid                 Smacker video (codec smackvideo)
V....D smc                      QuickTime Graphics (SMC)
V....D smvjpeg                  SMV JPEG
V....D snow                     Snow
V....D sp5x                     Sunplus JPEG (SP5X)
V....D speedhq                  NewTek SpeedHQ
V....D srgc                     Screen Recorder Gold Codec
V....D sunrast                  Sun Rasterfile image
V....D svq1                     Sorenson Vector Quantizer 1 / Sorenson Video 1 / SVQ1
V...BD svq3                     Sorenson Vector Quantizer 3 / Sorenson Video 3 / SVQ3
V....D targa                    Truevision Targa image
V....D targa_y216               Pinnacle TARGA CineWave YUV16
V....D tdsc                     TDSC
V....D eatgq                    Electronic Arts TGQ video (codec tgq)
V....D eatgv                    Electronic Arts TGV video (codec tgv)
VF..BD theora                   Theora
V....D thp                      Nintendo Gamecube THP video
V....D tiertexseqvideo          Tiertex Limited SEQ video
VF...D tiff                     TIFF image
V....D tmv                      8088flex TMV
V....D eatqi                    Electronic Arts TQI Video (codec tqi)
V....D truemotion1              Duck TrueMotion 1.0
V....D truemotion2              Duck TrueMotion 2.0
V....D truemotion2rt            Duck TrueMotion 2.0 Real Time
V....D camtasia                 TechSmith Screen Capture Codec (codec tscc)
V....D tscc2                    TechSmith Screen Codec 2
V....D txd                      Renderware TXD (TeXture Dictionary) image
V....D ultimotion               IBM UltiMotion (codec ulti)
VF...D utvideo                  Ut Video
```

```
VFS..D v210              Uncompressed 4:2:2 10-bit
V....D v210x             Uncompressed 4:2:2 10-bit
V....D v308              Uncompressed packed 4:4:4
V....D v408              Uncompressed packed QT 4:4:4:4
VFS..D v410              Uncompressed 4:4:4 10-bit
V....D vb                Beam Software VB
VF...D vble              VBLE Lossless Codec
V.S..D vbn               Vizrt Binary Image
V....D vc1               SMPTE VC-1
V..... vc1_v4l2m2m       V4L2 mem2mem VC1 decoder wrapper (codec vc1)
V....D vc1_qsv           VC1 video (Intel Quick Sync Video
                         ↳ acceleration) (codec vc1)
V..... vc1_cuvid         Nvidia CUVID VC1 decoder (codec vc1)
V....D vc1image          Windows Media Video 9 Image v2
V....D vcr1              ATI VCR1
V....D xl                Miro VideoXL (codec vixl)
V....D vmdvideo          Sierra VMD video
V....D vmnc              VMware Screen Codec / VMware Video
VF..BD vp3               On2 VP3
VF..BD vp4               On2 VP4
V....D vp5               On2 VP5
V....D vp6               On2 VP6
V.S..D vp6a              On2 VP6 (Flash version, with alpha channel)
V....D vp6f              On2 VP6 (Flash version)
V....D vp7               On2 VP7
VFS..D vp8               On2 VP8
V..... vp8_v4l2m2m       V4L2 mem2mem VP8 decoder wrapper (codec vp8)
V....D libvpx            libvpx VP8 (codec vp8)
V..... vp8_cuvid         Nvidia CUVID VP8 decoder (codec vp8)
V....D vp8_qsv           VP8 video (Intel Quick Sync Video
                         ↳ acceleration) (codec vp8)
VFS..D vp9               Google VP9
V..... vp9_v4l2m2m       V4L2 mem2mem VP9 decoder wrapper (codec vp9)
V..... libvpx-vp9        libvpx VP9 (codec vp9)
V..... vp9_cuvid         Nvidia CUVID VP9 decoder (codec vp9)
V....D vp9_qsv           VP9 video (Intel Quick Sync Video acceleration)
                         ↳ (codec vp9)
VF...D wbmp              WBMP (Wireless Application Protocol Bitmap) image
V....D wcmv              WinCAM Motion Video
VF...D webp              WebP image
V...BD wmv1              Windows Media Video 7
V...BD wmv2              Windows Media Video 8
V....D wmv3              Windows Media Video 9
V....D wmv3image         Windows Media Video 9 Image
V....D wnv1              Winnov WNV1
V..... wrapped_avframe   AVPacket to AVFrame passthrough
V....D vqavideo          Westwood Studios VQA (Vector Quantized Animation) video
                         ↳ (codec ws_vqa)
V....D xan_wc3           Wing Commander III / Xan
V....D xan_wc4           Wing Commander IV / Xxan
V....D xbin              eXtended BINary text
V....D xbm               XBM (X BitMap) image
V....D xface             X-face image
```

```
V....D xpm                    XPM (X PixMap) image
V....D xwd                    XWD (X Window Dump) image
V....D y41p                   Uncompressed YUV 4:1:1 12-bit
VF...D ylc                    YUY2 Lossless Codec
V..... yop                    Psygnosis YOP Video
V....D yuv4                   Uncompressed packed 4:2:0
V....D zerocodec              ZeroCodec Lossless Video
VF...D zlib                   LCL (LossLess Codec Library) ZLIB
V....D zmbv                   Zip Motion Blocks Video
A....D 8svx_exp               8SVX exponential
A....D 8svx_fib               8SVX fibonacci
A....D aac                    AAC (Advanced Audio Coding)
A....D aac_fixed              AAC (Advanced Audio Coding) (codec aac)
A....D libfdk_aac             Fraunhofer FDK AAC (codec aac)
A....D aac_latm               AAC LATM (Advanced Audio Coding LATM syntax)
A....D ac3                    ATSC A/52A (AC-3)
A....D ac3_fixed              ATSC A/52A (AC-3) (codec ac3)
A....D acelp.kelvin           Sipro ACELP.KELVIN
A....D adpcm_4xm              ADPCM 4X Movie
A....D adpcm_adx              SEGA CRI ADX ADPCM
A....D adpcm_afc              ADPCM Nintendo Gamecube AFC
A....D adpcm_agm              ADPCM AmuseGraphics Movie
A....D adpcm_aica             ADPCM Yamaha AICA
A....D adpcm_argo             ADPCM Argonaut Games
A....D adpcm_ct               ADPCM Creative Technology
A....D adpcm_dtk              ADPCM Nintendo Gamecube DTK
A....D adpcm_ea               ADPCM Electronic Arts
A....D adpcm_ea_maxis_xa      ADPCM Electronic Arts Maxis CDROM XA
A....D adpcm_ea_r1            ADPCM Electronic Arts R1
A....D adpcm_ea_r2            ADPCM Electronic Arts R2
A....D adpcm_ea_r3            ADPCM Electronic Arts R3
A....D adpcm_ea_xas           ADPCM Electronic Arts XAS
A....D g722                   G.722 ADPCM (codec adpcm_g722)
A....D g726                   G.726 ADPCM (codec adpcm_g726)
A....D g726le                 G.726 ADPCM little-endian (codec adpcm_g726le)
A....D adpcm_ima_acorn        ADPCM IMA Acorn Replay
A....D adpcm_ima_alp          ADPCM IMA High Voltage Software ALP
A....D adpcm_ima_amv          ADPCM IMA AMV
A....D adpcm_ima_apc          ADPCM IMA CRYO APC
A....D adpcm_ima_apm          ADPCM IMA Ubisoft APM
A....D adpcm_ima_cunning      ADPCM IMA Cunning Developments
A....D adpcm_ima_dat4         ADPCM IMA Eurocom DAT4
A....D adpcm_ima_dk3          ADPCM IMA Duck DK3
A....D adpcm_ima_dk4          ADPCM IMA Duck DK4
A....D adpcm_ima_ea_eacs      ADPCM IMA Electronic Arts EACS
A....D adpcm_ima_ea_sead      ADPCM IMA Electronic Arts SEAD
A....D adpcm_ima_iss          ADPCM IMA Funcom ISS
A....D adpcm_ima_moflex       ADPCM IMA MobiClip MOFLEX
A....D adpcm_ima_mtf          ADPCM IMA Capcom's MT Framework
A....D adpcm_ima_oki          ADPCM IMA Dialogic OKI
A....D adpcm_ima_qt           ADPCM IMA QuickTime
A....D adpcm_ima_rad          ADPCM IMA Radical
```

```
A....D adpcm_ima_smjpeg      ADPCM IMA Loki SDL MJPEG
A....D adpcm_ima_ssi         ADPCM IMA Simon & Schuster Interactive
A....D adpcm_ima_wav         ADPCM IMA WAV
A....D adpcm_ima_ws          ADPCM IMA Westwood
A....D adpcm_ms              ADPCM Microsoft
A....D adpcm_mtaf            ADPCM MTAF
A....D adpcm_psx             ADPCM Playstation
A....D adpcm_sbpro_2         ADPCM Sound Blaster Pro 2-bit
A....D adpcm_sbpro_3         ADPCM Sound Blaster Pro 2.6-bit
A....D adpcm_sbpro_4         ADPCM Sound Blaster Pro 4-bit
A....D adpcm_swf             ADPCM Shockwave Flash
A....D adpcm_thp             ADPCM Nintendo THP
A....D adpcm_thp_le          ADPCM Nintendo THP (little-endian)
A....D adpcm_vima            LucasArts VIMA audio
A....D adpcm_xa              ADPCM CDROM XA
A....D adpcm_yamaha          ADPCM Yamaha
A....D adpcm_zork            ADPCM Zork
AF...D alac                  ALAC (Apple Lossless Audio Codec)
A....D amrnb                 AMR-NB (Adaptive Multi-Rate NarrowBand) (codec amr_nb)
A....D libopencore_amrnb     OpenCORE AMR-NB (Adaptive Multi-Rate Narrow-Band)
                             ↳ (codec amr_nb)
A....D amrwb                 AMR-WB (Adaptive Multi-Rate WideBand) (codec amr_wb)
A....D libopencore_amrwb     OpenCORE AMR-WB (Adaptive Multi-Rate Wide-Band)
                             ↳ (codec amr_wb)
A....D ape                   Monkey's Audio
A....D aptx                  aptX (Audio Processing Technology for Bluetooth)
A....D aptx_hd               aptX HD (Audio Processing Technology for Bluetooth)
A....D atrac1                ATRAC1 (Adaptive TRansform Acoustic Coding)
A....D atrac3                ATRAC3 (Adaptive TRansform Acoustic Coding 3)
A....D atrac3al              ATRAC3 AL (Adaptive TRansform Acoustic Coding 3
                             ↳ Advanced Lossless)
A....D atrac3plus            ATRAC3+ (Adaptive TRansform Acoustic Coding 3+)
                             ↳ (codec atrac3p)
A....D atrac3plusal          ATRAC3+ AL (Adaptive TRansform Acoustic Coding 3+
                             ↳ Advanced Lossless) (codec atrac3pal)
A....D atrac9                ATRAC9 (Adaptive TRansform Acoustic Coding 9)
A....D on2avc                On2 Audio for Video Codec (codec avc)
A....D binkaudio_dct         Bink Audio (DCT)
A....D binkaudio_rdft        Bink Audio (RDFT)
A....D bmv_audio             Discworld II BMV audio
A....D comfortnoise          RFC 3389 comfort noise generator
A....D cook                  Cook / Cooker / Gecko (RealAudio G2)
A....D derf_dpcm             DPCM Xilam DERF
A....D dfpwm                 DFPWM1a audio
A....D dolby_e               Dolby E
A.S..D dsd_lsbf              DSD (Direct Stream Digital), least
                             ↳ significant bit first
A.S..D dsd_lsbf_planar       DSD (Direct Stream Digital), least
                             ↳ significant bit first, planar
A.S..D dsd_msbf              DSD (Direct Stream Digital), most
                             ↳ significant bit first
A.S..D dsd_msbf_planar       DSD (Direct Stream Digital), most
                             ↳ significant bit first, planar
```

```
A....D dsicinaudio        Delphine Software International CIN audio
A....D dss_sp             Digital Speech Standard - Standard Play mode (DSS SP)
A....D dst                DST (Digital Stream Transfer)
A....D dca                DCA (DTS Coherent Acoustics) (codec dts)
A....D dvaudio            Ulead DV Audio
A....D eac3               ATSC A/52B (AC-3, E-AC-3)
A....D evrc               EVRC (Enhanced Variable Rate Codec)
A....D fastaudio          MobiClip FastAudio
AF...D flac               FLAC (Free Lossless Audio Codec)
A....D g723_1             G.723.1
A....D g729               G.729
A....D gremlin_dpcm       DPCM Gremlin
A....D gsm                GSM
A....D libgsm             libgsm GSM (codec gsm)
A....D gsm_ms             GSM Microsoft variant
A....D libgsm_ms          libgsm GSM Microsoft variant (codec gsm_ms)
A....D hca                CRI HCA
A....D hcom               HCOM Audio
A....D iac                IAC (Indeo Audio Coder)
A....D ilbc               iLBC (Internet Low Bitrate Codec)
A....D libilbc            iLBC (Internet Low Bitrate Codec) (codec ilbc)
A....D imc                IMC (Intel Music Coder)
A....D interplay_dpcm     DPCM Interplay
A....D interplayacm       Interplay ACM
A....D mace3              MACE (Macintosh Audio Compression/Expansion) 3:1
A....D mace6              MACE (Macintosh Audio Compression/Expansion) 6:1
A....D metasound          Voxware MetaSound
A....D mlp                MLP (Meridian Lossless Packing)
A....D mp1                MP1 (MPEG audio layer 1)
A....D mp1float           MP1 (MPEG audio layer 1) (codec mp1)
A....D mp2                MP2 (MPEG audio layer 2)
A....D mp2float           MP2 (MPEG audio layer 2) (codec mp2)
A....D mp3float           MP3 (MPEG audio layer 3) (codec mp3)
A....D mp3                MP3 (MPEG audio layer 3)
A....D mp3adufloat        ADU (Application Data Unit) MP3 (MPEG audio layer 3)
                          ↳ (codec mp3adu)
A....D mp3adu             ADU (Application Data Unit) MP3 (MPEG audio layer 3)
A....D mp3on4float        MP3onMP4 (codec mp3on4)
A....D mp3on4             MP3onMP4
A....D als                MPEG-4 Audio Lossless Coding (ALS) (codec mp4als)
A....D msnsiren           MSN Siren
A....D mpc7               Musepack SV7 (codec musepack7)
A....D mpc8               Musepack SV8 (codec musepack8)
A....D nellymoser         Nellymoser Asao
A....D opus               Opus
A....D libopus            libopus Opus (codec opus)
A....D paf_audio          Amazing Studio Packed Animation File Audio
A....D pcm_alaw           PCM A-law / G.711 A-law
A....D pcm_bluray         PCM signed 16|20|24-bit big-endian for Blu-ray media
A....D pcm_dvd            PCM signed 16|20|24-bit big-endian for DVD media
A....D pcm_f16le          PCM 16.8 floating point little-endian
A....D pcm_f24le          PCM 24.0 floating point little-endian
A....D pcm_f32be          PCM 32-bit floating point big-endian
```

```
A....D pcm_f32le          PCM 32-bit floating point little-endian
A....D pcm_f64be          PCM 64-bit floating point big-endian
A....D pcm_f64le          PCM 64-bit floating point little-endian
A....D pcm_lxf            PCM signed 20-bit little-endian planar
A....D pcm_mulaw          PCM mu-law / G.711 mu-law
A....D pcm_s16be          PCM signed 16-bit big-endian
A....D pcm_s16be_planar   PCM signed 16-bit big-endian planar
A....D pcm_s16le          PCM signed 16-bit little-endian
A....D pcm_s16le_planar   PCM signed 16-bit little-endian planar
A....D pcm_s24be          PCM signed 24-bit big-endian
A....D pcm_s24daud        PCM D-Cinema audio signed 24-bit
A....D pcm_s24le          PCM signed 24-bit little-endian
A....D pcm_s24le_planar   PCM signed 24-bit little-endian planar
A....D pcm_s32be          PCM signed 32-bit big-endian
A....D pcm_s32le          PCM signed 32-bit little-endian
A....D pcm_s32le_planar   PCM signed 32-bit little-endian planar
A....D pcm_s64be          PCM signed 64-bit big-endian
A....D pcm_s64le          PCM signed 64-bit little-endian
A....D pcm_s8             PCM signed 8-bit
A....D pcm_s8_planar      PCM signed 8-bit planar
A....D pcm_sga            PCM SGA
A....D pcm_u16be          PCM unsigned 16-bit big-endian
A....D pcm_u16le          PCM unsigned 16-bit little-endian
A....D pcm_u24be          PCM unsigned 24-bit big-endian
A....D pcm_u24le          PCM unsigned 24-bit little-endian
A....D pcm_u32be          PCM unsigned 32-bit big-endian
A....D pcm_u32le          PCM unsigned 32-bit little-endian
A....D pcm_u8             PCM unsigned 8-bit
A....D pcm_vidc           PCM Archimedes VIDC
A....D qcelp              QCELP / PureVoice
A....D qdm2               QDesign Music Codec 2
A....D qdmc               QDesign Music Codec 1
A....D real_144           RealAudio 1.0 (14.4K) (codec ra_144)
A....D real_288           RealAudio 2.0 (28.8K) (codec ra_288)
A....D ralf               RealAudio Lossless
A....D roq_dpcm           DPCM id RoQ
A....D s302m              SMPTE 302M
A....D sbc                SBC (low-complexity subband codec)
A....D sdx2_dpcm          DPCM Squareroot-Delta-Exact
A....D shorten            Shorten
A....D sipr               RealAudio SIPR / ACELP.NET
A....D siren              Siren
A....D smackaud           Smacker audio (codec smackaudio)
A....D sol_dpcm           DPCM Sol
A..X.D sonic              Sonic
A....D speex              Speex
A....D libspeex           libspeex Speex (codec speex)
AF...D tak                TAK (Tom's lossless Audio Kompressor)
A....D truehd             TrueHD
A....D truespeech         DSP Group TrueSpeech
AF...D tta                TTA (True Audio)
A....D twinvq             VQF TwinVQ
```

```
A....D vmdaudio            Sierra VMD audio
A....D vorbis              Vorbis
A..... libvorbis          libvorbis (codec vorbis)
A....D wavesynth          Wave synthesis pseudo-codec
AFS..D wavpack            WavPack
A....D ws_snd1            Westwood Audio (SND1) (codec westwood_snd1)
A....D wmalossless        Windows Media Audio Lossless
A....D wmapro            Windows Media Audio 9 Professional
A....D wmav1             Windows Media Audio 1
A....D wmav2             Windows Media Audio 2
A....D wmavoice          Windows Media Audio Voice
A....D xan_dpcm          DPCM Xan
A....D xma1              Xbox Media Audio 1
A....D xma2              Xbox Media Audio 2
S..... ssa               ASS (Advanced SubStation Alpha) subtitle (codec ass)
S..... ass               ASS (Advanced SubStation Alpha) subtitle
S..... dvbsub            DVB subtitles (codec dvb_subtitle)
S..... libzvbi_teletextdec Libzvbi DVB teletext decoder (codec dvb_tele text)
S..... dvdsub            DVD subtitles (codec dvd_subtitle)
S..... cc_dec            Closed Caption (EIA-608 / CEA-708) (codec eia_608)
S..... pgssub            HDMV Presentation Graphic Stream subtitles (codec
                         L hdmv_pgs_subtitle)
S..... jacosub           JACOsub subtitle
S..... microdvd          MicroDVD subtitle
S..... mov_text          3GPP Timed Text subtitle
S..... mpl2              MPL2 subtitle
S..... pjs               PJS subtitle
S..... realtext          RealText subtitle
S..... sami              SAMI subtitle
S..... stl               Spruce subtitle format
S..... srt               SubRip subtitle (codec subrip)
S..... subrip            SubRip subtitle
S..... subviewer         SubViewer subtitle
S..... subviewer1        SubViewer1 subtitle
S..... text              Raw text subtitle
S..... vplayer           VPlayer subtitle
S..... webvtt            WebVTT subtitle
S..... xsub              XSUB
```

Annexure 3: Sample List of Encoders

This annexure contains sample output for the command `ffmpeg -encoders`.

```
Encoders:
V..... = Video
A..... = Audio
S..... = Subtitle
.F.... = Frame-level multithreading
..S... = Slice-level multithreading
...X.. = Codec is experimental
```

```
....B. = Supports draw_horiz_band
.....D = Supports direct rendering method 1
------
V....D a64multi              Multicolor charset for Commodore 64 (codec a 64_multi)
V....D a64multi5             Multicolor charset for Commodore 64, extended with
                             ⌐ 5th color (colram) (codec a64_multi 5)
V....D alias_pix             Alias/Wavefront PIX image
V..... amv                   AMV Video
V....D apng                  APNG (Animated Portable Network Graphics) image
V....D asv1                  ASUS V1
V....D asv2                  ASUS V2
V....D libaom-av1            libaom AV1 (codec av1)
V....D librav1e              librav1e AV1 (codec av1)
V..... libsvlav1             SVT-AV1(Scalable Video Technology for AV1)
                             ⌐ encoder (codec av1)
V....D avrp                  Avid 1:1 10-bit RGB Packer
V....D libxavs2              libxavs2 AVS2-P2/IEEE1857.4 (codec avs2)
V..X.D avui                  Avid Meridien Uncompressed
V....D ayuv                  Uncompressed packed MS 4:4:4:4
VF...D bitpacked             Bitpacked
V....D bmp                   BMP (Windows and OS/2 bitmap)
VF...D cfhd                  GoPro CineForm HD
V....D cinepak               Cinepak
V....D cljr                  Cirrus Logic AccuPak
V.S..D vc2                   SMPTE VC-2 (codec dirac)
VFS..D dnxhd                 VC3/DNxHD
V....D dpx                   DPX (Digital Picture Exchange) image
VFS..D dvvideo               DV (Digital Video)
VF...D exr                   OpenEXR image
V.S..D ffv1                  FFmpeg video codec #1
VF...D ffvhuff               Huffyuv FFmpeg variant
V....D fits                  Flexible Image Transport System
V....D flashsv               Flash Screen Video
V....D flashsv2              Flash Screen Video Version 2
V..... flv                   FLV / Sorenson Spark / Sorenson H.263 (Flash Video)
                             ⌐ (codec flv1)
V....D gif                   GIF (Graphics Interchange Format)
V..... h261                  H.261
V..... h263                  H.263 / H.263-1996
V..... h263_v4l2m2m          V4L2 mem2mem H.263 encoder wrapper (codec h263)
V.S... h263p                 H.263+ / H.263-1998 / H.263 version 2
V....D libx264               libx264 H.264 / AVC / MPEG-4 AVC
                             ⌐ / MPEG-4 part 10 (codec h264)
V....D libx264rgb            libx264 H.264 / AVC / MPEG-4 AVC
                             ⌐ / MPEG-4 part 10 RGB (codec h264)
V..... h264_v4l2m2m          V4L2 mem2mem H.264 encoder wrapper (codec h264)
V....D h264_vaapi            H.264/AVC (VAAPI) (codec h264)
V....D h264_amf              AMD AMF H.264 Encoder (codec h264)
V....D h264_mf               H264 via MediaFoundation (codec h264)
V....D h264_nvenc            NVIDIA NVENC H.264 encoder (codec h264)
V..... h264_qsv              H.264 / AVC / MPEG-4 AVC / MPEG-4 part 10 (Intel Quick
                             ⌐ Sync Video acceleration) (codec h264)
V.S..D hap                   Vidvox Hap
```

```
VF...D hdr                  HDR (Radiance RGBE format) image
V....D libx265              libx265 H.265 / HEVC (codec hevc)
V..... hevc_v4l2m2m         V4L2 mem2mem HEVC encoder wrapper (codec hevc)
V....D hevc_vaapi           H.265/HEVC (VAAPI) (codec hevc)
V....D hevc_amf             AMD AMF HEVC encoder (codec hevc)
V....D hevc_mf              HEVC via MediaFoundation (codec hevc)
V....D hevc_nvenc           NVIDIA NVENC hevc encoder (codec hevc)
V..... hevc_qsv             HEVC (Intel Quick Sync Video
                            ↳ acceleration) (codec hevc)
VF...D huffyuv              Huffyuv / HuffYUV
V....D jpeg2000             JPEG 2000
VF.... libopenjpeg          OpenJPEG JPEG 2000 (codec jpeg2000)
VF...D jpegls               JPEG-LS
V..... libjxl               libjxl JPEG XL (codec jpegxl)
VF...D ljpeg                Lossless JPEG
VF...D magicyuv             MagicYUV video
VFS... mjpeg                MJPEG (Motion JPEG)
V....D mjpeg_vaapi          MJPEG (VAAPI) (codec mjpeg)
V..... mjpeg_qsv            MJPEG (Intel Quick Sync Video acceleration) (codec mjpeg)
V.S... mpeg1video           MPEG-1 video
V.S... mpeg2video           MPEG-2 video
V....D mpeg2_vaapi          MPEG-2 (VAAPI) (codec mpeg2video)
V..... mpeg2_qsv            MPEG-2 video (Intel Quick Sync Video acceleration)
                            ↳ (codec mpeg2video)
V.S... mpeg4                MPEG-4 part 2
V....D libxvid              libxvidcore MPEG-4 part 2 (codec mpeg4)
V..... mpeg4_v4l2m2m        V4L2 mem2mem MPEG4 encoder wrapper (codec mpeg4)
V..... msmpeg4v2            MPEG-4 part 2 Microsoft variant version 2
V..... msmpeg4              MPEG-4 part 2 Microsoft variant version 3
                            ↳ (codec msmpeg4v3)
V..... msvideo1             Microsoft Video-1
V....D pam                  PAM (Portable AnyMap) image
V....D pbm                  PBM (Portable BitMap) image
V....D pcx                  PC Paintbrush PCX image
V....D pfm                  PFM (Portable FloatMap) image
V....D pgm                  PGM (Portable GrayMap) image
V....D pgmyuv               PGMYUV (Portable GrayMap YUV) image
V....D phm                  PHM (Portable HalfFloatMap) image
VF...D png                  PNG (Portable Network Graphics) image
V....D ppm                  PPM (Portable PixelMap) image
VF...D prores               Apple ProRes
VF...D prores_aw            Apple ProRes (codec prores)
VFS... prores_ks            Apple ProRes (iCodec Pro) (codec prores)
VF...D qoi                  QOI (Quite OK Image format) image
V....D qtrle                QuickTime Animation (RLE) video
V....D r10k                 AJA Kona 10-bit RGB Codec
V....D r210                 Uncompressed RGB 10-bit
VF...D rawvideo             raw video
V....D roqvideo             id RoQ video (codec roq)
V....D rpza                 QuickTime video (RPZA)
V..... rv10                 RealVideo 1.0
V..... rv20                 RealVideo 2.0
V....D sgi                  SGI image
```

```
V....D smc              QuickTime Graphics (SMC)
V....D snow             Snow
V..... speedhq          NewTek SpeedHQ
V....D sunrast          Sun Rasterfile image
V....D svq1             Sorenson Vector Quantizer 1 / Sorenson Video 1 / SVQ1
V....D targa            Truevision Targa image
V....D libtheora        libtheora Theora (codec theora)
VF...D tiff             TIFF image
VF...D utvideo          Ut Video
VF...D v210             Uncompressed 4:2:2 10-bit
V....D v308             Uncompressed packed 4:4:4
V....D v408             Uncompressed packed QT 4:4:4:4
V....D v410             Uncompressed 4:4:4 10-bit
V.S. D vbn              Vizrt Binary Image
V....D libvpx           libvpx VP8 (codec vp8)
V..... vp8_v4l2m2m      V4L2 mem2mem VP8 encoder wrapper (codec vp8)
V....D vp8_vaapi        VP8 (VAAPI) (codec vp8)
V....D libvpx-vp9       libvpx VP9 (codec vp9)
V....D vp9_vaapi        VP9 (VAAPI) (codec vp9)
V..... vp9_qsv          VP9 video (Intel Quick Sync Video
                        ↳ acceleration) (codec vp9)
VF...D wbmp             WBMP (Wireless Application Protocol Bitmap) image
V....D libwebp_anim     libwebp WebP image (codec webp)
V....D libwebp          libwebp WebP image (codec webp)
V..... wmv1             Windows Media Video 7
V..... wmv2             Windows Media Video 8
V..... wrapped_avframe  AVFrame to AVPacket passthrough
V....D xbm              XBM (X BitMap) image
V....D xface            X-face image
V....D xwd              XWD (X Window Dump) image
V....D y41p             Uncompressed YUV 4:1:1 12-bit
V....D yuv4             Uncompressed packed 4:2:0
VF...D zlib             LCL (LossLess Codec Library) ZLIB
V....D zmbv             Zip Motion Blocks Video
A....D aac              AAC (Advanced Audio Coding)
A....D libfdk_aac       Fraunhofer FDK AAC (codec aac)
A....D aac_mf           AAC via MediaFoundation (codec aac)
A....D ac3              ATSC A/52A (AC-3)
A....D ac3_fixed        ATSC A/52A (AC-3) (codec ac3)
A....D ac3_mf           AC3 via MediaFoundation (codec ac3)
A....D adpcm_adx        SEGA CRI ADX ADPCM
A....D adpcm_argo       ADPCM Argonaut Games
A....D g722             G.722 ADPCM (codec adpcm_g722)
A....D g726             G.726 ADPCM (codec adpcm_g726)
A....D g726le           G.726 little endian ADPCM ("right-justified")
                        ↳ (codec adpcm_g726le)
A....D adpcm_ima_alp    ADPCM IMA High Voltage Software ALP
A....D adpcm_ima_amv    ADPCM IMA AMV
A....D adpcm_ima_apm    ADPCM IMA Ubisoft APM
A....D adpcm_ima_qt     ADPCM IMA QuickTime
A....D adpcm_ima_ssi    ADPCM IMA Simon & Schuster Interactive
A....D adpcm_ima_wav    ADPCM IMA WAV
A....D adpcm_ima_ws     ADPCM IMA Westwood
```

```
A....D adpcm_ms             ADPCM Microsoft
A....D adpcm_swf            ADPCM Shockwave Flash
A....D adpcm_yamaha         ADPCM Yamaha
A....D alac                 ALAC (Apple Lossless Audio Codec)
A....D libopencore_amrnb    OpenCORE AMR-NB (Adaptive Multi-Rate Narrow-Band)
                            ↳ (codec amr_nb)
A....D libvo_amrwbenc       Android VisualOn AMR-WB (Adaptive Multi-Rate Wide-Band)
                            ↳ (codec amr_wb)
A....D aptx                 aptX (Audio Processing Technology for Bluetooth)
A....D aptx_hd              aptX HD (Audio Processing Technology for Bluetooth)
A....D comfortnoise         RFC 3389 comfort noise generator
A....D dfpwm                DFPWM1a audio
A..X.D dca                  DCA (DTS Coherent Acoustics) (codec dts)
A....D eac3                 ATSC A/52 E-AC-3
A....D flac                 FLAC (Free Lossless Audio Codec)
A....D g723_1               G.723.1
A....D libgsm               libgsm GSM (codec gsm)
A....D libgsm_ms            libgsm GSM Microsoft variant (codec gsm_ms)
A....D libilbc              iLBC (Internet Low Bitrate Codec) (codec ilbc)
A..X.D mlp                  MLP (Meridian Lossless Packing)
A....D mp2                  MP2 (MPEG audio layer 2)
A....D mp2fixed             MP2 fixed point (MPEG audio layer 2) (codecmp2)
A....D libtwolame           libtwolame MP2 (MPEG audio layer 2) (codec mp2)
A....D libmp3lame           libmp3lame MP3 (MPEG audio layer 3) (codec mp3)
A....D libshine             libshine MP3 (MPEG audio layer 3) (codec mp3)
A....D mp3_mf               MP3 via MediaFoundation (codec mp3)
A....D nellymoser           Nellymoser Asao
A..X.D opus                 Opus
A....D libopus              libopus Opus (codec opus)
A....D pcm_alaw             PCM A-law / G.711 A-law
A....D pcm_bluray           PCM signed 16|20|24-bit big-endian for Blu-ray media
A....D pcm_dvd              PCM signed 16|20|24-bit big-endian for DVD media
A....D pcm_f32be            PCM 32-bit floating point big-endian
A....D pcm_f32le            PCM 32-bit floating point little-endian
A....D pcm_f64be            PCM 64-bit floating point big-endian
A....D pcm_f64le            PCM 64-bit floating point  little-endian
A....D pcm_mulaw            PCM mu-law / G.711 mu-law
A....D pcm_s16be            PCM signed 16-bit big-endian
A....D pcm_s16be_planar     PCM signed 16-bit big-endian planar
A....D pcm_s16le            PCM signed 16-bit little-endian
A....D pcm_s16le_planar     PCM signed 16-bit little-endian planar
A....D pcm_s24be            PCM signed 24-bit big-endian
A....D pcm_s24daud          PCM D-Cinema audio signed 24-bit
A....D pcm_s24le            PCM signed 24-bit little-endian
A....D pcm_s24le_planar     PCM signed 24-bit little-endian planar
A....D pcm_s32be            PCM signed 32-bit big-endian
A....D pcm_s32le            PCM signed 32-bit little-endian
A....D pcm_s32le_planar     PCM signed 32-bit little-endian planar
A....D pcm_s64be            PCM signed 64-bit big-endian
A....D pcm_s64le            PCM signed 64-bit little-endian
A....D pcm_s8               PCM signed 8-bit
A....D pcm_s8_planar        PCM signed 8-bit planar
A....D pcm_u16be            PCM unsigned 16-bit big-endian
```

```
A....D pcm_u16le          PCM unsigned 16-bit little-endian
A....D pcm_u24be          PCM unsigned 24-bit big-endian
A....D pcm_u24le          PCM unsigned 24-bit little-endian
A....D pcm_u32be          PCM unsigned 32-bit big-endian
A....D pcm_u32le          PCM unsigned 32-bit little-endian
A....D pcm_u8             PCM unsigned 8-bit
A....D pcm_vidc           PCM Archimedes VIDC
A....D real_144           RealAudio 1.0 (14.4K) (codec ra_144)
A....D roq_dpcm           id RoQ DPCM
A..X.D s302m              SMPTE 302M
A....D sbc                SBC (low-complexity subband codec)
A..X.D sonic              Sonic
A..X.D sonicls            Sonic lossless
A....D libspeex           libspeex Speex (codec speex)
A..X.D truehd             TrueHD
A....D tta                TTA (True Audio)
A..X.D vorbis             Vorbis
A....D libvorbis          libvorbis (codec vorbis)
A....D wavpack            WavPack
A....D wmav1              Windows Media Audio 1
A....D wmav2              Windows Media Audio 2
S..... ssa                ASS (Advanced SubStation Alpha) subtitle (codec ass)
S..... ass                ASS (Advanced SubStation Alpha) subtitle
S..... dvbsub             DVB subtitles (codec dvb_subtitle)
S..... dvdsub             DVD subtitles (codec dvd_subtitle)
S..... mov_text           3GPP Timed Text subtitle
S..... srt                SubRip subtitle (codec subrip)
S..... subrip             SubRip subtitle
S..... text               Raw text subtitle
S..... ttml               TTML subtitle
S..... webvtt             WebVTT subtitle
S..... xsub               DivX subtitles (XSUB)
```

Annexure 4: Sample List of Filters

This annexure contains sample output for the command `ffmpeg -filters`.

```
Filters:
T.. = Timeline support
.S. = Slice threading
..C = Command support
A = Audio input/output
V = Video input/output
N = Dynamic number and/or type of input/output
| = Source or sink filter
... abench              A->A        Benchmark part of a filtergraph
..C acompressor         A->A        Audio compressor
... acontrast           A->A        Simple audio dynamic range compression/
                                    └ expansion filter
... acopy               A->A        Copy the input audio unchanged to the output
```

```
... acue              A->A     Delay filtering to match a cue
... acrossfade        AA->A    Cross fade two input audio streams
.S. acrossover        A->N     Split audio into per-bands streams
T.C acrusher          A->A     Reduce audio bit resolution
TS. adeclick          A->A     Remove impulsive noise from input audio
TS. adeclip           A->A     Remove clipping from input audio
TS. adecorrelate      A->A     Apply decorrelation to input audio
T.C adelay            A->A     Delay one or more audio channels
TSC adenorm           A->A     Remedy denormals by adding extremely low-level noise
T.. aderivative       A->A     Compute derivative of input audio
TSC adynamicequalizer A->A     Apply Dynamic Equalization of input audio
T.C adynamicsmooth    A->A     Apply Dynamic Smoothing of input audio
... aecho             A->A     Add echoing to the audio
TSC aemphasis         A->A     Audio emphasis
T.. aeval             A->A     Filter audio signal according to a specified
                               ↳ expression
T.C aexciter          A->A     Enhance high frequency part of audio
T.C afade             A->A     Fade in/out input audio
TSC afftdn            A->A     Denoise audio samples using FFT
TS. afftfilt          A->A     Apply arbitrary expressions to samples in
                               ↳ frequency domain
.SC afir              N->N     Apply Finite Impulse Response filter with supplied
                               ↳ coefficients in additional stream(s)
... aformat           A->A     Convert the input audio to one of the
                               ↳ specified formats
TSC afreqshift        A->A     Apply frequency shifting to input audio
TSC afwtdn            A->A     Denoise audio stream using Wavelets
T.C agate             A->A     Audio gate
.S. aiir              A->N     Apply Infinite Impulse Response filter
                               ↳ with supplied coefficients
T.. aintegral         A->A     Compute integral of input audio
... ainterleave       N->A     Temporally interleave audio inputs
T.. alatency          A->A     Report audio filtering latency
T.C alimiter          A->A     Audio lookahead limiter
TSC allpass           A->A     Apply a two-pole all-pass filter
... aloop             A->A     Loop audio samples
... amerge            N->A     Merge two or more audio streams into a
                               ↳ single multi-channel stream
T.. ametadata         A->A     Manipulate audio frame metadata
..C amix              N->A     Audio mixing
... amultiply         AA->A    Multiply two audio streams
TSC anequalizer       A->N     Apply high-order audio parametric multiband
                               ↳ equalizer
TSC anlmdn            A->A     Reduce broadband noise from
                               ↳ stream using Non-Local Means
TSC anlmf             AA->A    Apply Normalized Least-Mean-Fourth algorithm to
                               ↳ first audio stream
TSC anlms             AA->A    Apply Normalized Least-Mean-Squares algorithm to
                               ↳ first audio stream
... anull             A->A     Pass the source unchanged to the output
T.. apad              A->A     Pad audio with silence
T.C aperms            A->A     Set permissions for the output audio frame
... aphaser           A->A     Add a phasing effect to the audio
```

TSC	aphaseshift	A->A	Apply phase shifting to input audio
TSC	apsyclip	A->A	Audio Psychoacoustic Clipper
...	apulsator	A->A	Audio pulsator
..C	arealtime	A->A	Slow down filtering to match realtime
...	aresample	A->A	Resample audio data
...	areverse	A->A	Reverse an audio clip
TSC	arnndn	A->A	Reduce noise from speech using Recurrent Neural ↳ Networks
...	asdr	AA->A	Measure Audio Signal-to-Distortion Ratio
...	asegment	A->N	Segment audio stream
...	aselect	A->N	Select audio frames to pass in output
...	asendcmd	A->A	Send commands to filters
...	asetnsamples	A->A	Set the number of samples for each output audio ↳ frames
...	asetpts	A->A	Set PTS for the output audio frame
...	asetrate	A->A	Change the sample rate without altering the data
...	asettb	A->A	Set timebase for the audio output link
...	ashowinfo	A->A	Show textual information for each audio frame
T..	asidedata	A->A	Manipulate audio frame side data
TSC	asoftclip	A->A	Audio Soft Clipper
.S.	aspectralstats	A->A	Show frequency domain statistics about audio frames
...	asplit	A->N	Pass on the audio input to N audio outputs
.S.	astats	A->A	Show time domain statistics about audio frames
..C	astreamselect	N->N	Select audio streams
TSC	asubboost	A->A	Boost subwoofer frequencies
TSC	asubcut	A->A	Cut subwoofer frequencies
TSC	asupercut	A->A	Cut super frequencies
TSC	asuperpass	A->A	Apply high order Butterworth band-pass filter
TSC	asuperstop	A->A	Apply high order Butterworth band-stop filter
..C	atempo	A->A	Adjust audio tempo
TSC	atilt	A->A	Apply spectral tilt to audio
...	atrim	A->A	Pick one continuous section from the in put, ↳ drop the rest
...	axcorrelate	AA->A	Cross-correlate two audio streams
...	azmq	A->A	Receive commands through ZMQ and broker ↳ them to filters
TSC	bandpass	A->A	Apply a two-pole Butterworth band-pass filter
TSC	bandreject	A->A	Apply a two-pole Butterworth band-reject filter
TSC	bass	A->A	Boost or cut lower frequencies
TSC	biquad	A->A	Apply a biquad IIR filter with the given ↳ coefficients
...	bs2b	A->A	Bauer stereo-to-binaural filter
...	channelmap	A->A	Remap audio channels
...	channelsplit	A->N	Split audio into per-channel streams
...	chorus	A->A	Add a chorus effect to the audio
...	compand	A->A	Compress or expand audio dynamic range
T.C	compensationdelay	A->A	Audio Compensation Delay Line
T.C	crossfeed	A->A	Apply headphone crossfeed filter
TSC	crystalizer	A->A	Simple audio noise sharpening filter
T..	dcshift	A->A	Apply a DC shift to the audio
T..	deesser	A->A	Apply de-essing to the audio
T.C	dialoguenhance	A->A	Audio Dialogue Enhancement
...	drmeter	A->A	Measure audio dynamic range

T.C	dynaudnorm	A->A	Dynamic Audio Normalizer
...	earwax	A->A	Widen the stereo image
...	ebur128	A->N	EBU R128 scanner
TSC	equalizer	A->A	Apply two-pole peaking equalization (EQ) filter
T.C	extrastereo	A->A	Increase difference between stereo audio channels
..C	firequalizer	A->A	Finite Impulse Response Equalizer
...	flanger	A->A	Apply a flanging effect to the audio
...	haas	A->A	Apply Haas Stereo Enhancer
...	hdcd	A->A	Apply High Definition Compatible Digital (HDCD) ↳ decoding
.S.	headphone	N->A	Apply headphone binaural spatialization with HRTFs ↳ in additional streams
TSC	highpass	A->A	Apply a high-pass filter with 3dB point frequency
TSC	highshelf	A->A	Apply a high shelf filter
...	join	N->A	Join multiple audio streams into multi-channel ↳ output
..C	ladspa	N->A	Apply LADSPA effect
...	loudnorm	A->A	EBU R128 loudness normalization
TSC	lowpass	A->A	Apply a low-pass filter with 3dB point frequency
TSC	lowshelf	A->A	Apply a low shelf filter
...	mcompand	A->A	Multiband Compress or expand audio dynamic range
...	pan	A->A	Remix channels with coefficients (panning)
...	replaygain	A->A	ReplayGain scanner
..C	rubberband	A->A	Apply time-stretching and pitch-shifting
..C	sidechaincompress	AA->A	Sidechain compressor
T.C	sidechaingate	AA->A	Audio sidechain gate
...	silencedetect	A->A	Detect silence
...	silenceremove	A->A	Remove silence
.S.	sofalizer	A->A	SOFAlizer (Spatially Oriented Format for Acoustics)
T.C	speechnorm	A->A	Speech Normalizer
T.C	stereotools	A->A	Apply various stereo tools
T.C	stereowiden	A->A	Apply stereo widening effect
...	superequalizer	A->A	Apply 18 band equalization filter
.S.	surround	A->A	Apply audio surround upmix filter
TSC	tiltshelf	A->A	Apply a tilt shelf filter
TSC	treble	A->A	Boost or cut upper frequencies
T..	tremolo	A->A	Apply tremolo effect
T..	vibrato	A->A	Apply vibrato effect
T.C	virtualbass	A->A	Audio Virtual Bass
T.C	volume	A->A	Change input volume
...	volumedetect	A->A	Detect audio volume
...	aevalsrc	|->A	Generate an audio signal generated by an expression
...	afirsrc	|->A	Generate a FIR coefficients audio stream
...	anoisesrc	|->A	Generate a noise audio signal
...	anullsrc	|->A	Null audio source, return empty audio frames
...	flite	|->A	Synthesize voice from text using libflite
...	hilbert	|->A	Generate a Hilbert transform FIR coefficients
...	sinc	|->A	Generate a sinc kaiser-windowed low-pass, high-pass, ↳ band-pass, or band-reject FIR coefficients
...	sine	|->A	Generate sine wave audio signal
...	anullsink	A->|	Do absolutely nothing with the input audio
...	addroi	V->V	Add region of interest to frame

...	alphaextract	V->V	Extract an alpha channel as a grayscale image ↳ component
T..	alphamerge	VV->V	Copy the luma value of the second input into the ↳ alpha channel of the first input
TSC	amplify	V->V	Amplify changes between successive video frames
...	ass	V->V	Render ASS subtitles onto input video using the ↳ libass library
TSC	atadenoise	V->V	Apply an Adaptive Temporal Averaging Denoiser
T.C	avgblur	V->V	Apply Average Blur filter
...	avgblur_opencl	V->V	Apply average blur filter
...	avgblur_vulkan	V->V	Apply avgblur mask to input video
T.C	bbox	V->V	Compute bounding box for each frame
...	bench	V->V	Benchmark part of a filtergraph
TSC	bilateral	V->V	Apply Bilateral filter
T..	bitplanenoise	V->V	Measure bit plane noise
.S.	blackdetect	V->V	Detect video intervals that are (almost) black
...	blackframe	V->V	Detect frames that are (almost) black
TSC	blend	VV->V	Blend two video frames into each other
..C	blend_vulkan	VV->V	Blend two video frames in Vulkan
...	blockdetect	V->V	Blockdetect filter
...	blurdetect	V->V	Blurdetect filter
TS.	bm3d	N->V	Block-Matching 3D denoiser
T..	boxblur	V->V	Blur the input
...	boxblur_opencl	V->V	Apply boxblur filter to input video
TS.	bwdif	V->V	Deinterlace the input image
TSC	cas	V->V	Contrast Adaptive Sharpen
...	chromaber_vulkan	V->V	Offset chroma of input video ↳ (chromatic aberration)
TSC	chromahold	V->V	Turns a certain color range into gray
TSC	chromakey	V->V	Turns a certain color into transparency. ↳ Operates on YUV colors
...	chromakey_cuda	V->V	GPU accelerated chromakey filter
TSC	chromanr	V->V	Reduce chrominance noise
TSC	chromashift	V->V	Shift chroma
...	ciescope	V->V	Video CIE scope
T..	codecview	V->V	Visualize information about some codecs
TSC	colorbalance	V->V	Adjust the color balance
TSC	colorchannelmixer	V->V	Adjust colors by mixing color channels
TSC	colorcontrast	V->V	Adjust color contrast between RGB components
TSC	colorcorrect	V->V	Adjust color white balance selectively for blacks ↳ and whites
TSC	colorize	V->V	Overlay a solid color on the video stream
TSC	colorkey	V->V	Turns a certain color into transparency. Operates ↳ on RGB colors
...	colorkey_opencl	V->V	Turns a certain color into transparency. Operates ↳ on RGB colors
TSC	colorhold	V->V	Turns a certain color range into gray. Operates on ↳ RGB colors
TSC	colorlevels	V->V	Adjust the color levels
TSC	colormap	VVV->V	Apply custom Color Maps to video stream
TS.	colormatrix	V->V	Convert color matrix
TS.	colorspace	V->V	Convert between colorspaces
TSC	colortemperature	V->V	Adjust color temperature of video

253

```
TSC convolution         V->V      Apply convolution filter
... convolution_opencl V->V       Apply convolution mask to input video
TS. convolve            VV->V     Convolve first video stream
                                  ↳ with second video stream
... copy                V->V      Copy the input video unchanged to the output
... cover_rect          V->V      Find and cover a user specified object
..C crop                V->V      Crop the input video
T.. cropdetect          V->V      Auto-detect crop size
... cue                 V->V      Delay filtering to match a cue
TSC curves              V->V      Adjust components curves
.SC datascope           V->V      Video data analysis
T.C dblur               V->V      Apply Directional Blur filter
TS. dctdnoiz            V->V      Denoise frames using 2D DCT
TSC deband              V->V      Debands video
T.C deblock             V->V      Deblock video
... decimate            N->V      Decimate frames (post field matching filter)
TS. deconvolve          VV->V     Deconvolve first video stream
                                  ↳ with second video stream
TS. dedot               V->V      Reduce cross-luminance and cross-color
TSC deflate             V->V      Apply deflate effect
... deflicker           V->V      Remove temporal frame luminance variations
... deinterlace_vaapi V->V        Deinterlacing of VAAPI surfaces
... deinterlace_qsv     V->V      QuickSync video deinterlacing
... dejudder            V->V      Remove judder produced by pullup
T.. delogo              V->V      Remove logo from input video
... denoise_vaapi       V->V      VAAPI VPP for de-noise
T.. derain              V->V      Apply derain filter to the input
... deshake             V->V      Stabilize shaky video
... deshake_opencl      V->V      Feature-point based video stabilization filter
TSC despill             V->V      Despill video
... detelecine          V->V      Apply an inverse telecine pattern
TSC dilation            V->V      Apply dilation effect
... dilation_opencl     V->V      Apply dilation effect
T.. displace            VVV->V    Displace pixels
... dnn_classify        V->V      Apply DNN classify filter to the input
... dnn_detect          V->V      Apply DNN detect filter to the input
... dnn_processing      V->V      Apply DNN processing filter to the input
.S. doubleweave         V->V      Weave input video fields into
                                  ↳ double number of frames
T.C drawbox             V->V      Draw a colored box on the input video
... drawgraph           V->V      Draw a graph using input video metadata
T.C drawgrid            V->V      Draw a colored grid on the input video
T.C drawtext            V->V      Draw text on top of video frames using libfreetype
                                  ↳ library
T.. edgedetect          V->V      Detect and draw edge
... elbg                V->V      Apply posterize effect, using the ELBG algorithm
T.. entropy             V->V      Measure video frames entropy
.S. epx                 V->V      Scale the input using EPX algorithm
T.C eq                  V->V      Adjust brightness, contrast, gamma, and saturation
TSC erosion             V->V      Apply erosion effect
... erosion_opencl      V->V      Apply erosion effect
TSC estdif              V->V      Apply Edge Slope Tracing deinterlace
```

TSC	exposure	V->V	Adjust exposure of the video stream
...	extractplanes	V->N	Extract planes as grayscale frames
TS.	fade	V->V	Fade in/out input video
..C	feedback	VV->VV	Apply feedback video filter
TSC	fftdnoiz	V->V	Denoise frames using 3D FFT
TS.	fftfilt	V->V	Apply arbitrary expressions to pixels in frequency ↳ domain
...	field	V->V	Extract a field from the input video
...	fieldhint	V->V	Field matching using hints
...	fieldmatch	N->V	Field matching for inverse telecine
T..	fieldorder	V->V	Set the field order
T.C	fillborders	V->V	Fill borders of the input video
...	find rect	V->V	Find a user specified object
...	flip_vulkan	V->V	Flip both horizontally and vertically
T..	floodfill	V->V	Fill area with same color with another color
...	format	V->V	Convert the input video to one of the specified ↳ pixel formats
...	fps	V->V	Force constant framerate
...	framepack	VV->V	Generate a frame packed stereoscopic video
.S.	framerate	V->V	Upsamples or downsamples progressive source ↳ between specified frame rates
T..	framestep	V->V	Select one frame every N frames
...	freezedetect	V->V	Detects frozen video input
...	freezeframes	VV->V	Freeze video frames
T.C	frei0r	V->V	Apply a frei0r effect
T..	fspp	V->V	Apply Fast Simple Post-processing filter
TSC	gblur	V->V	Apply Gaussian Blur filter
...	gblur_vulkan	V->V	Gaussian Blur in Vulkan
TS.	geq	V->V	Apply generic equation to each pixel
T..	gradfun	V->V	Debands video quickly using gradients
...	graphmonitor	V->V	Show various filtergraph stats
TS.	grayworld	V->V	Adjust white balance using LAB gray world algorithm
TS.	greyedge	V->V	Estimates scene illumination by grey edge ↳ assumption
TSC	guided	N->V	Apply Guided filter
TSC	haldclut	VV->V	Adjust colors using a Hald CLUT
TS.	hflip	V->V	Horizontally flip the input video
...	hflip_vulkan	V->V	Horizontally flip the input video in Vulkan
T..	histeq	V->V	Apply global color histogram equalization
...	histogram	V->V	Compute and draw a histogram
TSC	hqdn3d	V->V	Apply a High Quality 3D Denoiser
.S.	hqx	V->V	Scale the input by 2, 3 or 4 using the ↳ hq*x magnification algorithm
.S.	hstack	N->V	Stack video inputs horizontally
TSC	hsvhold	V->V	Turns a certain HSV range into gray
TSC	hsvkey	V->V	Turns a certain HSV range into transparency. ↳ Operates on YUV colors
T.C	hue	V->V	Adjust the hue and saturation of the input video
TSC	huesaturation	V->V	Apply hue-saturation-intensity adjustments
...	hwdownload	V->V	Download a hardware frame to a normal frame
...	hwmap	V->V	Map hardware frames
...	hwupload	V->V	Upload a normal frame to a hardware frame
...	hwupload_cuda	V->V	Upload a system memory frame to a CUDA device

T..	hysteresis	VV->V	Grow first stream into second stream by ↳ connecting components
TS.	identity	VV->V	Calculate the Identity between two video streams
...	idet	V->V	Interlace detect Filter
T.C	il	V->V	Deinterleave or interleave fields
TSC	inflate	V->V	Apply inflate effect
...	interlace	V->V	Convert progressive video into interlaced
...	interleave	N->V	Temporally interleave video inputs
...	kerndeint	V->V	Apply kernel deinterlacing to the input
TSC	kirsch	V->V	Apply kirsch operator
TSC	lagfun	V->V	Slowly update darker pixels
T..	latency	V->V	Report video filtering latency
TSC	lenscorrection	V->V	Rectify the image by correcting for lens distortion
TS.	lensfun	V->V	Apply correction to an image based on info ↳ derived from the lensfun database
..C	libplacebo	V->V	Apply various GPU filters from libplacebo
...	libvmaf	VV->V	Calculate the VMAF between two video streams
TSC	limitdiff	N->V	Apply filtering with limiting difference
TSC	limiter	V->V	Limit pixels components to the specified range
...	loop	V->V	Loop video frames
TSC	lumakey	V->V	Turns a certain luma into transparency
TSC	lut	V->V	Compute and apply a lookup table to the RGB/YUV ↳ input video
TSC	lut1d	V->V	Adjust colors using a 1D LUT
TSC	lut2	VV->V	Compute and apply a lookup table from two ↳ video inputs
TSC	lut3d	V->V	Adjust colors using a 3D LUT
TSC	lutrgb	V->V	Compute and apply a lookup table to the RGB ↳ input video
TSC	lutyuv	V->V	Compute and apply a lookup table to the YUV ↳ input video
TSC	maskedclamp	VVV->V	Clamp first stream with second stream and ↳ third stream
TSC	maskedmax	VVV->V	Apply filtering with maximum difference of ↳ two streams
TSC	maskedmerge	VVV->V	Merge first stream with second stream using third ↳ stream as mask
TSC	maskedmin	VVV->V	Apply filtering with minimum difference ↳ of two streams
TSC	maskedthreshold	VV->V	Pick pixels comparing absolute difference of two ↳ streams with threshold
TSC	maskfun	V->V	Create Mask
TSC	median	V->V	Apply Median filter
...	mergeplanes	N->V	Merge planes
...	mestimate	V->V	Generate motion vectors
T..	metadata	V->V	Manipulate video frame metadata
T..	midequalizer	VV->V	Apply Midway Equalization
...	minterpolate	V->V	Frame rate conversion using Motion Interpolation
TSC	mix	N->V	Mix video inputs
TSC	monochrome	V->V	Convert video to gray using custom color filter
T.C	morpho	VV->V	Apply Morphological filter
...	mpdecimate	V->V	Remove near-duplicate frames
TS.	msad	VV->V	Calculate the MSAD between two video streams

TSC	multiply	VV->V	Multiply first video stream with second video stream
TSC	negate	V->V	Negate input video
TS.	nlmeans	V->V	Non-local means denoiser
...	nlmeans_opencl	V->V	Non-local means denoiser through OpenCL
TSC	nnedi	V->V	Apply neural network edge directed inte rpolation ⌊ intra-only deinterlacer
...	noformat	V->V	Force libavfilter not to use any of the specified ⌊ pixel formats for the input to the next filter
TS.	noise	V->V	Add noise
T.C	normalize	V->V	Normalize RGB video
...	null	V->V	Pass the source unchanged to the output
T.C	oscilloscope	V->V	2D Video Oscilloscope
TSC	overlay	VV->V	Overlay a video source on top of the input
...	overlay_opencl	VV->V	Overlay one video on top of another
...	overlay_vaapi	VV->V	Overlay one video on top of another
...	overlay_qsv	VV->V	Quick Sync Video overlay
...	overlay_vulkan	VV->V	Overlay a source on top of another
...	overlay_cuda	VV->V	Overlay one video on top of another using CUDA
T..	owdenoise	V->V	Denoise using wavelets
...	pad	V->V	Pad the input video
...	pad_opencl	V->V	Pad the input video
...	palettegen	V->V	Find the optimal palette for a given stream
...	paletteuse	VV->V	Use a palette to downsample an input video stream
T.C	perms	V->V	Set permissions for the output video frame
TS.	perspective	V->V	Correct the perspective of video
T.C	phase	V->V	Phase shift fields
...	photosensitivity	V->V	Filter out photosensitive epilepsy seizure-inducing ⌊ flashes
...	pixdesctest	V->V	Test pixel format definitions
TSC	pixelize	V->V	Pixelize video
T.C	pixscope	V->V	Pixel data analysis
T.C	pp	V->V	Filter video using libpostproc
T..	pp7	V->V	Apply Postprocessing 7 filter
TS.	premultiply	N->V	PreMultiply first stream with first plane of ⌊ second stream
TSC	prewitt	V->V	Apply prewitt operator
...	prewitt_opencl	V->V	Apply prewitt operator
...	procamp_vaapi	V->V	ProcAmp (color balance) adjustments for hue, ⌊ saturation, brightness, contrast
...	program_opencl	N->V	Filter video using an OpenCL program
TSC	pseudocolor	V->V	Make pseudocolored video frames
TS.	psnr	VV->V	Calculate the PSNR between two video streams
...	pullup	V->V	Pullup from field sequence to frames
T..	qp	V->V	Change video quantization parameters
...	random	V->V	Return random frames
TSC	readeia608	V->V	Read EIA-608 Closed Caption codes from input video ⌊ and write them to frame metadata
...	readvitc	V->V	Read vertical interval timecode and write it to ⌊ frame metadata
..C	realtime	V->V	Slow down filtering to match realtime
.S.	remap	VVV->V	Remap pixels
...	remap_opencl	VVV->V	Remap pixels using OpenCL
TS.	removegrain	V->V	Remove grain

T..	removelogo	V->V	Remove a TV logo based on a mask image
...	repeatfields	V->V	Hard repeat fields based on MPEG repeat field flag
...	reverse	V->V	Reverse a clip
TSC	rgbashift	V->V	Shift RGBA
TSC	roberts	V->V	Apply roberts cross operator
...	roberts_opencl	V->V	Apply roberts operator
TSC	rotate	V->V	Rotate the input image
T..	sab	V->V	Apply shape adaptive blur
..C	scale	V->V	Scale the input video size and/or convert the ↳ image format
...	scale_vaapi	V->V	Scale to/from VAAPI surfaces
...	scale_cuda	V->V	GPU accelerated video resizer
...	scale_qsv	V->V	QuickSync video scaling and format conversion
...	scale_vulkan	V->V	Scale Vulkan frames
..C	scale2ref	VV->VV	Scale the input video size and/or convert the ↳ image format to the given reference
...	scdet	V->V	Detect video scene change
TSC	scharr	V->V	Apply scharr operator
TSC	scroll	V->V	Scroll input video
...	segment	V->N	Segment video stream
...	select	V->N	Select video frames to pass in output
TS.	selectivecolor	V->V	Apply CMYK adjustments to specific color ranges
...	sendcmd	V->V	Send commands to filters
...	separatefields	V->V	Split input video frames into fields
...	setdar	V->V	Set the frame display aspect ratio
...	setfield	V->V	Force field for the output video frame
...	setparams	V->V	Force field, or color property for the output ↳ video frame
...	setpts	V->V	Set PTS for the output video frame
...	setrange	V->V	Force color range for the output video frame
...	setsar	V->V	Set the pixel sample aspect ratio
...	settb	V->V	Set timebase for the video output link
...	sharpness_vaapi	V->V	VAAPI VPP for sharpness
TSC	shear	V->V	Shear transform the input image
...	showinfo	V->V	Show textual information for each video frame
...	showpalette	V->V	Display frame palette
T..	shuffleframes	V->V	Shuffle video frames
TS.	shufflepixels	V->V	Shuffle video pixels
T..	shuffleplanes	V->V	Shuffle video planes
T..	sidedata	V->V	Manipulate video frame side data
.S.	signalstats	V->V	Generate statistics from video analysis
...	signature	N->V	Calculate the MPEG-7 video signature
...	siti	V->V	Calculate spatial information (SI) and temporal ↳ information (TI)
T..	smartblur	V->V	Blur the input video without impacting the outlines
TSC	sobel	V->V	Apply sobel operator
...	sobel_opencl	V->V	Apply sobel operator
...	split	V->N	Pass on the input to N video outputs
T.C	spp	V->V	Apply a simple post processing filter
...	sr	V->V	Apply DNN-based image super resolution to the input
TS.	ssim	VV->V	Calculate the SSIM between two video streams
.S.	stereo3d	V->V	Convert video stereoscopic 3D view
..C	streamselect	N->N	Select video streams

258

...	subtitles	V->V	Render text subtitles onto input video using the ↳ libass library
.S.	super2xsai	V->V	Scale the input by 2x using the Super2x SaI ↳ pixel art algorithm
T.C	swaprect	V->V	Swap 2 rectangular objects in video
T..	swapuv	V->V	Swap U and V components
TSC	tblend	V->V	Blend successive frames
...	telecine	V->V	Apply a telecine pattern
...	thistogram	V->V	Compute and draw a temporal histogram
TSC	threshold	VVVV->V	Threshold first video stream using other video ↳ streams
T..	thumbnail	V->V	Select the most representative frame in a given ↳ sequence of consecutive frames
...	thumbnail_cuda	V->V	Select the most representative frame in a given ↳ sequence of consecutive frames
...	tile	V->V	Tile several successive frames together
...	tinterlace	V->V	Perform temporal field interlacing
TSC	tlut2	V->V	Compute and apply a lookup table from two successive ↳ frames
TSC	tmedian	V->V	Pick median pixels from successive frames
T..	tmidequalizer	V->V	Apply Temporal Midway Equalization
TSC	tmix	V->V	Mix successive video frames
.S.	tonemap	V->V	Conversion to/from different dynamic ranges
...	tonemap_opencl	V->V	Perform HDR to SDR conversion with tone mapping
...	tonemap_vaapi	V->V	VAAPI VPP for tone-mapping
...	tpad	V->V	Temporarily pad video frames
.S.	transpose	V->V	Transpose input video
...	transpose_opencl	V->V	Transpose input video
...	transpose_vaapi	V->V	VAAPI VPP for transpose
...	transpose_vulkan	V->V	Transpose Vulkan Filter
...	trim	V->V	Pick one continuous section from the in put, drop ↳ the rest
TS.	unpremultiply	N->V	UnPreMultiply first stream with first plane of ↳ second stream
TS.	unsharp	V->V	Sharpen or blur the input video
...	unsharp_opencl	V->V	Apply unsharp mask to input video
...	untile	V->V	Untile a frame into a sequence of frames
.SC	v360	V->V	Convert 360 projection of video
T..	vaguedenoiser	V->V	Apply a Wavelet based Denoiser
TSC	varblur	VV->V	Apply Variable Blur filter
..C	vectorscope	V->V	Video vectorscope
T..	vflip	V->V	Flip the input video vertically
...	vflip_vulkan	V->V	Vertically flip the input ↳ video in Vulk an
...	vfrdet	V->V	Variable frame rate detect filter
TSC	vibrance	V->V	Boost or alter saturation
...	vidstabdetect	V->V	Extract relative transformations, pass 1 of 2 for ↳ stabilization (see vidstab transform for pass 2)
...	vidstabtransform	V->V	Transform the frames, pass 2 of 2 for ↳ stabilization (see vidstabdetect for pass 1)
TS.	vif	VV->V	Calculate the VIF between two video streams
T..	vignette	V->V	Make or reverse a vignette effect
...	vmafmotion	V->V	Calculate the VMAF Motion score

```
...  vpp_qsv            V->V     Quick Sync Video VPP
.S.  vstack             N->V     Stack video inputs vertically
TSC  w3fdif             V->V     Apply Martin Weston three field deinterlace
.SC  waveform           V->V     Video waveform monitor
.S.  weave              V->V     Weave input video fields into frames
.S.  xbr                V->V     Scale the input using xBR algorithm
TS.  xcorrelate         VV->V    Cross-correlate first video stream with second video
                                 ↳ stream
.S.  xfade              VV->V    Cross fade one video with another video
...  xfade_opencl       VV->V    Cross fade one video with another video
TSC  xmedian            N->V     Pick median pixels from several video inputs
.S.  xstack             N->V     Stack video inputs into custom layout
TS.  yadif              V->V     Deinterlace the input image
T..  yadif_cuda         V->V     Deinterlace CUDA frames
TSC  yaepblur           V->V     Yet another edge preserving blur filter
...  zmq                V->V     Receive commands through ZMQ
                                 ↳ and broker them to filters
...  zoompan            V->V     Apply Zoom & Pan effect
.SC  zscale             V->V     Apply resizing, colorspace
                                 ↳ and bit depth conversion
...  allrgb             |->V     Generate all RGB colors
...  allyuv             |->V     Generate all yuv colors
...  cellauto           |->V     Create pattern generated by an elementary cellular
                                 ↳ automaton
..C  color              |->V     Provide an uniformly colored input
...  colorchart         |->V     Generate color checker chart
...  colorspectrum      |->V     Generate colors spectrum
...  ddagrab            |->V     Grab Windows Desktop images
                                 ↳ using Desktop Duplication API
...  frei0r_src         |->V     Generate a frei0r source
.S.  gradients          |->V     Draw a gradients
...  haldclutsrc        |->V     Provide an identity Hald CLUT
...  life               |->V     Create life
...  mandelbrot         |->V     Render a Mandelbrot fractal
...  mptestsrc          |->V     Generate various test pattern
...  nullsrc            |->V     Null video source, return
                                 ↳ unprocessed video frames
...  openclsrc          |->V     Generate video using an OpenCL program
...  pal75bars          |->V     Generate PAL 75% color bars
...  pal100bars         |->V     Generate PAL 100% color bars
...  rgbtestsrc         |->V     Generate RGB test pattern
.S.  sierpinski         |->V     Render a Sierpinski fractal
...  smptebars          |->V     Generate SMPTE color bars
...  smptehdbars        |->V     Generate SMPTE HD color bars
...  testsrc            |->V     Generate test pattern
...  testsrc2           |->V     Generate another test pattern
...  yuvtestsrc         |->V     Generate YUV test pattern
...  nullsink           V->|     Do absolutely nothing with the input video
...  abitscope          A->V     Convert input audio to audio
                                 ↳ bitscope video output
...  adrawgraph         A->V     Draw a graph using input audio metadata
...  agraphmonitor      A->V     Show various filtergraph stats
...  ahistogram         A->V     Convert input audio to histogram video output
```

... aphasemeter	A->N	Convert input audio to phase meter video output
.SC avectorscope	A->V	Convert input audio to vectorscope video output
..C concat	N->N	Concatenate audio and video streams
... showcqt	A->V	Convert input audio to a CQT (Constant/Clamped Q ↳ Transform) spectrum video output
... showfreqs	A->V	Convert input audio to a frequencies video output
.S. showspatial	A->V	Convert input audio to a spatial video output
.S. showspectrum	A->V	Convert input audio to a spectrum video output
.S. showspectrumpic	A->V	Convert input audio to a spectrum video output ↳ single picture
... showvolume	A->V	Convert input audio volume to video output
... showwaves	A->V	Convert input audio to a video output
... showwavespic	A->V	Convert input audio to a video output single picture
... spectrumsynth	VV->A	Convert input spectrum videos to audio output
... avsynctest	|->AV	Generate an Audio Video Sync Test
..C amovie	|->N	Read audio from a movie source
..C movie	|->N	Read from a movie source
... afifo	A->A	Buffer input frames and send them when they are ↳ requested
... fifo	V->V	Buffer input images and send them when they are ↳ requested
... abuffer	|->A	Buffer audio frames, and make them accessible to the ↳ filterchain
... buffer	|->V	Buffer video frames, and make them accessible to the ↳ filterchain
... abuffersink	A->|	Buffer audio frames, and make them available to the ↳ end of the filter graph
... buffersink	V->|	Buffer video frames, and make them available ↳ to the end of the filter graph

Annexure 5: Sample List of Formats

This annexure contains sample output for the command `ffmpeg -formats`.

```
File formats:
 D. = Demuxing supported
 .E = Muxing supported
 --
 D  3dostr        3DO STR
  E 3g2           3GP2 (3GPP2 file format)
  E 3gp           3GP (3GPP file format)
 D  4xm           4X Technologies
  E a64           a64 - video for Commodore 64
 D  aa            Audible AA format files
 D  aac           raw ADTS AAC (Advanced Audio Coding)
 D  aax           CRI AAX
 DE ac3           raw AC-3
 D  ace           tri-Ace Audio Container
 D  acm           Interplay ACM
 D  act           ACT Voice file format
```

261

```
D  adf           Artworx Data Format
D  adp           ADP
D  ads           Sony PS2 ADS
 E adts          ADTS AAC (Advanced Audio Coding)
DE adx           CRI ADX
D  aea           MD STUDIO audio
D  afc           AFC
DE aiff          Audio IFF
D  aix           CRI AIX
DE alaw          PCM A-law
D  alias_pix     Alias/Wavefront PIX image
DE alp           LEGO Racers ALP
DE alsa          ALSA audio output
DE amr           3GPP AMR
D  amrnb         raw AMR-NB
D  amrwb         raw AMR-WB
 E amv           AMV
D  anm           Deluxe Paint Animation
D  apc           CRYO APC
D  ape           Monkey's Audio
DE apm           Ubisoft Rayman 2 APM
DE apng          Animated Portable Network Graphics
DE aptx          raw aptX (Audio Processing Technology for Bluetooth)
DE aptx_hd       raw aptX HD (Audio Processing Technology for Bluetooth)
D  aqtitle       AQTitle subtitles
DE argo_asf      Argonaut Games ASF
D  argo_brp      Argonaut Games BRP
DE argo_cvg      Argonaut Games CVG
DE asf           ASF (Advanced / Active Streaming Format)
D  asf_o         ASF (Advanced / Active Streaming Format)
 E asf_stream    ASF (Advanced / Active Streaming Format)
DE ass           SSA (SubStation Alpha) subtitle
DE ast           AST (Audio Stream)
DE au            Sun AU
D  av1           AV1 Annex B
DE avi           AVI (Audio Video Interleaved)
 E avif          AVIF
D  avisynth      AviSynth script
 E avm2          SWF (ShockWave Flash) (AVM2)
D  avr           AVR (Audio Visual Research)
D  avs           Argonaut Games Creature Shock
DE avs2          raw AVS2-P2/IEEE1857.4 video
DE avs3          AVS3-P2/IEEE1857.10
D  bethsoftvid   Bethesda Softworks VID
D  bfi           Brute Force & Ignorance
D  bfstm         BFSTM (Binary Cafe Stream)
D  bin           Binary text
D  bink          Bink
D  binka         Bink Audio
DE bit           G.729 BIT file format
D  bitpacked     Bitpacked
D  bmp_pipe      piped bmp sequence
D  bmv           Discworld II BMV
```

```
 D  boa             Black Ops Audio
 D  brender_pix     BRender PIX image
 D  brstm           BRSTM (Binary Revolution Stream)
 D  c93             Interplay C93
  E caca            caca (color ASCII art) output device
DE  caf             Apple CAF (Core Audio Format)
DE  cavsvideo       raw Chinese AVS (Audio Video Standard) video
 D  cdg             CD Graphics
 D  cdxl            Commodore CDXL video
  E chromaprint     Chromaprint
 D  cine            Phantom Cine
DE  codec2          codec2 .c2 muxer
DE  codec2raw       raw codec2 muxer
 D  concat          Virtual concatenation script
  E crc             CRC testing
 D  cri_pipe        piped cri sequence
DE  dash            DASH Muxer
DE  data            raw data
DE  daud            D-Cinema audio
 D  dcstr           Sega DC STR
 D  dds_pipe        piped dds sequence
 D  derf            Xilam DERF
 D  dfa             Chronomaster DFA
DE  dfpwm           raw DFPWM1a
 D  dhav            Video DAV
DE  dirac           raw Dirac
DE  dnxhd           raw DNxHD (SMPTE VC-3)
 D  dpx_pipe        piped dpx sequence
 D  dsf             DSD Stream File (DSF)
 D  dshow           DirectShow capture
 D  dsicin          Delphine Software International CIN
 D  dss             Digital Speech Standard (DSS)
DE  dts             raw DTS
 D  dtshd           raw DTS-HD
DE  dv              DV (Digital Video)
 D  dvbsub          raw dvbsub
 D  dvbtxt          dvbtxt
  E dvd             MPEG-2 PS (DVD VOB)
 D  dxa             DXA
 D  ea              Electronic Arts Multimedia
 D  ea_cdata        Electronic Arts cdata
DE  eac3            raw E-AC-3
 D  epaf            Ensoniq Paris Audio File
 D  exr_pipe        piped exr sequence
DE  f32be           PCM 32-bit floating-point big-endian
DE  f32le           PCM 32-bit floating-point little-endian
  E f4v             F4V Adobe Flash Video
DE  f64be           PCM 64-bit floating-point big-endian
DE  f64le           PCM 64-bit floating-point little-endian
DE  fbdev           Linux framebuffer
DE  ffmetadata      FFmpeg metadata in text
  E fifo            FIFO queue pseudo-muxer
  E fifo_test       Fifo test muxer
```

```
DE film_cpk      Sega FILM / CPK
DE filmstrip     Adobe Filmstrip
DE fits          Flexible Image Transport System
DE flac          raw FLAC
D  flic          FLI/FLC/FLX animation
DE flv           FLV (Flash Video)
 E framecrc      framecrc testing
 E framehash     Per-frame hash testing
 E framemd5      Per-frame MD5 testing
D  frm           Megalux Frame
D  fsb           FMOD Sample Bank
D  fwse          Capcom's MT Framework sound
DE g722          raw G.722
DE g723_1        raw G.723.1
DE g726          raw big-endian G.726 ("left-justified")
DE g726le        raw little-endian G.726 ("right-justified")
D  g729          G.729 raw format demuxer
D  gdigrab       GDI API Windows frame grabber
D  gdv           Gremlin Digital Video
D  gem_pipe      piped gem sequence
D  genh          GENeric Header
DE gif           CompuServe Graphics Interchange Format (GIF)
D  gif_pipe      piped gif sequence
DE gsm           raw GSM
DE gxf           GXF (General eXchange Format)
DE h261          raw H.261
DE h263          raw H.263
DE h264          raw H.264 video
 E hash          Hash testing
D  hca           CRI HCA
D  hcom          Macintosh HCOM
D  hdr_pipe      piped hdr sequence
 E hds           HDS Muxer
DE hevc          raw HEVC video
DE hls           Apple HTTP Live Streaming
D  hnm           Cryo HNM v4
DE ico           Microsoft Windows ICO
D  idcin         id Cinematic
D  idf           iCE Draw File
D  iff           IFF (Interchange File Format)
D  ifv           IFV CCTV DVR
DE ilbc          iLBC storage
DE image2        image2 sequence
DE image2pipe    piped image2 sequence
D  imf           IMF (Interoperable Master Format)
D  ingenient     raw Ingenient MJPEG
D  ipmovie       Interplay MVE
 E ipod          iPod H.264 MP4 (MPEG-4 Part 14)
D  ipu           raw IPU Video
DE ircam         Berkeley/IRCAM/CARL Sound Format
 E ismv          ISMV/ISMA (Smooth Streaming)
D  iss           Funcom ISS
D  iv8           IndigoVision 8000 video
```

```
DE ivf              On2 IVF
D  ivr              IVR (Internet Video Recording)
D  j2k_pipe         piped j2k sequence
DE jacosub          JACOsub subtitle format
D  jpeg_pipe        piped jpeg sequence
D  jpegls_pipe      piped jpegls sequence
D  jpegxl_pipe      piped jpegxl sequence
D  jv               Bitmap Brothers JV
D  kux              KUX (YouKu)
DE kvag             Simon & Schuster Interactive VAG
 E latm             LOAS/LATM
D  lavfi            Libavfilter virtual input device
D  libcdio
D  libgme           Game Music Emu demuxer
D  libmodplug       ModPlug demuxer
D  libopenmpt       Tracker formats (libopenmpt)
D  live_flv         live RTMP FLV (Flash Video)
D  lmlm4            raw lmlm4
D  loas             LOAS AudioSyncStream
DE lrc              LRC lyrics
D  luodat           Video CCTV DAT
D  lvf              LVF
D  lxf              VR native stream (LXF)
DE m4v              raw MPEG-4 video
 E matroska         Matroska
D  matroska,webm    Matroska / WebM
D  mca              MCA Audio Format
D  mcc              MacCaption
 E md5              MD5 testing
D  mgsts            Metal Gear Solid: The Twin Snakes
DE microdvd         MicroDVD subtitle format
DE mjpeg            raw MJPEG video
D  mjpeg_2000       raw MJPEG 2000 video
 E mkvtimestamp_v2  extract pts as timecode v2 format, as
                    ↳ defined by mkv toolnix
DE mlp              raw MLP
D  mlv              Magic Lantern Video (MLV)
D  mm               American Laser Games MM
DE mmf              Yamaha SMAF
D  mods             MobiClip MODS
D  moflex           MobiClip MOFLEX
 E mov              QuickTime / MOV
D  mov,mp4,m4a,3gp,3g2,mj2 QuickTime / MOV
 E mp2              MP2 (MPEG audio layer 2)
DE mp3              MP3 (MPEG audio layer 3)
 E mp4              MP4 (MPEG-4 Part 14)
D  mpc              Musepack
D  mpc8             Musepack SV8
DE mpeg             MPEG-1 Systems / MPEG program stream
 E mpeg1video       raw MPEG-1 video
 E mpeg2video       raw MPEG-2 video
DE mpegts           MPEG-TS (MPEG-2 Transport Stream)
D  mpegtsraw        raw MPEG-TS (MPEG-2 Transport Stream)
```

```
 D  mpegvideo        raw MPEG video
DE  mpjpeg           MIME multipart JPEG
 D  mpl2             MPL2 subtitles
 D  mpsub            MPlayer subtitles
 D  msf              Sony PS3 MSF
 D  msnwctcp         MSN TCP Webcam stream
 D  msp              Microsoft Paint (MSP)
 D  mtaf             Konami PS2 MTAF
 D  mtv              MTV
DE  mulaw            PCM mu-law
 D  musx             Eurocom MUSX
 D  mv               Silicon Graphics Movie
 D  mvi              Motion Pixels MVI
DE  mxf              MXF (Material eXchange Format)
 E  mxf_d10          MXF (Material eXchange Format) D-10 Mapping
 E  mxf_opatom       MXF (Material eXchange Format) Operational Pattern Atom
 D  mxg              MxPEG clip
 D  nc               NC camera feed
 D  nistsphere       NIST SPeech HEader REsources
 D  nsp              Computerized Speech Lab NSP
 D  nsv              Nullsoft Streaming Video
 E  null             raw null video
DE  nut              NUT
 D  nuv              NuppelVideo
DE  obu              AV1 low overhead OBU
 E  oga              Ogg Audio
DE  ogg              Ogg
 E  ogv              Ogg Video
DE  oma              Sony OpenMG audio
 E  opengl           OpenGL output
 E  opus             Ogg Opus
DE  oss              OSS (Open Sound System) playback
 D  paf              Amazing Studio Packed Animation File
 D  pam_pipe         piped pam sequence
 D  pbm_pipe         piped pbm sequence
 D  pcx_pipe         piped pcx sequence
 D  pfm_pipe         piped pfm sequence
 D  pgm_pipe         piped pgm sequence
 D  pgmyuv_pipe      piped pgmyuv sequence
 D  pgx_pipe         piped pgx sequence
 D  phm_pipe         piped phm sequence
 D  photocd_pipe     piped photocd sequence
 D  pictor_pipe      piped pictor sequence
 D  pjs              PJS (Phoenix Japanimation Society) subtitles
 D  pmp              Playstation Portable PMP
 D  png_pipe         piped png sequence
 D  pp_bnk           Pro Pinball Series Soundbank
 D  ppm_pipe         piped ppm sequence
 D  psd_pipe         piped psd sequence
 E  psp              PSP MP4 (MPEG-4 Part 14)
 D  psxstr           Sony Playstation STR
DE  pulse            Pulse audio output
 D  pva              TechnoTrend PVA
```

```
D  pvf              PVF (Portable Voice Format)
D  qcp              QCP
D  qdraw_pipe       piped qdraw sequence
D  qoi_pipe         piped qoi sequence
D  r3d              REDCODE R3D
DE rawvideo         raw video
D  realtext         RealText subtitle format
D  redspark         RedSpark
D  rl2              RL2
DE rm               RealMedia
DE roq              raw id RoQ
D  rpl              RPL / ARMovie
D  rsd              GameCube RSD
DE rso              Lego Mindstorms RSO
DE rtp              RTP output
 E rtp_mpegts       RTP/mpegts output format
DE rtsp             RTSP output
DE s16be            PCM signed 16-bit big-endian
DE s16le            PCM signed 16-bit little-endian
DE s24be            PCM signed 24-bit big-endian
DE s24le            PCM signed 24-bit little-endian
DE s32be            PCM signed 32-bit big-endian
DE s32le            PCM signed 32-bit little-endian
D  s337m            SMPTE 337M
DE s8               PCM signed 8-bit
D  sami             SAMI subtitle format
DE sap              SAP output
DE sbc              raw SBC
D  sbg              SBaGen binaural beats script
DE scc              Scenarist Closed Captions
D  scd              Square Enix SCD
 E sdl,sdl2         SDL2 output device
D  sdp              SDP
D  sdr2             SDR2
D  sds              MIDI Sample Dump Standard
D  sdx              Sample Dump eXchange
 E segment          segment
D  ser              SER (Simple uncompressed video format for astronomical capturing)
D  sga              Digital Pictures SGA
D  sgi_pipe         piped sgi sequence
D  shn              raw Shorten
D  siff             Beam Software SIFF
D  simbiosis_imx    Simbiosis Interactive IMX
D  sln              Asterisk raw pcm
DE smjpeg           Loki SDL MJPEG
D  smk              Smacker
 E smoothstreaming  Smooth Streaming Muxer
D  smush            LucasArts Smush
DE sndio            sndio audio playback
D  sol              Sierra SOL
DE sox              SoX native
DE spdif            IEC 61937 (used on S/PDIF - IEC958)
 E spx              Ogg Speex
```

```
DE srt               SubRip subtitle
D  stl               Spruce subtitle format
 E stream_segment,ssegment streaming segment muxer
 E streamhash        Per-stream hash testing
D  subviewer         SubViewer subtitle format
D  subviewer1        SubViewer v1 subtitle format
D  sunrast_pipe      piped sunrast sequence
DE sup               raw HDMV Presentation Graphic Stream subtitles
D  svag              Konami PS2 SVAG
 E svcd              MPEG-2 PS (SVCD)
D  svg_pipe          piped svg sequence
D  svs               Square SVS
DE swf               SWF (ShockWave Flash)
D  tak               raw TAK
D  tedcaptions       TED Talks captions
 E tee               Multiple muxer tee
D  thp               THP
D  tiertexseq        Tiertex Limited SEQ
D  tiff_pipe         piped tiff sequence
D  tmv               8088flex TMV
DE truehd            raw TrueHD
DE tta               TTA (True Audio)
 E ttml              TTML subtitle
D  tty               Tele-typewriter
D  txd               Renderware TeXture Dictionary
D  ty                TiVo TY Stream
DE u16be             PCM unsigned 16-bit big-endian
DE u16le             PCM unsigned 16-bit little-endian
DE u24be             PCM unsigned 24-bit big-endian
DE u24le             PCM unsigned 24-bit little-endian
DE u32be             PCM unsigned 32-bit big-endian
DE u32le             PCM unsigned 32-bit little-endian
DE u8                PCM unsigned 8-bit
 E uncodedframecrc uncoded framecrc testing
D  v210              Uncompressed 4:2:2 10-bit
D  v210x             Uncompressed 4:2:2 10-bit
D  vag               Sony PS2 VAG
D  vbn_pipe          piped vbn sequence
DE vc1               raw VC-1 video
DE vc1test           VC-1 test bitstream
 E vcd               MPEG-1 Systems / MPEG program stream (VCD)
D  vfwcap            VfW video capture
DE vidc              PCM Archimedes VIDC
DE video4linux2,v4l2 Video4Linux2 output device
D  vividas           Vividas VIV
D  vivo              Vivo
D  vmd               Sierra VMD
 E vob               MPEG-2 PS (VOB)
D  vobsub            VobSub subtitle format
DE voc               Creative Voice
D  vpk               Sony PS2 VPK
D  vplayer           VPlayer subtitles
D  vqf               Nippon Telegraph and Telephone Corporation (NTT) TwinVQ
```

```
DE w64                Sony Wave64
DE wav                WAV / WAVE (Waveform Audio)
 D  wc3movie          Wing Commander III movie
  E webm              WebM
  E webm_chunk        WebM Chunk Muxer
DE webm_dash_manifest WebM DASH Manifest
  E webp              WebP
 D  webp_pipe         piped webp sequence
DE webvtt             WebVTT subtitle
DE wsaud              Westwood Studios audio
 D  wsd               Wideband Single-bit Data (WSD)
 D  wsvqa             Westwood Studios VQA
DE wtv                Windows Television (WTV)
DE wv                 raw WavPack
 D  wve               Psion 3 audio
 D  x11grab           X11 screen capture, using XCB
 D  xa                Maxis XA
 D  xbin              eXtended BINary text (XBIN)
 D  xbm_pipe          piped xbm sequence
 D  xmv               Microsoft XMV
 D  xpm_pipe          piped xpm sequence
  E xv                XV (XVideo) output device
 D  xvag              Sony PS3 XVAG
 D  xwd_pipe          piped xwd sequence
 D  xwma              Microsoft xWMA
 D  yop               Psygnosis YOP
DE yuv4mpegpipe       YUV4MPEG pipe
```

Index

A

Apple Mac
    download, installation, 6
Audacity, 32, 34, 116, 120, 121, 123,
       125, 139, 140
Audio
    album art, 39, 64, 155–157,
       160, 162
    beep, 202, 203
    bitrate, 19, 48, 51, 55
    bleep, 204
    capture, 193, 194, 196
    channels
       channel maps, 44
       downmix, 126
       filters, 44
       merge, 44
       mix, 42, 43
       move, 42, 126, 129, 130
       mute, 41, 42
       out-of-phase, 130, 131
       split, 44, 126, 129
       swap, 128
    codec, 17–19, 56
    compression, 19, 173, 231, 242
    concatenate, 94, 171, 261
    conversion
       5.1 to stereo, 134
       from MIDI, 120
       mono to stereo, 133
       stereo to mono, 131, 132
       from text, 138
       two stereo to one
         stereo, 134–136
       from video, 119
       visual waveforms, 136–138
    copy, 42, 55, 56
    cut, 78, 79
    decoder, 18, 19, 48, 231
    downmix (*see* Channels,
       downmix)
    echo, 250
    encoder, 18, 19, 48, 55
    espeak (*see* libflite)
    extraction, 55, 56
    fading, 105
    hardware, 164
    libflite (*see* espeak)
    metadata, 23, 25, 38, 39, 155,
       158, 164, 260
    microphone, 19, 192–194
    MIDI, 47
    mono, 24, 42, 43, 129, 131,
       133, 135
    multi-channel, 126, 250
    noise, 102, 139, 252